Leisure and Its Use

Some International Observations

BY

HERBERT L. MAY

AND

DOROTHY PETGEN

NEW YORK

A. S. BARNES AND COMPANY

1928

CONTENTS

AN INTIMATE FOREWORD

In the spring of 1926, the Playground and Recreation Association of America requested that I organise and direct a study of leisure time activities in the principal countries of Europe. Scope and method were left entirely to my judgment. I selected as my assistants, Miss Dorothy Petgen and Miss Margaret Lawson. Miss Lawson accompanied Miss Petgen during the first six months of the study in Europe, and has given further valuable assistance in consultations over the collected material, in America. Miss Petgen devoted a year and a half to the study. As it was necessary for me to be in other parts of the world on another investigation, I was in Europe only a portion of this time, making Paris my headquarters during the study; however, a considerable previous residence abroad and familiarity with conditions enabled me to keep in close touch with the progress of the work. Nevertheless, it early developed that the assistant was better informed than the director, so that whatever of value there is in this resulting volume is largely due to Miss Petgen's ability as an interviewer, a student, and an interpreter of conditions.

A complete study of the uses of leisure in various parts of the world would involve excursions into the racial, social and economic history of each country, would take years to accomplish and volumes to report. Even in the relatively brief and superficial investigation possible for us there were numerous difficulties to be

encountered. In the fall of 1927 I undertook to direct
the arrangement and transcription of material (personal notes and collected publications) in Paris. At
my request, Miss Petgen wrote from Berlin during
this time the following letter, in an attempt to summarise the actual development of the study and to
provide a record somewhat more human than the im-
personal outlines which were guiding the arrangement
of material.

"You want a sort of Pilgrim's Progress of the recreation study?

"When it was undertaken there existed hardly any
plan. We had in the beginning—that is, when we
started for Europe—an amazing list of questions and
topics for investigation. These derived from numerous
and probably rather too varied sources, and represented immensely differing viewpoints and types of interest in the matter of the use of leisure. Our own
curiosities further complicated the matter. So far as
we could find out, the field, internationally considered,
was utterly new: there was literally nothing for us to
go by. The first, most important step, then, was to
attempt to bring these disconcertingly various questions into some sort of order, so that we could make
our own approach with a degree of orderliness. It
was not easy. The persons responsible for the list
(their faith was lovely) wanted apparently to inquire
into everything. Their curiosity extended to nearly
every department of human interest or activity which
might possibly provide means for the employment of
free time. Interesting enough, certainly, but immensely intimidating. On the other hand, in the matter
of the technicalities of recreation—the questions intended to apply to formal, conscious recreational de-

velopments—the thirst for statistical information of
the interested persons was no less appalling. In conversations over the classifying of all the suggested
questions we came to some tentative decisions influencing the conduct of the study. We agreed that
exhaustive statistical information as to activities, organisation, methods, equipment, and so on, would have
little practical value for any one in America. Even
for the purpose of pure comparison, little was to be
gained, since the greater body of such information,
were it collected, would inevitably be well out of date
by the time the study could be reported on in the
United States. We (even I) at least knew that in
most of these matters the United States could have
very little to learn from Europe. As a matter of fact,
actual methods in community recreation, playground
leadership, directed children's play, and 'educative'
propaganda in Europe may be said always to resemble
American methods or to approach or imitate them.
And after all, is much variation or innovation actually
possible in such matters? The exceptions are cases
where some recreational activity is a peculiar out-
growth of the racial temperament or national spirit of
a given people. In these cases, while description of the
activity may be interesting to America, it is obviously
not feasible to attempt transplanting. In view of all
this, we tacitly decided to slight the practical questions
regarding activities and to concentrate on what we
cheerfully called the 'fundamentals' of the recreation
problem.

"Without exception, the questions applying to the
'fundamentals' or general aspects of the leisure problem indicated that they had grown out of a belief
in the superiority of European life. (I am using the

word *life* in its proper sense, which has little to do with open plumbing.) At that time American consciousness of recreation was just setting in. A belief had grown up that there exists in Europe a unique *savoir vivre*, extending throughout all classes. This superstition has vast credence among well-to-do Americans who are in the habit of visiting Europe when— and where—it is loveliest, and among the people who read the magazines which pretend to the higher intellectual levels: they think that personal liberty exists all over Europe, and that every day labourer in Germany can whistle you the principal motifs of the *Ring*. The influence of the superstition was strong on the 'fundamentals' question of the list. For instance:

Why do Europeans appreciate good music and singing more than Americans?

The art of conversation . . . what has caused its decline in America?

Is religiosity responsible for bad use of leisure (in America)?

Why is beauty left out of American life?

Europe still has family life . . . we do not . . . why?

Now it is apparent to me that such questions originated from inaccurate and incomplete impressions and information. But in the beginning I was awfully innocent; I had the superstition, too. It was nice to think that somewhere this quintessence of dust enjoyed pleasures simpler, higher, purer, than in our crude and artificised society, and that one was on the point

of ferreting out the secret of this recreational nobility
and innocency.

"Of another element apparent in certain of these
questions I was more sceptical. That was the evangelical note. I was quite ready to admit the probable
esthetic superiority of some folk music to some jazz
but I could not fall in with the tendency, apparent in
some of the questions, to make a morality of recreation.
I thought we had better leave all questions of *quality*
of pleasure to metaphysicians. For practical purposes
the pleasure of an individual in dancing is probably no
different whether he dances a folk dance or a fox trot.
The fox trot is simply a folk dance which has the bad
luck to be contemporary. Another province where
moral judgment intrudes itself (and this is by no means
confined to American opinion) is that of 'passive'
recreation: to consider that the tendency to observe
rather than to participate is a social danger. This
attitude of course derives from the evidence of history
that such a tendency is apt to be associated with decadence. However, since the association is that of a
symptom rather than a cause, the tendency is hardly
subject to contemporary direction or control.

"We can say, then, that our first decision was to
make a psychological rather than a statistical survey,
and that our purpose was to look in Europe for beautiful ways of life. We approached with the utmost
humility—which, for American 'investigators,' is not
monotonously usual. And we expected to find material
for a recreational lesson for America.

"To the degree that we phrased our purpose at this
time, we considered the 'fundamentals' rather as follows: whether simpler, more natural, more wholesome
methods were employed by the formal 'recreation

movement' (where such existed) in Europe; whether
the people were responsive to the recreation movement;
whether the life of the people, for whatever reasons,
provided greater possibilities of satisfaction, occupation, and pleasure during free time than in America.
Nevertheless, we had not yet been daring enough to
discard entirely the practical and technical questions.
We retained them, or at any rate, their practical and
technical implications, in a place of second honour.
But, blinded by the vision of The Better Life of
Europe, we had not considered them of sufficient importance to attempt to reconcile them with the general
and abstract aspects of the inquiry.

"We went first to England. Perhaps, if we had gone
first to Germany we might have managed to keep to the
'fundamentals,' and might even have done very well
with them under the benign and talkative Teutonic
influences. But England is the worst place in the
world to approach with a half-formed idea, and with
such words as 'psychological' and 'sociological.' For
this sort of thing the first-rate Englishman has too
much sense of humour, and the second-rate Englishman
too little imagination. Here the dual nature of the
inquiry ran us into constant difficulty. It seemed that
the simple and rugged British mind would have nothing
to do with an inquiry which demanded in the same
breath information on paid recreation-leaders and on
the racial characteristics responsible for the 'Anglo-
Saxon play spirit.' In England, body and soul of
public movements seem to be kept jealously separate.
If your interests apply to both, you had better make
separate inquiries. Concrete statistical inquiry was
inevitably well-received (and we had no plans for it!),
but when we set forth the 'fundamentals' of the inquiry,

the Britons either doubted our sanity or gave way to
uncontrollable amusement. It became apparent that
something would have to be done toward reconciling
the two aspects of the inquiry if we were ever to get
anywhere in England. Eventually we agreed upon an
elaborate statement of our intentions:—That we were
making an inquiry regarding recreational activities;
that we desired to know what this particular organisation or agency actually did; that we desired also, and
perhaps primarily, to know what motives were involved,
and what response was obtained. Naturally it was
much easier to get the first sort of information than
the second. Very often officials or workers of an organisation showed a very slight grasp of the underlying
motives of their activity, and generally, no conception
whatever of the actual or possible relation of their
particular 'movement' to any general 'leisure problem.'
So far as response was concerned, that is a matter
upon which very few workers in 'movements' are happy
to be candid. Where our beloved 'fundamentals' were
concerned, then, we met almost always with disap-
pointment and defeat. We hardly ever encountered
any signs of a realisation in any large bodies of public
opinion, of a problem of leisure occupation and its
various dangers and possibilities. Recreational provision in industry might be considered as indicating
such a realisation, but generally one got the impression
that it was much more the product of the traditional paternalistic-philanthropic attitude of the upper
classes.

"There is plenty of explanation of this lack in the
conditions of organisation and temperament of the
agencies actually at work in the recreational field.
There is the characteristic single-mindedness and

energy, with attendant lack of centralisation and co-
operation, and the overlapping of activities. The English boast of their 'individualism' even as the French
do, but they call it 'independence.' They tell you that
they are not easily swayed by movements and mob enthusiasms, yet they will on occasion combine in the
common interest and for a common purpose; they may
be said to be socially-minded without being gregarious.
(In some cases the brother's keeper type of consciousness of social responsibility seems to be actually over-
developed—our heritage in the States!) Officially,
outside the very intelligent and inclusive support of
adult education enterprises by the Board of Education, there exists a system of nominal Royal patronage
and occasional official aid to certain worthy individual
movements, but on the whole almost everything depends
on private initiative and backing. And it is not necessary to go abroad to learn the defects of this system.
Since a great part of the provision existing has a
definitely *philanthropic* origin, it is very apt to appear
superimposed, and thus to alienate or fail to attract
large portions of the population who could greatly
benefit by it. This perhaps accounts for the fact that
it was possible to spend two months in England, with
the utmost attentiveness, without ever being made
aware of *the people* as a force in the leisure problem.
And it was with *the people,* after all, that our 'fundamentals' were concerned. Most of our conclusions as
to the actual 'life of the people' had to be arrived at
by inference. Our prejudice against much of what we
called 'superimposed' or 'provided' recreation was confirmed by certain Britishers, brutally critical, who
pointed out the phlegmatic response of the people to
many provided activities, and who, furthermore, were

strongly disposed to object to any efforts to influence or direct the lives of their fellow-citizens for whatever purpose. We were temperamentally inclined to share this view. Nevertheless, we were not at any time able to discover anything among the English people—certainly nothing among the 'working classes' —which could indicate that English life without provided recreation was better or more satisfactory than that of America similarly unprovided. It was here then that we turned against the superstition of The Better Life of Europe—here, you might say, that we began to bite the hand that fed us.

"We proceeded to the Continent. Here, to our immense relief, we found that there was at least pretty general recognition of a 'leisure problem.' It was even considered reasonable that one should inquire in the same interview into both the technical and the psychological aspects of the problem. Here it seemed to us that we had suddenly come into contact with the principal—and troubled—currents of European society. The study became less bewildering but more than a little awe-inspiring.

"It is naturally in the countries where the eight-hour day has been adopted or approached in legislation that the widest public concern has arisen over the leisure problem. And therefore the American student will be perhaps a little startled to find that to a Continental 'the leisure problem' means primarily almost always the specific problem of *workers' leisure*. The formal studies of the use of leisure which are in existence on the Continent have been made from this standpoint. Leisure occupation is here recognised as a powerful instrument for proselytising to various social movements. Leisure is therefore provided for in some degree by various agencies—principally, those of politics and religion. Under these conditions the whole problem has infinitely wider implications. And the question of the people and the life of peoples becomes somewhat more tangible. Here, then, it seemed that we would be able to make some headway with our 'fundamentals.'

"France, our first Continental country, was the ideal place to test not only the fundamental questions, but the Superstition underlying them. One was acquainted with the universal legend of the French talent for living, French hedonism, French lightness of spirit, the traditional strength of the family, and so on. Surely, if any people could find satisfactory uses for their leisure without organisation and direction, it should be the French.

"We were told by everybody that organisation and direction were almost non-existent. Later discoveries, however, lead one to believe that there is perhaps more organised and directed recreation, or at least more formal recreational activity as we understand it, than most foreigners living in France or great numbers of the French themselves are aware of. The difficulties admitted by native investigators (both official and non-official) in getting any exact or statistical information of such movements are enough to show how little public knowledge there is of the subject. In the activities which come readily to the attention, the hard typical Continental divisions are evident: division of youth and sport movements between Catholics and Protestants, with duplicate institutions of the type of the 'patron-age' or community centre; provision by employers; and provision and movements of various political origins. Only, in France, the official type of provision is scarcely to be found.

"Still concentrating on the 'fundamentals,' we did not concern ourselves here to any extent with the leisure problem from the standpoint of organisation, methods, activities, and general statistics. We knew that however much of this sort of thing existed, it was indubitably less than in, for instance, England or Germany. Our intention was to observe the natural individualistic uses of leisure—or enjoyment of leisure —which we believed especially beautiful in France, expecting to find certain superiorities to set against the defects of the philanthropic or strongly paternalistic recreation systems. But for all our zeal and faith, there was no evidence whatever to be found that the life of the French *people* was any more satisfactory than the life of any other people. Why should it be, individual Frenchmen would inquire; how could it be— *under similar economic conditions?* Here all intelligent people to whom we talked emphasised immediately the economic interpretation of the leisure problem. Here, too, we were made always to take into account the tremendous effects of the war (and of the 'peace') on the ways of life of present-day Europe. The French tend to overdo this in talking to an American, but at this point it was an excellent influence upon our attitude. The evidence which we did find, in print and in conversation, indicated very clearly that there exists an acute need for much of the organised sort of provision where it is lacking.

"Our observations in England had made us sceptical of the superstition of The Better Life of Europe; the study in France forced us finally to discard it altogether. It remained only to accept the evidence that a good use of leisure is not a geographical matter, and to prepare a realistic and objective account of the *need* for formal provision, where its evidence existed; of its causes; of existing provision, and of the motives behind the provision.

"We crossed to Germany. En route we visited Belgium, where following the introduction of the eight-hour day, it had been considered necessary to organise for a proper use of the leisure time of the masses every native activity from pig raising to music. From France, Germany is, of course, the recreational extreme. . . . During the time spent in actual inquiry in Germany, and during subsequent visits to Denmark, Czecho-Slovakia, and Austria, more nearly definite plans for the final report began to take shape. By this time observation of national tendencies and systems had resulted in the acceptance of certain changes and new emphasis in our group of 'fundamentals.' These and the knowledge from which they grew soon began to crystallise into the skeleton of a more nearly final plan.

"In the summer, after examining in Geneva all the material on the leisure problem available in the library and among the publications of the International Labour Office, I faced the collected material and the necessity of actually preparing some sort of report. But the humility which had distinguished us when we set out toward Europe had increased in me in the course of the study. At the end, elaborate outlines appeared far too pretentious. They implied a report constructed as a criticism of Europe and a lesson to America. Obviously this, from me, would be an impertinence; the thing was a job for a philosopher, a social psychologist.

" . . . Now that the material is finally under construction, there are some things which ought to be kept

in mind, whether or not anything critical is to find
its way into the report. One is the primary importance
of the economic factor in considering the use of leisur
in any country. Recreational phenomena must be considered as products of economic levels and of the types
of national economy, and could be better understood
through study of social classes than of races and political units: *i.e.*,—the agricultural, the bourgeois, the
worker. The static economic class divisions of the
older civilisations are not always easily realised or
borne in mind by the lay American, and without understanding them it is impossible to understand thoroughly any contemporary popular phenomena of
Europe. Besides this, recent and more or less temporary conditions resulting from the war and the
peace must be taken into account as influencing all
current phenomena.

"And in comparing European and American conditions, it is necessary to remember that the one
eventual and adequate solution of the 'leisure problem'
is education. The importance of education is perhaps
more emphasised in this connection in Europe than in
America. The probable superiority of bourgeois tastes
in leisure occupation (voluntary) in Europe is to be
explained by superior education, in comparison with
the same class in America. Some of our deficiencies in
this regard might be mended by improving a school
system which most Europeans assure me is 'as bad as
it can possibly be,' but a great part of these deficiencies
are to be influenced only by that education which is the
result of environmental factors; for that we must wait
for some generations.

"In the matter of material facilities, observation in
Europe would seem to indicate that they should un-

questionably be supplied or supported by official means, to prevent their limitation to any particular classes or bodies of people; and their existence—playing-fields, public music and drama, adult education enterprises— should increase so far as humanly possible. But it is apparent that without education to enable intelligent individual selection and participation, all the provided facilities, direction and organisation in the world cannot satisfactorily fill the terrible emptiness which leisure must represent to the empty of mind."

The misgivings indicated in this letter we experienced frequently in the course of the study, as well as in the drafting of the report, where the chief difficulty was the selection of material from a trunk-full gathered in almost a dozen countries and in eight different languages. It finally became apparent that a report of the study would be of most value to Americans if an attempt were made to give a background, in the treatment of each country, of the special racial, social, economic or educational factors necessary to an understanding of the leisure problem in that country, and to go into detail as to activities only in such cases as indicated an approach differing from the American, or a phase of special interest. It was decided that the report should be subjective, in criticism of native attitudes toward the problem and the principal influencing factors, and objective in consideration of specific activities, quoting local opinion and documents wherever feasible or illuminating. A general consideration of the whole problem of leisure is followed by the specific reports on the countries visited. A brief article on recreation in America is added for the benefit of those who are not familiar with the developments there.

In a study of this kind nothing is more easy than generalisation,—and nothing more dangerous. And yet, to compress the material within reasonable limits, a certain amount of generalisation cannot very well be avoided. With this warning, the reader, it is hoped, will recognise a generalisation when one appears, and will make due allowances.

A word about translations: obviously many of the references and quotations in this report are from the originals in foreign languages. Free translations have been made; and in the case of names of organisations and titles of books the purpose has been to supply an equivalent easily understood, rather than to translate literally.

It would be altogether impossible adequately to express here our appreciation of the time and assistance so freely given us by a multitude of persons in America and the various countries visited. References in the text of the report to the names of persons interviewed or the books written by them will perhaps be some indication of the help rendered. To many, thanks were expressed in person. However, especial mention should be made of the invaluable assistance rendered by the Playground and Recreation Association of America, and more particularly, by Howard S. Braucher throughout the whole course of the study, by Roy Smith Wallace in reading and revising the manuscript and offering valuable suggestions, by J. W. Faust in the arrangement of contacts and interviews, and by Weaver W. Pangburn in the preparation of the article on the recreation situation in the United States. In Paris, a personal friend spent weeks in assisting in the selection of material, in shaping up the notes and helping to arrange the final report. Many organisations lent invaluable aid, but more especially the **Junior Red Cross** at various places in Europe in the matter of children's playgrounds, and the International Labour Office, both in Geneva and in its other European offices, in suggesting sources and furnishing material.

To the thanks given personally must be added the statement that without such help this report would have been valueless,—which it is our hope it may not prove to be—to those students of the problem who wish to continue where we have made a beginning.

HERBERT L. MAY.

PARIS, *October* 13, 1927.

PART I

THE LEISURE PROBLEM—GENERAL CONSIDERATIONS

PART I

THE LEISURE PROBLEM—GENERAL CONSIDERATIONS

SINCE this is a comparative study, we must reach an understanding of the words leisure and recreation which will apply to all countries. "Leisure" we shall use according to the definition of some students as the time surplus remaining after the practical necessities of life have been attended to. The word "recreation" as used in America has often the limited connotation of play, and etymologically has the suggestion of re-building from a subnormal condition; the equivalent of the word, when found in other languages, implies something different from the American sense. Since the place of this word is usually taken in other languages by the term "the use of leisure," and since in Europe adult education, cultural pursuits, and even political study and activity are considered a "recreational" use of leisure, we shall use the term "leisure time activities" as practically synonymous for our purpose with "recreation."

It may be useful to recall certain universal conditions of the question of leisure occupation. In general, the broad classifications of organised, and non-organised, may be applied to the current forms of leisure activity. Among the non-organised are to be considered, (a) the types followed in the home or garden; out-door life; wandering; traditional games, sports, etc., and (b) commercial recreation. Organised recreation may be divided into (a) the voluntary, such as is indulged in by clubs, and (b) the provided, such as is furnished, on the initiative of the few, by philanthropic bodies, industrial organisations, and governmental units. Intermediate are those cases where the State (or other agency) merely provides facilities which are used by voluntary organisations.

Comparison, point by point, of the various countries in matters of leisure activity is extremely difficult, since the use of leisure depends upon the general conditions of life in any given community or nation. In order thoroughly to understand the recreational scene, several important influencing factors must be kept in mind:

Social: First comes the time element; unless there is a time surplus there is no leisure. This inquiry leads us into the realm of working hours, whether fixed by legislation, agreement, or custom. Next, the physical element: an undernourished or overworked person is not fit for a proper use of leisure; and here we perceive the importance of social legislation. Further must be considered the effect of racial temperament and of climate on recreational tendencies and social customs—such as the strength of the family tie, and the gregariousness or individualism of a people. And it is even necessary to take the question of housing into account: obviously a "garden city" with the working-place close to the residence and facilities near by for outdoor activities, and with possibly a library, theatre, concert hall and community house provided, reduces the question of the use of leisure to its simplest terms.

Political: Certain political systems present characteristic recreational phenomena. In a country where a dictatorship exists, there are apt to be exhaustively organised superimposed recreation programmes, with little left to individual initiative. Under more individualistic systems where provision and organisation for leisure occupation are left largely to private initiative, there will usually be waste, overlapping of effort, and inadequacy to the public need. It must be remembered that where official agencies take an interest in providing facilities for the use of leisure a much higher uniformity and efficiency are attained, and the facilities are not restricted to class or confessional limitations. (The avoiding of these limitations is naturally of greater importance *at present* in Europe than in America, because of the intense class and religious antagonisms existing throughout the European countries.)

The above factors may be considered as "external." The principal "internal" factors influencing the individual's own conscious choice of the form of his leisure time activities are the economic, and the educational or cultural.

Economic: The trend of a country's recreation depends largely upon its economic standard—upon the average man's economic surplus, if any. The greater this surplus, the stronger is the tendency to buy one's pleasures. From this standpoint, the United States may figuratively be said to be in the automobile stage of recreation, and Europe in the bicycle stage.

Educational and cultural: Here we approach questions of the quality of leisure time activities. Whether or not leisure is put to a good use in the individual case depends largely upon the state of educational or cultural development which has been attained through study and environment. And by a good use of leisure we can here understand not only a use of leisure in which the individual avoids psychological and physical harm, but one in which—while satisfying himself— he incidentally "improves" himself: by enriching memory and imagination, or by developing physical strength and skill.

Clearly, the *problem* of the use of leisure arises when it becomes apparent that for one reason or another a people or a class tends not to put its leisure to good use. "Bad" use of leisure, so far as it is subject to observation, usually involves the more widespead and specious forms of commercial recreation.

Wherever there is elaborate development of commercial recreation it becomes evident that very few people who can afford to buy their leisure occupation will continue to be content with the simpler forms of unorganised recreation. Therefore it can be said that a problem of the use of leisure results immediately where there is well-developed commercial recreation. There is so much discussion of an American "recreation problem" in the United States at present that it is difficult to approach any study of European recreation without regard for the current American belief in a general European superiority in the use of leisure. However, the development in Europe of various movements seeking to introduce the Golden Age motif into recreation—such as the numerous "return to the soil" and "Youth" movements—are evidence enough that the passion for some of the vulgarities of commercial recreation is not peculiar to the United States alone. In attempting any comparison of America and Europe from this standpoint, it must be remembered that the elaborate commercial recreation-systems of the modern city (since they are the product of the present industrial system) are comparatively recent. In Europe, these influences have to contend with the forces of folk-habits and traditions of centuries-long pre-existence, and with environmental factors rich in historic associations. Since in the United States the commercial recreations have the field of public interest and habit practically clear for unlimited exploitation, it is not astonishing if American conduct during free time is sometimes less moderate and rational than that of Europe.

Whether one attempts to compare European leisure occupation with the American, or to compare with one another the countries of Europe, it must not be forgotten that similar classes will be found to have practically similar ways of life everywhere, and, in similar environments with similar facilities, different peoples will be found exercising fairly similar choices. There is, for example, the practical uniformity of modern bourgeois life, in contrast to the life of certain classes whose use of leisure depends upon their kind and place of work; the bourgeois uniformity, in its turn, being the result of economic standing assuring a fair amount of leisure, and of tastes formed by relatively higher education. The American estimate of the use of leisure in Europe is too often limited to observation of this bourgeois—or high-bourgeois—life; the comfortable burgher reading political articles and attending opera and the theatre with solemnity and a picnic lunch in Central Europe; retiring to the country to fish and keep a garden in France; walled into a suburban tennis-courted place in England. But only a part of the life of Europe is here; for a comprehensive picture of the use of leisure it is necessary to look at all classes. It is significant that one of the chief arguments of those opposed to the shortening of working time, in Europe as in America, has been that the people do not know what to do with their free time and tend generally to put it to unfortunate uses; and the reports of native students contain plenty of evidence to bear out this claim.

We come, then, to the question of the "working classes," and of the extent to which leisure actually exists, which is the question of working time. From an ideal standpoint, these large groups of the population merit special consideration in matters concerned with leisure and its uses. Under the present industrial system processes have been developed which deprive the worker of any possibility of finding a pleasurable interest in his work, or of exercising imagination or the creative faculty. In such conditions it is only in so far as he has leisure that the average human being can find any opportunity for reflection, self-expression, and the development and satisfaction of pleasurable interests and tastes—in short, for life itself. Much writing and talk both in Europe and in America indicate a purely altruistic attitude toward the "leisure problem"—an attitude which associates its existence entirely with the non-human monotonies of modern industrial processes, without taking into consideration the antiquity of the problem; for all but a little part of the labour necessary to the maintenance of existence and of the mechanisms of civilised societies has always been colourless and difficult and stultifying. The importance of the industrial system in the problem of leisure is not in the nature of its processes, but in its power to encroach upon necessary and desirable leisure. Therefore it will be found that the extraordinary amount of attention accorded the question of workers' leisure in Europe has a very practical basis, which is its connection to national and international effort to limit and decrease working time.

Where the working day is of some ten hours' duration and where transportation difficulties must often be taken into account, the actual free time, the "time to do as he pleases" of the worker is too limited to give rise to any significant problem of its use. It will perhaps be of some value to review something of the development of the working time problem in Europe. Before the war the shortening of working time was a fundamental of the trade union programmes in the principal industrial countries. During the war it became necessary to release the working time in many industries from all normal limitation. As interior political situations became progressively difficult in certain of the countries involved, various promises and assurances were given to labour that working time would be shortened or legally limited when hostilities should end. In 1918 Russia introduced legal restriction of working time, and, in the face of spreading Communist propaganda, shortly after the end of the war France, Germany, Austria, Italy, Belgium, Switzerland —practically all European countries except England— had found it expedient to take steps toward introducing legal restriction of working time on the basis of the eight-hour day or the forty-eight-hour week. Then came the creation of the International Labour Organisation, "moved by sentiments of justice and humanity as well as by the desire to secure the permanent peace of the world." It is not necessary here to discuss the obvious economic and political reasons underlying the beauty of this statement.

The first Labour Conference accepted a Convention limiting the hours of work in industrial undertakings to eight in the day and forty-eight in the week. According to the Convention, each member ratifying agreed to bring its provisions into operation not later than July first, 1921. These States ratified unconditionally: Czecho-Slovakia, Belgium, Bulgaria, Chile, Greece, India, and Rumania. These States ratified on condition that the big European industrial powers would ratify simultaneously and carry out the provisions: Austria, France, Italy, and Lithuania. England and Germany showed no signs of ratifying.

The conditional ratifications have of course no practical value, and at the Labour Conference of this year (1927), the commission charged to examine the reports of the governments to the International Labour Organisation concerning the actual application of the provisions of the Convention, stated that the seven countries which ratified unconditionally do not in fact apply the provisions of the Convention. So much, then, for the practical accomplishment of the Labour Organisation in this field. When it was advisable for interior political reasons to make some formal restrictions of working time, the various countries took such steps. When the pressure of these demands relaxed, and economic pressures came into ascendancy, the restrictions were discarded or trespassed.

Nevertheless, the moral values involved here are of the utmost importance. Not only has the work of the Labour Conference made it practically impossible for any country to increase its working time appreciably or to remain indifferent to the general movement for restriction, but it has resulted in the first international recognition of the question of the use of this leisure which it desires to increase and to maintain. Throughout Europe the Recommendation of the Labour Conference (1924) on the Development of Facilities for the Use of Workers' Leisure, and its questionnaire to the governments, have created a body of public interest and attention to the leisure problem in general in fields where its importance might not otherwise have been recognised, and have forced official attention to be formally directed upon the question of provision of facilities. Thus, in Europe, the problem of leisure has been brought into public and official consciousness, and it is obvious that from the resulting increase in interest and enlightenment of public opinion in general, and from the possibilties of practical result through stimulation of official interest in the provision of facilities, great future advantages in the use of leisure may be expected, not for the "workers" only, but for all classes of the populations.

THE INTERNATIONAL LABOUR OFFICE AND WORKERS' SPARE TIME

At the International Labour Conference of 1924, held in Geneva, the following draft recommendation concerning the utilisation of workers' spare time was adopted:

"Whereas in adopting at its First Session, held at Washington, a Convention on the subject of the eight-hour day and the forty-eight-hour week, the General Conference of the International Labour Organisation had as one of its principal aims to secure for workers, beyond the necessary hours for sleep, an adequate period during which such workers could 'do as they please,' or, in other words, an adequate period of 'spare time';

"And whereas during such spare time workers have the opportunity of developing freely, according to their individual taste, their physical, intellectual and moral powers, and such development is of great value from the point of view of the progress of civilisation;

"And whereas a well directed use of this spare time, by affording to the worker the means for pursuing more varied interests and by securing relaxation from the strain placed upon him by his ordinary work, may increase the productive capacity of the worker and increase his output, and may thus help to obtain a maximum of efficiency from the eight-hour day;

"And whereas, while giving full weight to the customs prevalent in the different countries and to local circumstances, it may nevertheless be useful to lay down the principles and methods which at the present time seem generally best adapted to secure the best use of periods of spare time, and it may also be instructive to make known for the benefit of all countries what has been done in this direction in other countries;

"And whereas the value of this information is particularly great at the moment when the ratification of the Convention on hours of work is being considered by the States Members of the Organisation;

"Now the General Conference hereby recommends that each Member of the Organisation should take into consideration the principles hereinafter mentioned:

"1. Preservation of Spare Time.

"Whereas it is agreed that if the States Members, in cases in which limitations have been placed on hours of work by means of legal measures, collective agreements or otherwise, wish to secure, both for wage-earners and for the community, all the benefits which may be expected from such measures, such Members must take steps to ensure that the workers shall have the undiminished enjoyment of the hours of spare time so secured to them as aforesaid;

"And whereas it is important that, on the one hand the workers should fully appreciate the value of the periods of spare time which have been secured to them and should do their utmost, in all circumstances, to keep and use this period as a period of spare time, and on the other hand, that employers should always aim at establishing wages corresponding sufficiently with the needs of the workers so as to make it unnecessary for them to have recourse during their periods of spare time to additional hours of paid work;

"Whilst recognising that legal prohibition against the continuance of paid work in their own occupation for the same or another employer in excess of the legal working day is difficult to enforce, and may even at times seem to infringe the workers' right of using their periods of spare time as they choose, the Conference nevertheless considers that it may be of some advantage to draw attention to the steps which have been taken in this direction in a number of countries;

"The Conference recommends that Governments should encourage and facilitate the conclusion of collective agreements which would ensure a normal standard of living to workers in exchange for the legal hours of work and which would determine, by voluntary agreement between employers and workers, the measures to be taken to prevent workers from having recourse to additional paid work.

"And whereas it is agreed that every facility should be given to the workers to enable them to make the best use of their periods of spare time so secured to them as aforesaid, the Conference recommends:

"(a) That each Member, whilst having due regard to the requirements of different industries, local customs, and the varying capacities and habits of the different kinds of workers, should consider the means of so arranging the working day as to make the periods of spare time as continuous as possible;

"(b) That by means of a well conceived transport system and by affording special facilities in regard to fares and time tables, workers should be enabled to reduce to the minimum the time spent in travelling between their homes and their work, and that employers' and workers' organisations should be extensively consulted by public transport authorities or private transport undertakings as to the best means of devising such a system.

"2. Spare Time and Social Hygiene.

"And whereas the utilisation of the workers' periods of spare time cannot be separated from the general measures adopted by the community for promoting the health and welfare of all classes of society, and without attempting to examine in detail each of the great welfare problems, the solution of which would contribute to improving the workers' status, the Conference recommends to the Members:

"(a) The encouragement of individual hygiene by the provision of public baths, swimming pools, etc.;

"(b) Legislative or private action against the misuse of alcohol, against tuberculosis, venereal disease and gambling.

"3. Housing Policy.

"Whereas it is of advantage to the workers and to the whole community to encourage everything tending to the harmonious development of the workers' family life;

"And whereas the most effective means of protecting the workers from the aforesaid dangers is to place within their reach a proper home;

"The Conference recommends the increase in number, if necessary in co-operation with the national or local authorities concerned, of healthy dwellings at low rentals in garden cities or urban communities under proper conditions of health and comfort.

"4. Institutions for the Utilisation of Spare Time.

"Without attempting to differentiate between the innumerable institutions which are able to afford to the workers opportunities of making free use of their activities according to their own personal tastes, the development of which is dependent on the manners and customs of each country or district, the Conference nevertheless draws the attention of the Members to the necessity of avoiding misplaced activities which may be caused by the establishment of institutions not called for by some well-defined need. The Conference desires to emphasise the importance of taking into account, in the establishment and development of these institutions, the desires, the tastes and the special requirements of the workers for whose use they are designed;

"At the same time, among the institutions which may both assist full and harmonious development of the individual and of the family and contribute to the general progress of the community, the Conference thinks it right to recommend those schemes which have for their object:

"(a) the improvement of the workers' domestic economy and family life (workers' gardens, allotments, poultry keeping, etc.), which combine the benefits of recreation with the feeling that some addition, however slight, is being made to the family resources;

"(b) the development of the physical health and strength of the workers by means of games and sports which enable young workers who are working under the highly specialised conditions prevalent in modern industry to give free play to their energies in a manner which encourages initiative and the spirit of emulation;

"(c) the extension of technical, domestic and general education (libraries, reading-rooms, lectures, technical courses, educational courses, etc.), which meets one of the workers' most keenly felt needs and affords the best means of progress to industrial communities;

"The Conference therefore recommends that Members should encourage these forms of activity by the grant of subventions to organisations concerned with the moral, intellectual and physical development of the workers.

"5. Freedom of Institutions and Co-ordination of Local Action.

"1. Whereas for many years past the workers in the great industrial countries have always sought to ensure that they may live their lives outside the factory or workshop in complete freedom and independence and they particularly resent any outside interference in their private affairs; and whereas this feeling is so strong as to provoke opposition to any attempts to deal either nationally or internationally with the question of the use of spare time for fear that it may possibly restrain their liberty;

"Whereas the Conference, while expressing appreciation of the motives which have led to the creation of institutions for the encouragement of the wise use of the spare time of the workers, suggests that Members should draw the attention of the promoters of such institutions to the

necessity of safeguarding the individual freedom of the
workers against any system or scheme which has for its
object any tendency towards compelling the workers directly or indirectly to use any particular institution:

"Whereas the most practicable and successful institutions are those which have been started and developed by
the workers themselves, the Conference, while recognising
that in many cases where public authorities or employers
lend financial or other assistance for the encouragement
of workers' allotments, games or educational institutions,
they consequently have a legitimate claim to take part in
their management;

"Recommends that every care should be taken to avoid
any encroachment on the liberty of those for whose use
such institutions are intended.

"2. While not contemplating any systematic organisation
of spare time occupations, but having in mind a number of successful efforts made to assist them, the Conference further recommends that each Member should consider the possibility of promoting the formation of district
or local committees, composed of representatives of the
public authorities, of employers' and workers' organisations, and of co-operative associations, for co-ordinating
and harmonising the activities of the various institutions
providing means of recreation.

"3. The Conference further recommends to the Members that an active and effective propaganda should be
undertaken in each country for the purpose of influencing
public opinion as to the necessity of the proper use of the
spare time of the workers.

"DRAFT RESOLUTION"

"The Conference invites the International Labour Office,
keeping in constant touch with the various Governments,
to collect and keep up to date information concerning
the use of spare time, and on the basis of the information communicated by the Members, or obtained from

other sources, to publish regularly studies of the action
taken and the results obtained in the different countries
in the application of measures which have for their object
the proper use of the workers' spare time."

During the years that the International Labour
Office has been functioning, it has gathered much interesting material on the recreational activities of working men in various countries. It may also be interesting to refer to the Director's Report of 1927:

"Close attention continues to be given to the question of
the utilisation of workers' spare time by all those who
realise the effects which the shortening of the working
day may have for civilisation generally. . . . The big
movement in favour of providing facilities for the utilisation of workers' spare time expanded considerably during
1926. Workers' educational centres are on the increase.
Every day sees the birth of new associations endeavouring
to provide the workers with the means of educating themselves and with recreation—libraries, lectures, theatres,
concerts, etc. More and more workers are finding in the
arts the means of utilising their spare time, and the successful district exhibitions held at Lyons and Lausanne
are being followed by Montpelier, which is going to organise an international exhibition of workers' art. Further, fresh impetus has been given to workers' sports
organisations. The different sports federations, there is
no need to recall, reckon on giving great importance to the
workers' Olympic Games which are to be held this summer
at Prague. On all sides the Office is being asked what the
International Labour Organisation can do to develop
sports, which are so beneficial for the health of the people
and the workers. Within the means at its disposal the
Office proposes to consult the organisations concerned
which could best suggest what it can do in this direction.

"Two relatively new factors, it would seem, are bound
to be of the utmost importance in the future in the utilisation of workers' spare time—wireless telephony and the

cinema. The short investigation which it undertook in connection with the International Cinema Congress held in September, 1926, at Paris has shown the Office how powerful an instrument for the education of the workers the cinema might be in the future. The cinema already renders invaluable services. Numbers of different bodies, workers' associations, and educational organisations possess a cinematograph apparatus. In some places endeavours are made to train voluntary operators from among the workers. In other places film libraries are being created and endeavours are being made to produce films. Undoubtedly there are considerable difficulties in the way, the chief one being perhaps the lack of good educative films, but it seems that these difficulties could be overcome by a certain amount of collaboration and organisation, and that big results can be expected from this admirable means of education. The Paris Congress was well aware of the possibilities and expressed the wish that the Office should continue its investigations on as broad a basis as the subject demands.

"Wireless telephony, which is a more recent development, is also full of promise for the future. It already occupies an important place in certain workers' centres. It has clearly not yet entered on its organisation stage, but as soon as it reaches that stage there is no doubt but that, as was suggested in last year's Report, it will effect a veritable revolution in the utilisation of workers' spare time.

"Increased interest is being taken by the Governments in the question of providing facilities for the utilisation of spare time. Unfortunately a number of Governments seem more disposed to wait for private initiative to lead the way than to stimulate private initiative where it is still wanting. Belgium and Italy are still the only countries which have applied one of the important suggestions contained in the Recommendation, viz., that district or local bodies should be created for encouraging action already being taken, to promote fresh action, and to co-ordinate the activities of the various institutions which aim at promoting healthy utilisation of the worker's spare time. The three provincial committees in Belgium have continued their activities in this direction, and the Italian national institution, Dopolavoro, will soon be at the end of its second year's work. It has developed its work in different directions—sport, education, theatres, cinemas—and will now draw a considerable income from the compulsory contributions imposed on the union funds by the administrative rules issued under the Trade Union Act and approved by a Royal Decree of July 1st, 1926.

"The Office continues to keep up to date with the action taken in the different countries. It will prepare reports which it has in mind on certain special aspects of the problem, such as the cinema, wireless telephony and sport. When these reports are finished it hopes to be able, with the help of the information which the different Governments may communicate in pursuance of the 1924 Recommendation, to publish at an early date a general review of the whole question, which, it need hardly be repeated, cannot be lost sight of without diminishing the value of the good effects which are legitimately expected of a reduction in the length of the working day. Action by the Office for the purpose of co-ordinating activities and spreading information can hardly be more beneficial than on the present subject."

NOTES ON CHILDREN'S PLAYGROUNDS

The reader of the detailed study of the various countries visited will note that but little is said of playgrounds for young children. It might suffice to say that America has nothing to learn from Europe in this matter, but an attempt may not be amiss at explanation of the tardiness of a recognition in Europe of the problem of young children's recreation. A writer in a recent issue of a Paris paper says: "One hears a great deal, since the eight-hour law came into effect, of workers' leisure. When will one begin to consider the question of school children's leisure?"

Let us generalise, remembering that we speak now of children between the ages of, say five and twelve, so as to exclude those that may be considered as coming within "youth movements." To begin with, comparing the American with the European child, the former has had and has a time surplus for leisure: his school hours are shorter, his home study less fatiguing; the economic condition of his family is less likely to require his labour. Again, industrialism in America went forward wth leaps and bounds at about the same time that the vacant lot in the heart of the city was built upon and the automobile made the street an unsafe place to play; and this was before the day of town planning. All this antedated the shorter day for workers, and social-minded America saw the leisure problem as one primarily of children, and the philanthropically inclined aligned themselves behind the playground movement. In Europe, generally speaking, not only were these factors largely absent, but there were social considerations to complicate the problem. In England, for example, sport was an "upper class" tradition, largely manifesting itself among the children of "pay schools"; in Latin countries, social tradition held the children more in the family group and the antigregarious tendency was not confined to adults. But most important of all, in Europe, the leisure problem as such, when recognised at all, came to the fore on a large scale only with the advent of the shorter working day at the close of the war, and the need for adult recreation absorbed the time, the money and the political activities of the "recreationists" at the expense of the child. This statement must be qualified by tak-

ing into account the influence of the "youth movement," particularly in Central Europe, upon recreation for adolescents; and further by a recognition of
the effect of town planning on comparatively new cities
like Berlin, where "open spaces" in the streets and in
interior courts in the newer sections of the city obvi-
ated to some extent the necessity for "playgrounds"
as that word is used in America.

Certain universal conditions must be remembered.
All old towns, large or small, naturally afford no free
or playing space for large numbers of the population,
and very often far from the requisite degree of light
and air for health. In this respect, in small ancient
towns and in the "old city" sections of the great cities,
conditions are very often deplorable. It is obvious
that the "quaint" and charming buildings adored of the
tourist can outdo the modern slum tenement in mis-
erable social conditions. Play space where it is most
needed could therefore only be provided by razing of
existing buildings. In all European countries there is
now effort in some degree to supply the need; playgrounds are being or have been provided, but because
of the economic difficulties, it frequently occurs that
playgrounds are constructed in districts where the need
of them is relatively slight. Problems of open space
also exist in the country; land-owners and farmers object to children's play on their properties. In England the Women's Institute movement established the
first rural playground. It would be interesting to
make a precise comparative study of public playground
facilities. From casual impressions one might say
that the countries in order of their provision of space
in proportion to population are probably: Germany,
Austria, England, Belgium, France and Italy. This
applies entirely to space officially provided. Some

post-war building developments in France and Italy include provision for children's (and adults') play; this is, however, usually in the case of special developments of "workers' garden cities," etc., and is usually due to private industrial initiative. In Vienna there are playground-courts in the large tenements that were built by the City to supply the housing shortage after the war; one of these tenements visited contained as well an indoor playroom large enough for games, for use in bad weather. Socialistic states or municipalities naturally adopt most readily methods of appropriation, condemnation, etc., in order to acquire space where it is needed. Under more conservative régimes improvement is generally the result of effort on the part of private philanthropic organisations and sport clubs, gifts of interested citizens, and intelligence on the part of employers, architects, and builders; which is to say, of a gradually more informed public opinion.

Where playgrounds exist, they are either to be found in connection with the schools, sometimes operated only during school holiday season, as in London through the Holiday Play Centre movement; or as detached grounds which may be visited by the children only in classes under the care of a teacher, as in Vienna. In such cases the visits to the playground constitute a part of the school work in physical training, and if the children have daily periods of physical training, these visits will occur two or three times a week, alternating with the indoor gymnastic training. There are also to be found municipal playgrounds open to all children, with or without supervision. It is rarely that such playgrounds have trained supervisors in the American manner. Very often teachers retired from teaching service are in charge; in such cases there can obviously be no efficient athletic leader-

ship. One may note here that there is a critical attitude in Europe toward the American type of playground operation with what they speak of as "its
constant directed activity": it is thought that the
children have their natural restlessness increased, and
run the danger of losing capacity and taste for quiet
or mental enjoyments.

The use of public parks, gardens, squares, and forests for children's play must be taken into consideration. Very often playground facilities exist in parks—
fields for games, apparatus, sand piles, and so on.
Many of the public squares of Berlin contain special
areas for the play of small children. The great public
forests are interesting also in this connection—as for
instance the "Bois" in Paris and the "Grunewald" in
Berlin. These are accessible to small children living
in distant points of the city only in so far as they
may be taken there in classes, in various group excursions, or in family outings, but a visit to any
European public forest in fine weather convinces one
that the citizens appreciate these lovely areas and
are willing to make some effort to avail themselves of
them. The presence of restaurants is probably a facili-
tating factor; whole families can spend a Sunday or
a holiday in the forests without troubling with the
question of the mid-day meal, which they would otherwise have to carry with them at the expense of some
trouble of preparation, or for which they would have
to return home, breaking the day's relaxation. This
does not mean that picnic-lunching does not exist.
In these forests small children may be seen playing
simple games, wandering, exploring, or—miraculous!—
simply being quiet.

The Berlin schools have grounds, but without the
play equipment in the American manner. There is a

holiday movement in Germany; children are taken by special workers for excursions, bathing, etc., during the school holidays. These special workers are employed by the Welfare Bureau of the community; children are sent in large groups under their care to the forests and bathing-places—this is a one-day version of the Vacation-home idea. The service is availed of by both the workers and the middle class.

In Austria, as in Germany, there are municipally-owned playgrounds, open to all, and subsidised grounds allotted to certain organisations. The Vienna playgrounds, aside from those in the possession of athletic clubs, are distributed by hours to the schools and associations by the Vienna Jugendhilfwerk. There are fourteen playgrounds throughout the different districts. The play hours allotted to the Deutsch-Oesterreichischer Jugendbund (German-Austrian Youth Federation) are divided among the affiliated groups at a special meeting of the leaders. These hours occur during the afternoons and evenings. (It is stated that "socialistic organisations which are in close relation to the present community-council get most of the play hours for their children.") There are few playgrounds for pupils of higher schools. A large playground was given by Duke Schwarzenberg to the Union of Catholic German Youth in the Lacypark in Neuwaldegg. In 1924 the German-Austrian Youth Federation applied to the government for the construction of a large playground, and was assured that the project would be carried out. The site of the proposed playground was to be in the Prater (the large public park). However, since it is also to be used for the schools, discussions have been in progress between the Ministry of Commerce which owns the ground, the Ministry of Social Welfare, and the Min-

istry of Education, and the conclusion of these negotiations is not yet in sight at the date of this report
(1927).

In France children's playgrounds such as are known
in America are practically non-existent.

It may be interesting to note that the League
of Nations has an Advisory Commission for the protection and welfare of children and young people, with
a special Child Welfare Committee. A glance at the
proceedings of the last session of this committee, held
at Geneva, May 11, 1927, indicates that it is making
a study of various phases of children's recreation. We
quote below one of the resolutions of that committee
at its last session:

"The Child Welfare Committee considers that it is
not necessary, at any rate for the present, to send
a questionnaire to the Governments on the question of
the mental and physical recreation of children.

"It decides to retain on its programme this question,
the importance of which it fully appreciates.

"The Committee appoints Dame Katharine Furse,
Dr. Matz and Dr. Humbert to act as Rapporteurs.
Their report, which will be examined at the next session, should mention the methods adopted in different
countries and the results already obtained. The Committee would be grateful to the International Labour
Office if the latter would communicate to the Secretariat any information it may possess regarding the
utilisation of workers' spare time in its relation to
child welfare."

PART II

SOME PHASES OF RECREATION IN FRANCE, GERMANY AND ENGLAND

PART II

SOME PHASES OF RECREATION IN FRANCE, GERMANY AND ENGLAND

In the Foreword is indicated in general the order in which the various countries were visited. Rather detailed studies were made in England, France and Germany, and much briefer ones in other countries. For the purpose of this report it seems best to ignore the chronological order and to treat, first, France, next Germany, then England; and to follow with notes on the other countries visited. Let it be remembered that no attempt at an exhaustive survey was made; those phases only were chosen which, it was believed, would be of special interest to the American student.

Where no special mention is made of playgrounds (other than the foregoing notes on children's playgrounds in Part I), or of Boy Scouts, Girl Guides, Y.M.C.A. work, etc., it may be assumed that it was considered that these activities, if existing at all, presented no specially interesting phenomena or developments differing from well known types.

FRANCE

GENERAL OBSERVATIONS

In France there is a notable indifference to recreation as a problem, and a conspicuous lack of widespread recreational and leisure provision, either ofcial or voluntary. As an instance of the official attitude it may be cited that the government, in response to the inquiries of the International Labour Office as to its policy in this matter, indicated that it considers provision for the leisure of its citizens to be no affair of the State. The explanation of this official and voluntary lack of provision for leisure must be sought in "the French temperament."

Individualism is a most marked characteristic of the Latin peoples, and the French in particular cultivate and pride themselves upon this quality. It is the French belief that the finest national culture is to be attained by the free development of the individual according to his own inclinations and talents. In social relationships, the Frenchman has all of the Englishman's independence, and little of the Englishman's gregarious instinct. The club-life of the Anglo-Saxon has no counterpart in France,* but its place is taken to some extent by the more elastic and informal social intercourse of the café.

The Frenchman's feeling of social responsibility does not in general extend beyond his immediate family. The family is the important social unit and its position is confirmed by law and custom. There are regular family gatherings. The common circumstance of all members of a family being engaged in a small business, or of husband and wife operating together a small trade or a shop, makes for family solidarity in a social stratum where it is elsewhere most often wanting. In these instances, family solidarity sometimes results in an extreme narrowness of the range of interests of the individual, and contributes to the French habit of mind which, in self-criticism, they term "parochial."

* It has been said in France that "a Frenchman is always happy to participate in any organisation of which he can be president."

An excellent indication of the moderation and sanity of the French sense of values is to be found in the French adage, "work a little, play a little, save a little." The Frenchman is apt not to suffer from a too strong differentiation between work and play hours: since in France industrial specialisation has not progressed as far as in England and America, he is very often an artisan or small proprietor who finds pleasurable interest in his work. In the matter of "saving a little," the ambition of the Frenchman is to retire, regardless of the fact that he may still be relatively young, as soon as he has achieved an adequate competence, and to devote his mature years to the more reflective types of recreation, and to the cultivation of a small place in the country. It must be remembered that the French concept of "play" differs in some respects from the Anglo-Saxon, as for instance in its greater emphasis upon the pleasures of the senses.

The café habit is an essential factor in French masculine life. As to its recreational value, opinions vary even among French students of the question. Some see in the café, at least so far as the working-man is concerned, a more or less deplorable result of unfortunate home conditions, and a symptom of poverty of the inner life of the people; while others maintain that it is at the café, where he meets with the stumulus and response of appreciative companionship, that the Frenchman is happy and at his best. The latter observers consider the café not only commendable but actually indispensable, since it furnishes an opportunity for the enjoyment of those conversational and social amenities which represent to the Frenchman some of the most desirable forms of recreation.

The investigator in France hears frequently, from persons with intimate knowledge of French conditions,

the statement that "there is no youth in France."
The French middle-class girl, for instance, has but
one ambition—to be "Madame"; for girls, marriage
is looked upon as the necessary economic and social
solution of their lives; in general, therefore, French
girls are given no opportunity to be "young people";
the freedom granted to American girls is unknown to
them, especially as regards their relationships with
the opposite sex. The tendency is to keep the French
girl a child until a relatively late age and then, almost overnight, require her to adopt the manners, the
interests, the dress, that go with being a woman.
With the boys it is the same, except that, in general,
the sudden change of interests comes earlier: at thirteen or fourteen the French boy suddenly becomes
a small adult; without having passed through any
transitional period, he is encouraged, by parents and by
social opinion, to take on all the habits of a grown
man. A large part of the explanation of the lack of
young people's recreation in France is to be found
in the fact of their sudden emergence, at about the
time of adolescence, into adulthood. Besides, it must
be remembered that in France the education of the
young is a singularly intensive and exhausting process
which, as many French observers are coming to believe,
probably tires and ages the children unduly; this fact
also doubtless contributes to the indifference of French
young people to almost all the livelier forms of recreation. It is only since the war that there has been
physical training in the elementary schools; and this
training is a matter of gymnastics rather than of
games.

It is perhaps salutary for the American investigator
to face the fact that what has here been said about
the French raises a pertinent question; namely, whether

American ideas about recreation and the use of leisure are the last word on the matter, when another important people has been able to achieve, not only a great civilisation, but a great culture as well, by a way of thinking and living that is rooted in assumptions which are, especially in the matter of recreation and leisure, diametrically opposite to those of the majority of American workers in that field.

It would, however, be misleading to give the impression that because the French in general, and most Frenchmen in particular, are indifferent to the recreation-and-leisure problem, there are no specific instances of social analysis grounded in the belief that there is need of leisure-time provision in France. There have indeed been some brilliant treatises on this matter by French writers. To the investigator these treatises are of interest because of the insight with which they approach the various aspects of their problem; but one must beware of regarding them as an indication in France of a growing "awareness of the leisure-problem" in the sense in which that term is used by Americans; these treatises are rather, in most instances,—and the statement is made without any implication of disparagement—a manifestation of the French love of rhetoric; they tend, in matters of social welfare and the related problems of leisure and recreation, more to academic essays than to practical altruism. This tendency does not of course invalidate the theories, findings, and contentions of the treatises; and the fact that it does not is sufficient justification for our mentioning several of the more important of them now, and later quoting from one or another whenever the quotations throw light on the particular matter being considered. Several of these treatises are: "La Corvée de Joie" (The Drudgery of Joy), by Paul

Rives, published by Les Presses Universitaires de France, 1924; "La Durée du Travail et L'Utilisation des Loisirs" (Working Time and the Use of Leisure), by Gaston Bouthol, Librairie Girard, 1924; a Bulletin of the Ministry of Labour on the use of leisure created by the eight-hour law, 1923, and another published in 1924; and "Enquête sur les Loisirs de L'Ouvrier Français" (Inquiry into the Leisure of the French Worker), a thesis by Jean Beaudemoulin for his doctorate degree. Each of these writers approaches his subject with a lucid perception that, "As the working day diminishes, the question of utilising leisure becomes more urgent."

In 1919 France legally adopted the eight-hour day. Nevertheless it is to be remembered that an eight-hour law proves nothing as to the number of hours actually worked. One must also keep in mind the workers' frequent desire, here as elsewhere, to increase their earnings by doing additional work in the extra hours. Neither can the technical number of hours in the working day be too readily accepted as an indication of the amount of useable leisure; the arrangement of the working day is here the determining factor. In many occupations, in France, as elsewhere on the Continent, the custom of the lengthy noon interval makes the whole problem of leisure different from that of the United States, besides having unquestionable bearing upon the whole mood of the workers concerned (by making them leisurely, although restricting possibilities of the *use* of leisure). It has also a certain influence upon home and family life.

In France there are fewer and less stringent child-labour regulations than in America, and such regulations as there are are not so generally obeyed and enforced as are the American child-labour laws.

Industrial Welfare.—In our survey of England the term Industrial Welfare will be used in a more specific sense than in the case of France. In England the many voluntary associations considered as a part of Adult Education include several organisations having to do with workers—the Workers' Educational Association, and the like; these are therefore considered under the heading of Adult Education. But in France, where there is no formulated Adult Education Movement, bodies analogous to the various workers' associations in England will be regarded as a part of Industrial Welfare, as will also a considerable amount of interesting French theory in regard to workers' leisure, whether or not that theory has ever been put into practice.

Some Theories and Conclusions of "La Corvée de Joie" (The Drudgery of Joy).—Before discussing the specific organisations described by him and others, let us consider a few of the theories and conclusions of Paul Rives in "La Corvée de Joie." At the outset he writes: "The worker must be detached from the material with which he is assimilated during his daily work; the whole question of social satisfaction lies there and nowhere else. Increase salaries? That amounts to giving a politeness of dress, not of manners; without the second the first is only a mask; it makes ridiculous without hiding anything. . . . The workers must therefore have leisure in which to improve themselves and acquire other interests apart from their daily toil." Later he develops the thought more fully: "What is the use of cleaning oneself up to lead the same kind of life as when one was dirty? The worker, freed from the material marks of toil, should not only penetrate into an abode healthy and bright, if not elegant, but also into a circle of collective life where the conversation exacts, without too much effort, a certain amount of care; that is at bottom what he goes and looks for at a cabaret, for lack of any other institution, or else at the house of ill-fame because the women there wear silk stockings and false jewels which create a certain illusion. Where will the worker find the same eager welcome, which will be moreover distinterested, honestly enticing, in order to lead him to the joys of refinement and not of debauch? The eight-hour law necessitates a law on the organisation of leisure." A few pages later he adds: "We shall see if sanctuaries of collective joy exist; and where; if they succeed, why they do or why they do not. Again, it is essential that they should be everywhere, that the worker should know where they are, know that he will find joy there and above all that he should learn to love what he finds there. The habit of disorder outlives all will to improve. Habits are fixed thus; after work there is the repose of sleep and eating; suppose a couple of unexpected hours of freedom intervene; they will be spent in sleep or feasting so long as the taste for utilising them in some other way has not been created. To create institutions is only half the need; to teach the use of them is the essential thing. 'What do I do when I am not at the factory or the estaminet? Well, I sleep— And when I don't sleep? . . . Then. . . . Say, wife, what do I do when I haven't anything to do?' Thus spoke a worker of thirty, with an assured salary. A whole education is needed of which the eight-hour law has just revealed the urgency. . . . The worker having no idea of how to utilise his leisure merely welcomes the eight-hour day because of the opportunity given for overtime work.

He frequently undertakes a second job as a sideline—even policemen have been known to employ their off hours as shop assistants."

The above statement might be misleading if left un-amplified. Mr. Rives elsewhere calls attention to the still-prevailing French trades-heredity, under which the ambition of each generation seems to be not to rise out of the paternal trade, but to improve, *within* it, general living conditions, personal well-being, oppor-tunities for education, etc. To fulfil this modest am-bition, however, salaries are nearly always inadequate; thence, overtime work and, often, a return to the old-time long working-day, leisure forfeited.

"By those whom it serves, the workers, the eight-hour law is only defended because it is possible to turn it from its true purpose; party spirit alone appears to keep for it its name as a banner in the social struggle, an employed symbol of a sincere reality; and that is just the danger. By those whom it harms or hinders, at least temporarily, the employers, the eight-hour law is sneered at, opposed systematically and assaulted; the employers prepare lists of figures and examples against it; works have already appeared which at-tempt to show its dangers; skirmishes before the final and more or less direct assault. Therefore why worry to organise what a probably ephemeral law has just created? Here fear paralyses initiative; there hope prolongs inaction. It is this situation of waiting, this preparation for battle around the eight-hour law which any enquiry into the utilisation of the workers' leisure would have to describe. However, here and there cer-tain tendencies are observable, for after all the law continues to exist; that therefore is what we must seize hold upon at the risk of slightly simplifying the design in order to see more clearly. The efforts undertaken, the aim of these attempts, the wish to render useless sacrifice which has the appearance of weakness, the ideas, the sentiments, the misgivings—such are the pictures which this outline of social psychology will contain."

For a detailed account of these "ideas, sentiments, misgivings," we must refer the reader to M. Rives' excellent though somewhat pessimistic book. As to the latter quality, we can well imagine that the exceptional Frenchman gifted or afflicted—according to one's point of view—with social consciousness, would find pessimism hard to avoid; for persons with such a consciousness, even in countries where it is not so exceptional, are seldom notably optimistic.

Later M. Rives proceeds to show that he is not alone in his belief that the leisure of workers is a serious problem. He writes: "A report presented by Doctor Hazemann (syndicate of social medicine) in the name of the commission charged with studying the utilisation of leisure (14th National Congress 15-20 Sept., 1919) points to certain conclusions which should be realised. The writer of the report insists upon the urgency of filling the six or eight hours of daily leisure which the worker enjoys at the present time: it is essential 'to perfect his intellectual, moral and artistic knowledge and to improve his physical side by every kind of sport.' The means recommended? The construction in every important locality of a Trades Union Institute (Maison des Syndicats), spacious, with library, lecture-room, theatre, cinema, bathrooms, sports grounds, medical and surgical department and dispensary attached. Certain indications follow on the question of housing reform, communal and individual homes, transport, hygiene; the organisation of workers' cities is foretold as being incumbent upon the community; finally a long chapter is devoted to the Federation of Amusements (Fédération des Spectacles) and to its proposal for providing the working class with a theatre "at once healthy, educational and cheap." M. Rives comments: "A fine programme, no doubt, but one finds no attempt, in Paris any more than in the provinces, to put it into systematic execution; no doubt through lack of funds; also through lack of perseverance and perhaps of true faith."

In regard to the employers as opposed to the workers, M. Rives points out that "the employers seem to realise better than any one the necessity of utilising the workers' leisure time, possibly because if the workers have nothing with which to occupy or amuse themselves they will become actively interested in politics. Amuse them and stop their thinking. Also, to a certain extent, the old idea of 'Noblesse oblige' has descended upon them from the feudal lords."

In summarising his observations concerning the use made by workers of the provisions made for their leisure, M. Rives writes: "Almost everywhere the restaurant and the canteen cover their expenses; the cinema does not make ends meet but the deficit remains insignificant; the library remains empty, the lectures are without listeners, doubtless a little because the worker lacks that desire for culture which one supposes ought to come to him as soon as he has the means of learning. . . . Probably the main reason is that it is imposed from above. The worker profoundly desires a centre of which he will be the master."

In conclusion, M. Rives expresses the belief that the workers "resist both the employers and the unions in their desire to organise their leisure because leisure is their one individual refuge. . . . If the workers' leisure is to be organised, there are three moral ob-

stacles to be overcome: the dignity of the worker, the
individualism of the worker and the laziness and ig-
norance of the people. . . . What must be created is
a 'school of the people' which will teach the love of
science, the respect for thought, the pride of a strong
conviction, the meaning of life, of social activity, and
of human destiny in this world."

French Industrial Welfare Situation in General.—
The agencies which have been most conspicuous in providing various facilities have been the big employers
or industries, the two large opposing church groups,
and the various labour groups themselves. It is obvious
that the motives of none of these are disinterested.
The reasons for the increase in industrial provision
are varied. When it became necessary to rebuild the
devastated regions, there was a natural desire to build
"model" towns, which should have decent houses with
gardens, and provision for meetings of the employés
and for their entertainment. In isolated communities
of purely industrial origin, it is of course necessary
to provide some recreational features in order to compete with the big towns for labour. It is to be recalled
that the eight-hour day became legal in 1919, and presented a great problem to the "over-classes"; with two
extra hours or thereabouts free time a day, it was
feared that the working people would rot with drink
or employ the time in activities of a revolutionary
nature. The pay was not increased when the working-
time was shortened, so there was little possibility for
the people to spend their new leisure in the more harm-
less and entertaining commercial recreations. Therefore, with the rebuilding of towns, and elsewhere, there
developed many new efforts on the part of industrials
to provide wholesome facilities for the increased free
time. Many of the efforts have apparently been most

elaborate, judging by the reports of the Ministry and various other investigators. Gymnasiums, athletic fields, theatres, music societies, clubrooms, swimming pools, etc., have been constructed, subsidies granted voluntary organisations among the workers, etc. In some cases the workers respond well; in others, they resent the continuing influence of the employer during free time, and the efforts are not appreciated. As for the religious agencies, these probably have the most money, and their efforts are most wide-spread. Evidence seems to indicate, however, that the odour of sanctity obtrudes even in the gymnasium and there is too much propaganda resulting from the intense antagonisms existing between Catholics and Protestants. In regard to "organising," French workers will often form voluntarily into organisations when community of interests is the only requirement; but regulations and restrictions necessitated for general order and convenience in large associations are intolerable to them.

"Enquête sur les Loisirs de L'Ouvrier Français" (Inquiry on the Leisure of the French Worker).— The above is the title of Jean Beaudemoulin's aforementioned treatise for his doctorate degree. M. Beaudemoulin addressed questions to various large employers in differing sections of France; his interest having been simple and practical, the material he gathered affords little of value as to motives or response, in the case of definite "patronal" (employers') provision. Let us simply summarise his findings in the various regions.

In the southeast region M. Beaudemoulin reports that in most cases the principal leisure-time activity is work in gardens; carpentry, too, is popular. The young people incline more and more to sports, he says. In many cases each household has an ample garden and large allotment near the city. M. Beaudemoulin sees, in this southeast region, "a life more harmoniously filled, less oppressive, more balanced, more airy, more largely humane! There they do not have the cabaret or the cinema, but the garden, the work table, the home and the family." Among the workers are various societies—brass band, choral, shooting, football, etc. Bicycling, mountain climbing, and winter sports, like skiing, are other forms of recreation.

In the central region, again gardening was found to be popular. There is also a growing love of sport. In one instance a Catholic group has bought a place called "The House of the People" (La Maison du Peuple), where lectures, plays and movies are given for the young people. With rare exceptions the workers here were said to use their time well; in the way of sports, they prefer football, though the weather limits the season for it. M. Beaudemoulin learned that workers under employers' provision for leisure feel as if still in the factory; they prefer other associations. Commenting on the attempt to provide for workers' leisure, M. Beaudemoulin remarks: "One would have to be a very penetrating psychologist to say what will please the workers or what will not." His opinion is that the majority is indifferent to both mental and physical culture; both require an effort of which they cannot see the immediate recompense. On the other hand, the cultivation of the garden or improvement of the house are projects which can win their enthusiasm.

In the southwest, M. Beaudemoulin found, as elsewhere, a love of gardening. In the fall of the year hunting and shooting are enormously popular. In winter there are public gatherings. He noted an increased tendency to attend the theatre and cinema. Here the games, pelote-basque and paume, are in great favour. In the country, he remarks, football has taken the place, with the great majority of workers, of the musical gatherings which were their distractions in the war. Here "little has been attempted to influence good use of time. Some say little response has greeted any such effort; that in this region the workers are too dispersed." One employer expressed the opinion that the solution lies in putting within reach of the workers the possession of their own homes and gardens.

In the centre of France, "the workers' house and garden suffice in themselves as solution of the social problem." Gardening is the favourite occupation. In this region M. Beaudemoulin remarks also on the sports club for the young, courses in household economics for girls 13 to 20 years old, and a choral society of 100.

In the west, too, gardening is prominent as a leisure activity of the workers, "the men give at least an hour a day to the café." And "according to the mentality of each his free time is differently employed."

In the region of Paris, although the actual workers do not much frequent the cabarets, they do frequent the cinemas and theatres. The workers who have gardens cultivate them assiduously; the young go in for sports. Photography is a common hobby. There is a great desire on the part of workers to own their own homes; this applies especially to the mechanic, "the élite of the working class." Some workers have bought a bit of ground in the suburbs which they cultivate and on which they erect a "baraque." Of those who have been given additional leisure by the eight-hour day, many simply dine earlier, go to bed earlier, or go out *en famille* after dinner. Few take professional courses.

In the east, "encouragement of gardening, stock-raising, etc., keeps the elders away from the cabaret and wholesomely employed, the young are too devoted to the cabaret and cinema to go in for evening courses; some go in for sports." Fishing is much loved. The gardening and pig-raising elders spend the extra time in winter in sleep. Such "practical" utilisation is "more adapted to their temperament and to their tastes than attending lectures or indulging in other intellectual occupations."

In the northwest, recreation among the married takes the form of care of the house, gardening, fishing, etc.; among the unmarried it takes almost entirely the form of sports—cycling, hunting, football, tennis, fishing. Here the country is eventful, with its forests and streams, its picturesque paths through valleys. The country is appreciated, and both the married and unmarried make frequent excursions into it.

Mining Communities.—In Pas-de-Calais, M. Beaudemoulin reports, some of the provision is organised, and some is not. The unorganised often takes the form of gardening and keeping poultry. Many of the workers show a fondness for learning to play wind-instruments. Sunday visits to cabarets are popular; and lengthy Sunday dinners seem to be the rule. They like the "café," but not so much for drink as for conversation, card games, etc. Another recreation is cock-fighting. Fishing is liked. The cinema is popular. Bicycle excursions are common. In the case of the organised or "patronal" provision, garden land is provided, and there are garden competitions. There are meeting-places, libraries, brass bands, provision for sports, such as football ground, running track, gymnasium, etc. There are also professional courses; but physical distractions hold a much greater place than the intellectual.

In Moselle, twenty-five per cent go in for music in

some form—accordion, mandolin or choral groups. The "cafés" with their decorated interiors are more attractive than elsewhere. On Sunday cinema attendance is general. Cheap novels are popular. In summer bicycling, often in groups, is the popular sport.

M. Beaudemoulin's Conclusion.—Interesting are some statements which are the heart of the conclusion reached by M. Beaudemoulin in the course of his inquiry: "It would be as false to say that all the workers completely employ their leisure as to say they make nothing at all of it. It would be as false to say that they employ all their leisure well as it would be to affirm the exact opposite. He who wishes to repose on formulas is in danger of losing reality."

Under Employer Auspices.—The material for this account comes from the previously mentioned 1923 "Bulletin of the Minister of Labour," containing an inquiry on the use of the leisure created by the eight-hour day. The Bulletin contains reports from numerous firms; only some of the most important are discussed here.

Conspicuous in their recreational accomplishments have been the Carmichael establishments, Ailly-sur-Somme, with 1,750 workers. Before the eight-hour law a sports club was in existence at Ailly-sur-Somme, but until 1920 there were not more than twenty or thirty members and very limited activities. Following the war and the eight-hour law, the committee of this association undertook an effort to intensify interest in games and sport. They made a wide programme, and *"as they hoped for little from the community,"* they appealed to the generosity of M. Carmichael, from whom they obtained a fine playing field, equipment and areas for various games, a canteen, etc., and "an avenue of flowers bordered with chestnut trees." For the winter season M. Carmichael put at their disposal a meeting hall, a place for practise of indoor games, a recreation room (for club purposes, cards, etc.), and reading room; also a cinema apparatus in a hall holding 400. As a result the club soon numbered several hundred members. (It is interesting to note that the report mentions with gusto the fact that the football teams of the club have a high standing and that it has furnished several champions in athletics.) M. Carmichael has also established shower baths, built workers' houses with gardens, and has assisted adult education courses in the vicinity.

Raffinerie Paix & Cie., Courchelettes (Nord), provides workers' houses with gardens, cultivates a farm of which the products are put in reach of the workers through a co-operative society, and subsidises a sports club. The young people are said to go in for games, while the elders prefer to attend concerts or instructive films in a festival hall belonging to the factory.

At the firm of Les Fils d'E. Lang, Nancy, with 600 workers, allotment gardens are provided. A music society, established by the management before the war, possesses a large hall for rehearsals and performances. On occasion this hall also serves as a theatre.

The Société Anonyme des Papeteries de Clairfontaine, Eitvel (Vosges), with 900 workers provides allotment gardens; has aided in founding a music society; has established a sport society which is provided with a hall suitable for physical training instruction.

The firm of Marcheville & Daguin, Meurthe-et-Moselle, with 400 workers, provides allotment gardens, and has created and subsidised a sports club, many of whose members do not belong to the personnel, for which it lends a playing field. The report states that the exhibitions, matches, etc., of this club interest greatly the population of the district. A music society was established before the war. A hall is available for public performances. Technical and vocational courses are also provided.

The Société des Biscuits Pernot, Dijon, with 900 workers, provides allotments adjacent to their factory. It has created a sports club with a budget divided for athletics, football, and the foundation of a little stadium. Also a choral society. It is worth noting that, to encourage these societies, the firm fixes the closing hour at 5:30 invariably. When length of working days varies, the hour for commencing work changes, so that these sport and music meetings may begin always between 5:30 and 5:45.

The Compagnie du Chemin de Fer d'Orléans has organised sports and music societies. Interest and participation in sports are encouraged especially among the apprentices; the heads of local branches are obliged to interest themselves in physical training enterprises and to provide facilities for creation of playing fields and halls for physical education; annual grants are given to sport societies formed by the agents of the company. Similar encouragement and subsidy are given music and artistic societies. Allotment gardens are provided. Professional courses are conducted and libraries established containing general as well as technical collections.

Main Trades Union Associations.—There are in France three main trades union associations. These are the C. G. T. Chrétienne (General Confederation of Christian Workers), the Confédération Générale du Travail Unitaire (General Confederation of Communist Workers, whose abbreviation is C. G. T. U.), and the Confédération Générale du Travail (General Confederation of Labour, whose abbreviation is C. G. T.).

C. G. T. Chrétienne.—Its avowed purpose is struggle on social and political ground against socialist and revolutionary tendencies. As to its influence in the field of leisure occupation, it has been said by critics that it should be ranked among religious agencies, and that its highest social achievements have been a furthering of hygiene and "the creation of a cult of resignation" in social concerns. Actually, it may be considered simply as a conservative influence upon the leisure of the workers whom it involves, emphasising the importance of a satisfactory home-life, the normal recreations of the family, and the romantic consolations of religion.

C. G. T. U.—The C. G. T. U. is a Communist body, attached to the Third Internationale. Its main purpose seems to be Communist propaganda. It does, however, resort to methods which are incidentally recreational: at one time it had a theatre, which has since gone bankrupt; it still has a pseudo-Montmartre cabaret. In one of its revolutionary cabarets, singers, men and women, gather each Sunday evening to sing songs and recite monologues on questions of current interest: wages, the hard lot of the workers, the class-struggle, industrial and political corruption. The C. G. T. U. has also undertaken the organisation of many big sporting rallies mainly for purposes of propaganda.

The C. G. T.—The C. G. T. has set to work with more will and competence; its action is double. First it seeks to group together scattered recreational efforts wherever they exist with a view to increasing their individual strength. This programme realised in the domain of sports, led M. Guillevic to the creation of the Workers' Sports Federation (Fédération Sportive du Travail); the intentions of this great sportive family were inspired by what had been accomplished in Czecho-Slovakia; the directing committee which made a journey of inquiry and amity brought back from Prague memories, which haunted their meetings; and from year to year, through ever-increasing additions, they pushed forward toward the idea of a festival more social than sportive where physical exercise would only be the excuse for a vast concourse of friendly persons.

The second side of C. G. T. activity is popular education. The workers' university comprises nine sections: (1) the trades union school; (2) the trades union study and action circle; (3) the co-operative school; (4) the Popular University (arts, science, philosophy); (5) sports and hygiene; (6) infant education; (7) statistic documentation; (8) school for party workers; (9) social and professional law.

Of the C. G. T., M. Rives writes: "Thus the activity of the C. G. T. turns toward the needs of education. It is certain that the most weighty difficulty lies in the indifference of the workers to all intellectual effort; although a number of workers found time during the war for reflecting upon certain ideas, the majority of them gained from it a taste for idleness."

Independent Unions and Co-operatives.—In addition to the three main bodies there are some independent unions. These organisations organise various kinds of outings and entertainments. The Co-operative Societies have somewhat similar aims; they usually possess a co-operative hall with restaurant, dance rooms, etc.

On the whole, however, as M. Rives has observed, "the working class refuses to be herded together into schemes of entertainment specially created for it." Having been with his fellows all day, the worker likes a little private enjoyment at night. The complaint of a miner is typical: "Leisure time, that is the only stretch when one can be oneself, and it's not to be wasted on pleasures identical for all."

Workers' Gardens.—No account of industrial welfare in France would be complete without an account of the workers' gardens movement.

According to Bouthoul, the origin of the first workers' gardens goes back to a time when, because the twelve-hour day was the rule, the question of leisure did not arise. They were established for the most part by mining associations whose works were far from populated centres at a time when the means of transport available was far from perfect. The heads of the enterprise proposed to attract workers and to keep them reasonably contented. They had at their disposal vast stretches of ground which the companies had bought in order to avoid, in case of land subsidence, costly legal proceedings with the proprietors. The existence of these lands made the installation of workers' gardens far easier. Until the introduction of the ten-hour day, only the women had the time to busy themselves with the cultivation and upkeep of these patches of ground, the men now and then devoting part of Sunday to them. With the establishment of this last measure the progress was marked. But it is above all since the application of the eight-hour law in 1919 that the movement seems to have taken a considerable extension. In the single company of Anzin in 1914 the workers shared among them 3,789 gardens; in 1922 this figure had mounted to 8,485, 5,091 of which were attached to their houses.

The "Ligue Française du Coin de Terre et du Foyer" (The French Home and Garden League), founded in 1897, consisted at first of sixteen branches with 655

gardens. From 1921 to 1922 the number of gardens
in cultivation had almost tripled. It had passed from
17,825 in 1912 up to nearly 50,000 in 1922.

Pantin-sur-Seine (Socialistic).—According to M.
Auray, Deputy Mayor of Pantin-sur-Seine, "French
socialism wishes to work in the interest of the working
class, *even in spite of itself.*" At Pantin an excellent
small park has been laid out, and the grounds of a
former manor-house not far distant have been converted into a community sport and play place. Associated with this is an open-air school for small children in need of special care. The athletic field contains
a running-track, ball grounds, spaces for exhibitions
of gymnastic drill, etc. As to educational and cultural
activities—lectures, varied courses, concerts—centre-
ing the town hall, the Mayor admitted that for the
present the programme is perhaps a little idealistic;
he is however firm in the conviction that once the people
have gained a little familiarity with the fine things
of art they will prefer them to more trivial distractions.

Garden Cities.—From the workers' gardens movement "garden cities" followed as a natural development. These garden cities are, it might be said, a conscious and directed attempt to build for large groups
of workers houses that shall be no less attractive than
the workers' gardens, and then, in turn, so to plan the
streets, open spaces, etc., that the result will be an
unusually attractive "city"; usually, of course, in
point of population, such a "city" is hardly larger
than a village. Garden Cities are often characterised
by carefully planned recreational facilities and almost
always by communal enterprises such as co-operative
stores.

In the garden city of "Les Lilas," near Paris, one
of the most impressing features noted was the robust-

ness and the happy aspect of the children, together with the fact that they were actually playing together in the open—a thing one too rarely sees in France. Obviously, parents must realise that, even when living there entails the discomfort and expense of commuting, life in a "cité jardin" has its manifest compensations.

Especially interesting and commendable are the garden cities of the Northern Railway Company. A noteworthy fact is that figures taken from them show that their infant mortality is far lower than that of the surrounding districts, while their birth rate is higher.

The relevancy of garden cities to a discussion of leisure hardly needs to be explained; in England it will be seen how bad housing conditions, rendering adequate open spaces and playing fields impossible, had created what the National Playing Fields Association of England termed "a really critical and indeed a tragic situation." Equally tragic situations tend to exist in other countries, especially in their large cities; and the garden city movement is obviously a noteworthy attempt to alleviate such conditions.

Commenting on the markedly desirable conditions as regards health and general well-being of workers and their families living in these garden cities, M. Bouthol writes: "This progress which results from the happy solution brought (in great part thanks to the eight-hour day) to the question of workers' housing contains in germ all the other methods of a satisfactory utilisation of leisure. Once the workers are grouped in agreeable cities and enjoy comfortable and bright home surroundings they will quite naturally be led to live far more in their own family circle and employ their time in reading and social intercourse. In addition between the inhabitants of the same city there quite naturally develops an active and profitable social

states, the increasing interest in sports has been prejudicial. Also, "literary and dramatic societies exist which hold recreational meetings and give performances. These are created by workers' organisations and industrial firms. Many of these also present special cinema showings."

It will thus be seen that there is in France a dearth of available material on those aims, interests and activities which are in England grouped together under the term Adult Education. There are, however, as has been indicated, somewhat analogous French developments, on a less extensive scale, recounted in the various aforementioned treatises having to do with leisure provision. These developments, because they are concerned mostly with workers, have been dealt with earlier.

Les Equipes Sociales (The Social Teams).—France is, relatively, not very far advanced in its settlement enterprises; there are surprisingly few active ones throughout the country. Of these a great many are denominational in organisation. One of the most typical of these, and one of the most active throughout the country, *Les Equipes Sociales,* is of Catholic origin. Two others of like character are called La Jeunesse Ouvrière Chrétienne (Young Christian Workers) and La Jeunesse Patriote (Patriot Youth). In spite of its religious origin, however, no mention at all is made in its catalogue regarding this, nor is the organisation characterised by any confessional restrictions or discriminations.

Les Equipes Sociales, in their present form, came as a result of the war. Their announced aim is to bring about "an understanding among workers of all classes by a common friendship." Their belief has been that, by means of education, the students of the large public schools—acting as instructors and lecturers—could easily be brought into contact with all types of workers, and that the resultant exchange of ideas, during the course of these lectures and classes, would be beneficial to all.

After three years' experience in a popular group, Robert Garric, an old student of the Ecole Normale, founded the first "équipes," or teams, of young men, in November, 1921. Their success and rapid extension in the provinces as well as in Paris proved that they met a distinct public need, and in March, 1923, "équipes" of young women were formed.

The first care of Les Equipes Sociales has been to ensure a solid and practical basis of education. Accordingly, they have organised technical classes, designing, electricity, engineering, etc., for young men; shorthand, languages, dressmaking and designing for girls and young women. Also the desire of many workmen to complete their primary studies impelled the "équipes" to commence classes in French and arithmetic, and study circles have been organised where current questions are discussed and enlarged upon. The "équipes" do not attempt to turn out specialists, but, by helping to develop the personality of students, to turn them into efficient men and to help them to shape their lives.

Recreation is not neglected. Walks, visits to museums, concerts, visits to theatres, open air games, courses on physical education, holiday camps, travel, etc., are all provided by Les Equipes.

The development of the work has forced them to embrace other activities. For instance, in certain surroundings it has been found necessary to form "*les coins des gosses*," or meetings for small boys, and the girls' "équipes" have their "*jardins d'enfants*," or children's clubs.

Also, the members of Les Equipes Sociales help in their work certain invalids; 'Auxilia," which was founded at Berck in February, 1926, and in operation in July of the same year, is an institution which follows up correspondence courses with invalids. The activities of this organisation have since been extended to other centres where tuberculosis of the bones is treated. "Auxilia" has drawn together more than 700 students and 250 teachers.

The movement comprises in Paris, one hundred "teams" with 2,000 young men and 2,000 young women; in the provinces, in the big towns such as Lille, Le Havre, Marseilles, or in small villages, more than 100 "teams" are in full activity, and their activities embrace some 4,000 to 5,000 young men and women.

Foyers Populaires Civils.—The "Foyers" grew out of French-American centres for soldiers' recreation. There are twenty-nine in existence in the provinces. (There is none in Paris.) The provisions and activities include libraries, restaurants, cinema, football, dramatic work, and various educational courses. Football is said to be played through this agency by more than 150,000 a month. There is a small membership fee of ten francs a year.

L'Aide Sociale.—Of the various settlements, L'Aide Sociale, a Community House at 6, Rue Clavel, Paris, is spoken of first by every one as one of the best pieces of social work in Paris. It fosters zealously all the various activities that have been described as characteristic of Les Equipes Sociales. It also carries on a creditable library service.

Settlements in General.—Les Equipes Sociales, and other organisations of like character have resulted in the establishment of a number of settlements. Many of these, like the one at Levallois-Perret, besides having playgrounds for the children, track, basket and football fields, gymnasiums, etc., have classes for children and adults in music, out of which choral societies are formed. They have also very popular dramatic societies. In the Spring they usually give, outdoors, what is called the "Fête du Printemps," a pageant affair, which is the occasion for much dancing, tableaux, music, etc.

Religious "Patronages."—Religious patronages are simply community settlement houses attached to various churches. They exist mainly for the young people. Usually the patronage adjoins the church itself. There are of course Catholic and Protestant patronages. In these are to be found the characteristic activities of the community house, but carried on with certain obvious religious influences. The very well-known Catholic patronage presided over by the pleasant and liberal-minded Abbé Viollet combines with such purely recreational enterprises as amateur drama and "family-evenings," a sort of system of ethical and biological education of young people for the more fundamental duties of life. In a few instances Protestant patronages are under the auspices of the Y.M.C.A. The patronages of both churches are equipped with gymnasiums, stages, etc., according to the funds available.

Voluntary Organisation for Sports.—Until the war, there was practically nothing—outside of charitable enterprises (which touched only a tiny proportion of the people)—in the way of organised recreation or organisations for promoting play, sport, community affairs, etc. Since the war there has been an increase in the number of such organisations, and often an increase in membership of those already in existence. But, even taking into account these additional organisations, there are, as might be expected, considerably fewer of them in France than in England; and their activities are neither so extensive nor so spiritedly maintained as are those of the English voluntary organisations. In France, they are under the auspices of three different public interests: religious, philanthropic and industrial. The following is a list of the more important of these French organisations devoted to sport and physical activities: Workers' Sport Federation; The Union of French Societies for Athletic Sports; Union of Gymnastic Societies of France; French Women's Federation of Gymnastics and Physical Training; Gymnastic and Sport Federation of Patronages; the three Scout organisations, Catholic, Protestant and neutral, to be mentioned later in connection with young people's recreation. There are also two organisations with directly military aims: the Union des Sociétés d'Equitation Militaire (League of Cavalry Associations), which represents all classes —workers, employers and students, and includes probably 700 Societies; and the Union des Sociétés d'Education Physique et de Préparation au Service Militaire (Union of Societies of Physical Education and of Preparation for Military Service), whose total membership is not known. Especially deserving of mention is the Junior American Red Cross in France; the nature of its work and ideals is too well known to Americans to need exposition.

Young People's Recreation.—Although, for reasons which we have attempted to explain, French young people tend to be indifferent to the livelier forms of recre-

ation, it is nevertheless true that the growth of sport
in France has begun to affect the older boys and young
men and is gradually building up their interest in
games, especially in football.   This growing interest
is reflected in the reply of a schoolboy of a province
town who was asked his opinion as to who was the
greatest Frenchman; he named the hero of a local
football team.   Also, the 1924 Bulletin of the Ministry of Labour remarks of football that "the game
attracts the youth" more than any other activity.
The Bulletin states that in many towns and villages
football is the only diversion, arousing keen interest
in the entire population; the youth go into training
at the age of 15 or 16, keen to arrive at length in the
classification of "vétéran," and in this training they
"spend the greater part of their free time."

As to the three Scout organisations already mentioned, the Bulletin reports: The neutral body, the
Fédération des Eclaireurs de France (Federation of
French Boy Scouts), founded in 1911, includes in its
memberships students and working youths; the Fédération des Scouts de France (Federation of French
Scouts), founded in 1920, took in at that time various
pre-existing Catholic Scout groups; and the (Protestant) Eclaireurs Unionistes de France (Unionist
Scouts of France), was founded by the Y.M.C.A. and
is directed on Baden-Powell lines.   Its growth has been
slow since the war, probably because of the elaborate
requirements for leaders, which exact conditions of
"ability and morality" and a statement of religious
belief; its membership is recruited especially from students, only secondarily from the working youth.

It is probable that many young people are represented in the various bodies that are listed in our
discussion of the Bulletin's report on non-industrial

recreation.   Certainly cycling is highly popular throughout France and one frequently sees groups of cyclists composed chiefly of young folk.

Growth of Sports.—It is apparent that sport, as we know it, as the English know it, is in France a recent phenomenon.   There is nevertheless something of an effort to transplant the "sporting tradition," or possibly more accurately, to develop one, in the new interest in games and competitive athletics.   Guillevic, with his previously mentioned Fédération Sportive, has had such a development in mind; he works toward the discouragement of professionalism, and his solution has been in a moderately successful (for France, perhaps remarkably successful) attempt to popularise group athletics, drill, rhythmic exercise, and so on, as an approach to the team spirit.   Here is a very definite impulse toward a conception of the game for its own sake, and loyalty to good playing, rather than personal rivalry, which approximates the Anglo-Saxon attitude.   In a certain American magazine, at the time of the tennis matches when Tilden was defeated, appeared this sentence, as a preface to an account of what might have seemed some singularly caddish and unsportsmanlike conduct on the part of a prominent French player: "There is in the French an intellectually honest, logical keenness which not only makes them want to win in sport but forces them to discard a vast amount of this sport-for-sport's sake bunk."   It may be well for Americans to be apprised of the fact that when tennis was discussed with a certain Frenchman, he observed that the French would be happy to make America a present of this player, his "prima donna" qualities having brought him unpopularity even in France.

The fact remains, that whatever the strength of the French desire for personal aggrandisement in sport, there are a number—limited possibly, but actual—of persons interested in the growth of sports and athletics, who take the Anglo-Saxon "sport-for-sport's sake" as much for granted as the playing rules of the games they have adopted, and who seem as sensible of the existence of such sporting values as any English public school product.

1924 Ministry of Labour Bulletin.—Perhaps the growth of sports in France is best reflected in the findings on the subject of non-industrial recreation, of the aforementioned 1924 Bulletin of the Ministry of Labour, with its "inquiry on the use of leisure created by the eight-hour law." The Bulletin states that physical exercise appears in the first rank of activities for leisure and sees in the growing habit of *attending* sports exhibitions of all kinds, a sign of an increasing tendency on the part of the French people (especially since the war) toward outdoor exercise; it believes that this tendency is indicated also in the growth of sport societies. In considering the influence of the eight-hour day on the increase of physical exercise, the Ministry of Labour consulted national federations or organisations which comprise associations scattered throughout France. These were able to provide general statistics sufficient to show the rising strength of the movement. The membership of these associations represents the most diverse social catagories. Besides these, there are more limited organisations of a local or professional nature, often created through workers' or employers' initiative. As to the big organisations, "it is not always without difficulty that it is possible to obtain useful information." Methods differ as to assembling statistics, and it was not possible to establish any exact general and comparative statistics from the data available. Nevertheless it transpired definitely that there has been a marked increase in membership in all these organisations since the end of the war. It is impossible to say with precision to what extent the working class is represented, but it is thought that they constitute the majority. This estimate has been corroborated by statements of certain federations regarding increase in membership when the eight-hour day and the "English week-end" have been introduced. Let us list a few of the agencies consulted by the Ministry.

The Union of French Societies for Athletic Sports states that the war contributed greatly to developing the taste for sport; also, that "sport has to some extent become a fashion." Summer time, the English week-end, and the eight-hour day have all exercised happy influences. The union comprised in 1924 some 12 "Fédérations," representing football, rugby, gymnastics, skating, cricket, winter sports, tennis, hockey, swimming, women's sports, "pelote basque," "longue paume," etc., and numbering about 6,000 societies. It is impossible to estimate the number of members involved, since some societies belong to more than one Federation: "Although they fulfil all conditions desirable for their work of physical education," the Bulletin remarks, "it is not always the same in their establishing of statistics." However, the secretary of the Union believes that each society has an average of 100 members.

The Union of Gymnastic Societies of France is estimated at some 2,000 societies; it is impossible to state the total membership number because of shifts in class work, etc. The president estimates the number roughly at 225,000. Here one may note the relative strength of numbers in the Alsace-Lorraine territory. "In Alsace many industrials are not content to subsidise gymnastic societies, but take part as well in their activities."

The French Woman's Federation of Gymnastics and Physical Training was founded in 1920 through the combination of two societies already existing, one dating from 1912. This latter association comprised but few societies before the war, but from 1919 on there was an increase in the number of affiliated societies. In November, 1923, the Federation included over 500 societies, each averaging 30 members. The Federation states that "it accords merited attention to *moderate* and *educational* practise of sports, considering it useless and even harmful to exalt individual ability."

The Gymnastic and Sport Federation of Patronages groups not only the association of patronages, but all Catholic sports organisations which give it their support. In 1923 there were over 200,000 active members and over 2,000 societies.

Also cited in the report of the Bulletin are such Societies as the Union Vélocipédique (Bicycle Union), "for encouragement of sport and preparation for military cycling," with 118,000 members; the National Federation of Societies of Physical Culture and Preparation for the Military Service of France and Her Colonies, with probably over 110,000 members; and the National Federation of the Societies of Physical Culture, of Target Practice and of Sport, with about 45,000 members.

Children's Recreation: American Junior Red Cross Playground Movement in France.—Practically the only organised provision for the recreation of French children has been made by the American Junior Red Cross. Unfortunately, the only definite information as to their playgrounds in France is contained in a report covering a period that, in recreational matters, seems far back —from March, 1921, to October, 1921.   The report relates that at that time exposition playgrounds modelled on the American plan had been established in many places, among them Roubaix, Tourcoing, and Lille.   One of the most interesting things in the report is its quoting Madame Gouraud-Morris, the then champion woman athlete of France, and M. Raoul Peoli, the then champion weight thrower and football player, as saying: "We realise that the children of France have been neglected in our scheme of athletics and we want to remedy it."   Although the report expresses great optimism as to the probable growth of the playground movement in France, our observation has been that on the whole the playgrounds established by the American Red Cross have been apparently unappreciated, and are neglected or unused.

Music and the Theatre.—Several indications have already been given of the place the theatre holds in the life of the French people.   Theatre attendance is especially marked in the bigger cities.   The cinema is increasingly popular.   In the theatres, the French public seems to care more for smooth, competent acting than for a high quality of play; a person sensitive to subject matter in the theatre tends to weary of its everlasting employment of "the eternal triangle" as the theme of its plays.   For the rest, in the words of M. Jacques Valdour, "The theatre holds the public only if it offers rapid, even precipitous action, and either sentimental, comic, or licentious types."

As to music in France, the French themselves admit that they are not musical. In the schools, for instance, music, in comparison with the plastic arts, is neglected. Consulted as to the preferences of French people, a prominent concert director stated that they have no great fondness for oratorio; "violin recitals sell better than singers," he said, "and pianists best of all." In opera, "the people like the standard repertoire of the two Paris houses because they can whistle the tunes, but it is suicidal to attempt putting on a new work at the opera—the house will be empty." In spite of the fact that the most notable of the modern schools of composition has flourished in Paris, there is little interest in its products outside a very restricted group; "one cannot fill the halls for anything more advanced than Debussy and Ravel; the audiences tend to regard the extremists with suspicion of their artistic sincerity." The French, or at least the Parisians, at present greatly admire Russian music in every form.

As to orchestras, in France an orchestra must prove itself attractive to a substantial audience before it can obtain a subsidy. The orchestras in Paris at the present time are co-operative bodies of musicians; they must secure a sufficient advance subscription to assure their season in order to get their state assistance. This assistance is not tremendous. Because the men put through four or five rehearsals and a performance for a total fee of about five dollars, they are obliged to spend most of their spare time in teaching or whatever hackwork they can get.

There is only one specially built concert hall in Paris; various other auditoriums are used in addition. Although conditions are not ideal, there has been a definite improvement since the war; before that, men of the standing of Bauer or Cortot were known to give recitals to unfilled halls. But in spite of the improved conditions in Paris, foreign musicians and first-rate French ones cannot afford to penetrate the country, for the reason that it is impossible to get adequate audiences in the provincial towns, with the exception of the Côte d'Azur.

As to the radio, examination of the current French programmes indicates that they are about the level of the average in America; that is, semi-classical, semi-popular and jazz.

Governmental Action.—In this direction scarcely anything is done. But according to M. Rives: "The work, however, of an energetic prefect of the Seine Inférieure, M. Lallemand, shows what could be accomplished. He decided that various 'offices' should be created: (1) health; (2) cheap habitations; (3) popular education and utilisation of leisure. Each service to have a specialist: Doctor, Architect, Professor, at the head. The members of the council refused to vote the money. The prefect cunningly made his most vigorous opponents the 'reporters' on the various projects and through pride they became staunch supporters of the work they had to explain and the money was voted. For popular education 150 thousand francs was voted annually. Its objects were (1) to encourage the development of sporting association; (2) to encourage the work of the societies managing workers' gardens; (3) to develop education. The work in this department was very successful, especially in the country districts where there was no competition with ordinary amusements."

In the communes (villages), M. Rives reports, there is usually an annual fête lasting three days. There are several communes near Rouen where workers have organised an entertainment hall.

GERMANY

GENERAL OBSERVATIONS

It is necessary to warn against a casual American tendency to disregard the fact that Germany is a federation of states. Some misapprehension has been created in the United States by occasional press accounts of various laws and conditions exisiting "in Germany," without the more exact information that the subjects under discussion are peculiar only to a certain State of the Reich. It is equally important to remember the variety of temperament comprised in "the German people"; since it is possible for a Prussian to differ in character from a Bavarian almost as markedly as a Bavarian from a Frenchman.

In contrast to the French, and, to a lesser degree, to the English, the Germans are fundamentally gregarious. This quality has certain obvious influences upon their entire society, and it assumes a particular importance in relation to the use of leisure.

The German docility under authority, and their veneration of and amenability to discipline, make them a people especially inclined to institute and to support state direction and control in social concerns. The German tendency to organise stands in obvious relationship to their gregariousness and amenability, and is another important factor in the German recreational scene. Here may be noted also the temperamental susceptibility of the Germans to "movements" (industrial, political, philosophical, religious: movements of every conceivable kind and for the most various purposes), and what may be termed a sort of crusading spirit, a spirit concerned as much with the crusade

for its own sake—as a means of expression for a rest-
less and virile will—as with whatever social or moral
reforms it undertakes to accomplish.

Probably no people of the western world is endowed
with a stronger social consciousness than the Germans. This consciousness is to some extent a heritage
from the paternalistic influences of the former governmental system, but the original source is deep in the
character of the race; it is one of the most marked
of German attributes and its evidences are conspicuous
in every important aspect of German life. In the matter of recreation and leisure the thought of Germany
has been more thorough, more far-reaching, and more
profound than that of any other European nation: it
has been more widely concerned with what we have
termed the "fundamentals" of the problem.

This German social consciousness is admirably reflected in Dr. Stresemann's speech of September 15,
1926, in reply to the welcome given him and other
members of the German delegation to the Assembly
of the League of Nations on the occasion of their
visit to the International Labour Office in Geneva.
Certain excerpts from Dr. Stresemann's speech not
only show the German social consciousness at its best,
but serve to indicate facts which have been contribu-
tive to present conditions in Germany. Many of his
statements should be of special interest here because
of their equal applicability to the American scene.

"In hardly any country," said Dr. Stresemann, "has
the development from a self-supporting agrarian State
to a State of great cities, wage earners, and industry
taken place with such rapidity and suddenness as in
Germany. It is possible to entertain very different
opinions as to whether it is a gain for the world that,
here in Europe and in America and in other countries,

we have become peoples of great cities. I personally have grave misgivings as to this development. I see that human individuality suffers under mass suggestion and mass psychosis, and I see in the concentration of hundreds and thousands and millions of men on the soil of a single city a hindrance and a check to the development of the individual spirit. . . . I see, too, in the transition from the ancient handicrafts to our present-day undertakings, carried on with millions of capital, a decline of the personal labour which has contributed so much to the culture of humanity, in favour of a Taylor system under which a man is no longer himself, but is in danger of becoming a mere part of the machine. And just because I see this danger, just because I do not believe that human culture has gained by the fact that great cities and great undertakings have become essential constituents of the nations, I think it all the more important that a far-seeing social policy should protect the great interests of the State and of the peoples against what would otherwise be dangerous in this development. . . . We speak to-day of the rationalising of industry; that rationalising is bound up with a development which sees only undertakings with millions of capital on one side and entirely dependent human beings on the other side. In speaking of dependent things I am thinking not only of workers, but much more of the personal initiative of the worker, the struggle for one's own work, which has brought us so much technical progress and which can never be psychologically replaced by vast streams of capital. . . . For these reasons it is the duty of the States, in a period of such development as this, to see to it that developments of this kind do not in the long run become a curse to humanity. And since we have entered on this development, which shows itself to-day in what we call the 'Americanising' of the world, it is undoubtedly, in my opinion, an honour for Germany that, at the very beginning of this development, she set before herself the idea of social welfare as one of the principal functions of the State. To hold out the hand of the State to those classes who are in danger of going under and of losing their personal freedom and their power of raising themselves, in order that they shall not go under, is one of the highest duties of humanity."

It is hardly necessary to state that the German social consciousness is not grounded in pure altruism. It rises rather from the desire and purpose to improve the race—more widely evident than in the case of England, and in profound contrast to France—which in Germany may be regarded as a primary type of patriotism.

Goethe has said that to be German is to be able to do a thing for its own sake. The German possesses an ability to interest himself in whatever must be done which contributes largely to his capacity for satisfaction in life. Thoroughness and industriousness are not only racial qualities; they are objectified into national ideals. The Germans are attracted and intrigued by "things" in themselves, and their racial vitality expresses itself in the power of concentration. Hence it is possible that they are somewhat better fitted than certain other peoples for mechanical and industrial civilisation. Discipline for its own sake and the discipline of circumstances have taught them something of contenting themselves in the face of environmental imperfections. All these factors tend to some extent to reduce in Germany the gravity of the formal "leisure problem" generally attending modern industrial conditions.

Sports, in the sense of games, are a post-war phenomenon in Germany, as elsewhere on the continent. Pre-war American commentators on German recreation stressed the apparent lack of elasticity and lively activity in leisure occupation, the encroaching on after work leisure occasioned by the arrangement of the working day with its two-hour lunch period, the indulgence in "gregarious eating and drinking" and the milder forms of exercise in preference to energetic outdoor games. All this is in most striking contrast to the present scene, with its flourishing workers' sport movement, its hundreds of thousands of adolescents participating in games, and the vigorous games-and-sports propaganda of official and voluntary bodies. However in preoccupation with the question of the extent of sports the student must not disregard the importance as a leisure influence of the ancient German love of the outdoors. In his free time the German turns instinctively to the infinite house of forest and sky, and is perhaps more at home there than in any four walls of brick and stone, since this spontaneous tendency arises from a tradition of forest life, tree worship, and wandering longer than history. Thus the wandering youth of Germany to-day sing, besides the ancient folk-songs, the romantic "Lieder" which arose a hundred years ago from the old forest-wandering tradition.

German opinion of American tendencies in the use of leisure follows the general trend of the opinion of Europe, although it is natural that it does not include the indictment of intensive organisation, propaganda, and mass action in the field of provided recreation—all of which may be found in the same field in present-day Germany—which is characteristic of the thought of peoples of more individualistic temperament. German criticism is more concerned with the influence on the use of leisure of forces unrelated to the formal recreation movement and generally considered in Europe as characteristic products of American society. The German observer has a keen appreciation of the peculiar economic basis of the present trends in the (undirected) American use of leisure, and tends to transfer his criticism of them to their underlying causes —the accession to leisure and high wages of great numbers of people before any firm national culture has been established to influence taste and provide adequately for the employment of the new free time and the new economic surplus; the "standardisation" in all departments of life which Europeans believe to result from the processes—and the material products—of the American industrial system; and the emphasis on material comforts and possessions (and hence, on artificial recreations), upon which the whole industrial system is to some extent dependent. The philanthropic and "elevating" aspects of the formal recreation in America, where they imply an attitude of condescension, have been criticised, as well as the absence of any strong educational or cultural leisure movements. From this standpoint, one observer remarked that "all American recreation suggests a kindergarten."

Germany, then, appears as a country with strong official appreciation of the leisure problem, and a general tendency to organise to meet all recreational needs and to utilise all possibilities to provide for a good use of leisure. The German official attitude in social matters may be considered an expression of the German social consciousness, with origins in the traditions, historical influences, and temperament of the German people. In general, its purpose may be defined as the building of the physical life of the people and espe-

cially of the youth—the latter purpose having come
into especial prominence as a result of after-war developments—and the supplying of wholesome and cultural influences. Specific expressions of various aspects of this purpose will be given in connection with
instances of applications of the official attitude which
we shall consider here: Youth Welfare (and incidentally
the Youth Movement) ; Universities for Physical Training; various subsidies; official or semi-official structures
such as wandering-shelters, local clubhouses, stadiums,
athletic fields, etc.; and existing and proposed legislation for open space. But because certain important
agencies in Germany, incidentally influential on the
use of leisure, have more significance from the standpoint of social welfare than from that of recreation,
they will not be considered here.

Everywhere in Germany, and especially in unofficial
organisations and movements, are to be found political,
social, and religious divisions. The German Red Cross
finds it necessary to strive constantly in all its activities to eliminate political and religious considerations,
particularly in the work with youth, and to work
toward establishing some co-operation and sympathy
among the various religious, trade, political, and class
divisions. According to an official of the German
Junior Red Cross, the Catholics did not co-operate
before the war to any extent in physical training and
playground movements, but contended that the body
was in danger of being considered at the expense of
the soul; after the war the need for such activities
was so indisputable that this extreme attitude had to
be abandoned, but the Church is still (as elsewhere)
unsympathetic to movements which tend to bring the
leisure of the people, and especially of the children,
under non-Catholic influences. A difficult attitude in

such matters is by no means peculiar to any one religious body, and is readily comprehended in Germany when the strength and power of the anti-religious Socialist leisure movements are taken into consideration. As elsewhere in Europe, the fundamental divisions into social classes must be taken into account, and here again the strength of German socialism has been responsible for a heightening of class-consciousness. It is sometimes difficult for an American unacquainted with internal conditions in European countries to realise the prevailing importance of class-division even in technically democratised nations. Particularly in Germany, class division and antagonism must be remembered as important factors in the development of welfare and free-time movements. In Germany also, as elsewhere in Europe, leisure occupation has been recognised as an instrument for winning converts to various political or religious movements. These facts must be kept in mind in our discussion of the various voluntary leisure organisations, since nearly all voluntary movements, sports, adult education, youth activities, military training movements, etc., appear in Germany in from two to half a dozen manifestations, indicating degrees left and right, or varying religious sympathies.

A tremendous increase in voluntary organised recreation has occurred since the war in Germany, especially in the field of sports. It is hard to estimate to what extent this increase has been the expression of a new direction in public taste and to what extent it has been stimulated from above by popular leaders—organisations and individuals—who see in sport a substitute for the former military training. There are certainly a good number of agencies for sport and athletic development which have the definite purpose of providing actual military drill, or sports and athletics approached purely as a substitute for the former compulsory military training; and a military implication is inevitably suggested by the widespread conversion of drill fields into athletic grounds.

Patriotic and Military Associations.—All of these voluntary patriotic and military organisations, whether they belong to the Right side or to the Left, have for their avowed purpose "the old dream—(of the creation of)—a greater Germany." To attempt here to describe the differences between these numerous organisations would require too much space; suffice to say that they all, as part of their military instruction, include sports and allied recreational activities which justify their being mentioned in this report. The associations on the Right side, then are: the Stahlhelm, with 1,000,000 members; the Frontring, with 250,000 members; the Wehrwolf, with 250,000 members; and many other groups of less importance; in all, the Right has some 2,500,000 of the youth in organisations of this type. The associations on the Left include the Reichsbanner, with 3,500,000 members, an organisation including socialists, "democrats," and the left wing of the Catholic party, devoted to the purpose of sustaining the republican form of government; this is a virtual militia, a sort of unarmed national guard; it is said to have arisen as a countermovement after various disclosures of reactionary or Communist activities, secret societies, arsenals, etc.; it gives its members military drill (without arms) and physical training. There is lastly, the Communist group, Roter Frontkampfverbund, with 120,000 members. In addition there is the Jungdeutscher Orden, with about 200,000 members; this is an absolutely non-political organisation, belonging neither to Right nor Left, and has as its purpose the destroying of political and class demarcations among the youth.

Deutsche Reichsausschuss fuer Leibesuebungen (German National Committee for Physical Training).— One of the most important influences in the German recreation movement is the Deutsche Reichsausschuss fuer Leibesuebungen. Semi-official and state-subsidised, it is the head organisation of the various German athletic societies, and is governed by a board composed of people actually at the head of or appointed by affiliated societies. Thus it centralises all sports clubs, playground effort, etc.

Its publications are among the best sources of general and statistical information, while its work of educative propaganda and agitation for open-space legislation is of inestimable value to the leisure time movement.

It will be noted that this institution and affiliated bodies are often referred to in this report. Dr. Carl Diem, the head of the organisation, is one of the outstanding figures in Germany in the recreational field.

One of the aims of the organisation is: "three square metres (32 sq. ft.) playground space per capita." This aim incites rivalry among towns, and competition to excel in playground and stadium provision. In this connection some averages may be interesting. Koenigsberg has 1.49 metres per capita; Leipzig, Köln, Dresden, 4 square metres; while Berlin is relatively backward, with only something between 1½ and 1¾ square metres per capita.

Types of Playing Field—Financial Aid.—No country surpasses Germany in its realisation of the importance of the need for adequate open space for playing fields, gardens and the like. Municipal provision for playing space was already well developed throughout Germany in the nineties. To-day the amount of existing and proposed legislation for open space is striking, as is the abundant evidence of far-seeing German thought on the matter.

In Germany there are two types of play or athletic ground. The first, or Staedtische (Municipal) are open to all; they are used by schools, etc., and a supervisor is maintained. The second are grounds sustained by private organisations on land granted by the municipality; naturally these groups must be of considerable size and achievement to obtain such a grant.

The Prussian Minister of Welfare, writes, in his "State Welfare Work in Prussia, 1919-1923": "The establishment of recreation grounds and halls has been largely undertaken in Prussia, in such a manner that, according to their financial requirements, different communities, associations and other organisations have been granted subsidies for the purpose of construction or for the maintenance and improvement of establishments already in existence. This includes the provision of all sorts of appliances. Grants have been allowed from the Central Fund for 454 gymnasiums, games and sports grounds, 89 gymnasium halls, 110 shelters for juveniles and pedestrian excursionists, 71 bathing and swimming places, 18 boat-houses. *In order to avoid misunderstandings, it should once more be emphasised that the expenses are mainly borne by funds received from Subscribers and that the State has only been responsible for a fraction of the costs, taken from the Central Fund. Although the State gives material assistance to constructive schemes, it is* *with the understanding that the funds are chiefly to be supplied by third parties. This system of obtaining opportunities for physical culture has been very successful.**

"Attention should also be drawn to the fact that, in establishing recreation places and shelters for pedestrian excursionists, the underlying principle was that these institutions should serve all classes of the population to the greatest possible extent.

"Further, the Government Presidents granted subsidies out of the national funds placed at their disposal, for the purposes of 1,520 playing grounds, 130 gymnasiums, 161 shelters, 111 bathing and swimming establishments, and small grants for 14,811 athletic, games and sports clubs and thousands of Committees on Juvenile Welfare and Leagues of Youth.

"Considerable contributions have been given to the laying out of drill grounds and playing fields by the authorities in charge of the care of the unemployed.

"On occasions it was necessary to exercise the right of confiscation of land, in order to protect the public against private interests."

As an example of subsidised recreation may be cited the case of the German National Board of Youth Associations. Here German paternalism does not confine itself to expressions of sympathy and approval; the official interest also takes the form of substantial annual subsidies. The same is true of the German College of Physical Education. In its Report on the College's activities from the first of April to the 31st of March, 1926, occurs the following acknowledgment: "Our gratitude is due to the Government authorities, especially the Home Office, which have granted us subsidies

* Italics our own.

during the year covered by this Report amounting to 75,000 marks."

Some General Facts About Sport in Germany.—No German child is allowed to leave school without having learned to swim. There are five hours of physical training weekly in the schools—two game and three gymnastic periods or vice versa. The young spend a great part of their free time in sport, with few other comparably keen interests; and it is estimated that some 5,000,000 adults—from fifteen years up—throughout Germany are connected with sport organisations. One-fourth of this membership is female, and half of it is over twenty years of age. Throughout Germany there is a great love for tennis but difficulty in getting courts. Football is popular. Boxers, wrestlers, and cyclists are the only professionals in German sports. It is probable that Germany has less tendency to sport hero-worship than the United States or England.

A Suggested Playing-fields Bill.—Notable among the publications of the Deutsche Reichsausschuss fuer Leibesuebungen is a Proposed Playing-fields Bill. The General Secretariat of the above organisation prepared an interesting "Draft of a Federal and State Bill."

The suggested National Bill follows:

"1. The Federal Chancellor is empowered to grant, from the national finances, over a period of 30 years, to municipalities and like bodies, subsidies totalling up to 10 million marks a year for the establishment and equipment of gymnasiums, playing-fields and sports grounds for the youth at schools and universities and for athletic associations.

"2. The yearly subsidies afforded should generally not exceed 20 per cent of the costs of establishment, payable according to the means already existing, or the fifth part of the interest payment on the capital involved. They should be granted only on the understanding that the State Governments and their subdivisions shall assist with yearly subsidies of at least equal amount.

"3. In respect of the State Governments and their subdivisions, the granting of the national subsidy can be made subject to the fulfilment of special conditions; and in particular an undertaking can be exacted that local authorities shall be compelled to set aside at least 3 square meters per head of population of practicable playing ground for the sports of children and adolescents, either within their own spheres of jurisdiction or within reasonable distance from them, and that the installation of these playgrounds, in this proportion, shall take place within at the most thirty years from the passing of this Bill.

"4. The fulfilment of the conditions imposed by the Federal Government, and the employment of the monetary assistance supplied, shall be under the control of the State Governments, who will report to the Federal Government every three years on the use made of the monetary assistance afforded.

"5. The Federal exchequer (Military and Naval administration) is bound to place state-owned areas and barrack grounds free of charge at the disposal of local authorities for the use of school children and athletic societies, so far as this is compatible with military requirements.

"6. The regulation concerning the administration of small parks and small common lands of July 31, 1919, also applies to the procuring of areas for playing fields."

The draft of the State Bill contains only three sections:

"1. The State Government is empowered to grant to local authorities subsidies up to a sum of ——— Marks (varying according to the size of each province, and on the basis of a total sum of ten million Marks) out of the State exchequer for the establishment and equipment of gymnasiums, playing-fields and sports-fields for the youth at schools and universities and for the athletic associations.

"2. Every district and local administration is bound to establish and maintain playing-fields for free use in relation to the size of its population. The equipment and establishment of gymnasiums, playing-fields and sports-grounds must fulfil certain minimum requirements concerning which special executory conditions are set forth.

"3. The procuring and equipment of the necessary gymnasiums, playing-fields and sports-grounds must be carried out within a period of construction not exceeding thirty years."

The draft also contains provisions, of a most painstaking and thorough nature, as to "Grounds of Calculation," "Smallest Practicable Playing Areas," "Minimum Equipment of Playing Fields," "Minimum Size of Playing Fields," etc. Following the draft is the "Argument" on its behalf: it is another instance of the widespread recognition in Germany of what we have termed the "Fundamentals" of the recreational problem. Excerpts from the "Argument" follow:

"Care for the maintenance and strengthening of succeeding generations of the nation, care for the Youth of Germany, no less demands the attention of State and local authorities than the decrease in the excess of births over deaths and the other problems of population that embrace the fundamental strength of the nation. It must even be said that a practical population policy can only be carried through on the foundation of the thorough bodily and spiritual efficiency of German Youth. The youth in the struggle of a game, the girl playing on the grass, is the father, is the mother, of a generation to come. It is therefore the highest possible task of the legislation to afford to the younger sections of the nation freedom for healthy development, and to enable them to have the necessary breathing space on playing fields and sports-grounds.

"The isolation from nature of dwellers in the big towns has made the need for playing-fields and sports-grounds situated as near as possible to their dwellings into an elementary necessity of life. The radius of dwelling places in a town of over 100,000 inhabitants is over two kilometres.* Open spaces, suitable for the games of young people, should, even where there is a three and four kilometre radius, be within half or three-quarters of an hour's distance. In towns that attain to millions, such as Hamburg and Greater Berlin, open country can only be reached after half an hour's railway journey. For the masses it is only possible occasionally and in a limited degree to escape the stony wilderness of human dwellings and offices. A concentrated substitute for free exercise in open country in the form of adequately large and suitably arranged playing-fields and sports-grounds is therefore a fundamental conditon of existence in the life of a big town.

"Quite apart from this need of space, this lack of room to breathe, physical training on playing-fields and sports-grounds is a necessary physiological reagent against the increased demand on bodily and nervous strength made by the life of a big town. It is no accident that the banding together of young people into games, sports and gymnastic societies should have taken place at a time when the congregation into big towns was sharply on the upgrade. Systematic strengthening of the body was, and is to-day in a higher degree, the only assurance against the exhaustion of body and spirit. If at one time the danger of overtried strength loomed only as a threatening cloud on the horizon, now, after the monstrous losses on the battlefield and with the special need of strength for the next ten years of peace, it takes its place in the forefront of present-day life. We should no longer allow ourselves the luxury of delivering to waste the strength and life of our Youth in popular cafés, beer halls and doubtful pleasure resorts. A healthy social scheme for the use of the na-

* A kilometre is about five-eighths of a mile.

tional physical resources excludes any such frittering away of the most valuable asset.

"Recognising that 'to live' does not merely mean to be alive, but to be healthy, the healthy kernel of the youth of the big towns has for decades organised itself for bodily exercise in reaction against the deadening and soul-depressing life offered by a big town to young people. This awakening of youthful spirit and strength must not be restricted. The maintenance of the State requires that the public authorities should foster and encourage it. Youth makes its demand for room to live! It will and must have its playing-fields and sports-grounds. Without these the greatest strength of the nation is suspended literally, in mid-air. Breathing space on the playing-fields is the condition of bodily and spiritual efficiency in the younger generation.

"It will be the direct purpose of the Playing-fields Bill to lend grace and dignity to bodily efficiency. Playing-fields and sports-grounds must be centres of culture as are our schools; practical purpose and artistic form must be united in them at the highest level. State assistance should take such form as to ensure that the affiliation and absorption of the centres of physical education, restoration and amusement into the public welfare system may be considerably hastened and carried on in such a manner as to avoid vexations and annoyances. To desire to make nothing more of the new nurseries for the physical culture of Youth than drab gravel-patches with a small gymnastic equipment would be to waste the national resources. Unfortunately town society still knows very little of how to set up town playing-fields, although there is no lack of experts or of examples both in the country and abroad. Only a short time before the war the German National Committee for Physical Training issued a pointer for the building of playing-fields and sports-grounds. It requires for one playing-field a piece of grass land of adequate size, suitable for all such games as football, hockey, lacrosse, etc. Moreover for sports 100 metre and 450 metre running tracks are necessary. The necessary dressing-rooms, washing accommodation, accommodation for spectators, etc., are evident requirements. Besides this absolutely essential equipment of the playing-field it is to the purpose to add gymnasiums and swimming-baths, partly open and partly covered, to the practice-grounds for organised games, and to bring the children's games on grass and sand into organised relation with the whole.

"If these plans cannot be realised to the extent indicated above, and in any idealistic form, it is none the less certain that the establishment of playing-fields must take place on a scale far more carefully considered and more suited to the many-sided requirements of Youth than has hitherto been the case if they are to enter into competition with the attractions of the streets, the dance-halls, the cinemas, bars and cafés. Playing-fields must become centres of attraction if they are to fulfil their most important social function. The bare gravel-patch with a few benches is no manner of use. The playing-field must occupy the whole individual; not only the body, but also brain, imagination, heart, eye—in short, everything that tends to develop the highest energies. This principle assumes that the design of playing-fields shall not be placed in the hands of an underground building expert or a market gardener, but of qualified park experts working in conjunction with the societies for the furtherance of physical culture."

The Lippe Playing-ground Law.—In Germany there exists one instance of legislation making playing grounds compulsory; that instance is in the little State of Lippe. The law was passed on November 26, 1922; we quote it from the Lippe Law Gazette, Detmold, December 9, 1922, and the Regulations (dated March 31, 1924) as to its administration, from the same journal, April 2, 1924.

The Playing-ground Law follows:

1.

"The Local Authorities (Municipal and Rural) are obliged to lay out, arrange and maintain spaces for gymnastic exercises, games and sports (playing grounds) for public use by young people of the age for compulsory school or higher education, in proportion to their population. These facilities for exercise must conform to certain minimum requirements. The details will be settled by further regulations.

2.

"The laying out and arranging of the necessary playing grounds must be completed within ten years. It is for the Landespraesidium to decide if a playing-ground has to be furnished in less than ten years.

3.

"The Landespraesidium is empowered to grant subsidies to the Local Authorities, from funds available for the purpose, to facilitate the laying-out and furnishing of playing-grounds. In general, such subsidies are not to exceed 33⅓ per cent of the cost of the work or of the interest on the capital employed on the undertaking. It is the business of the Local Authorities to obtain the necessary ground. The Landespraesidium may grant a subsidy for this also, in the case of districts particularly in need of assistance.

4.

"Districts of more than 500 inhabitants are bound to install playing-grounds. Several neighbouring districts may combine to make and maintain common playing-grounds.

"The Landespraesidium is empowered to further the administration of this law by ordering several districts to combine to form a joint playing-ground, or by issuing other orders in consonance with this Law, always taking into consideration the resources of the districts concerned.

5.

"The Order with regard to Small Holdings and Allotments of 31st of July, 1919 (Reichsgesetzblatt P. 1371), and the Orders in force in Lippe in connection with the administration of the said Order, are also applicable to the obtaining of land for playing-grounds, but with the proviso that the final decision rests with the Landespraesidum. The dispossessed owners shall be credited as having handed over property as if for the purposes of small holdings, allotments or settlements.

6.

"This law comes into force on the day of its promulgation. The Orders as to its administration will be issued by the Landespraesidium.

> "Detmold, 28th November, 1922.
>
> "Lippe Landespraesidium."

And the following are the Regulations as to the law's administration:

"Art. 1.

"(referring to No. 2 of the Law)

"(1) The Communities shall undertake the obtaining and preparation of the necessary playing-grounds. Playing-grounds shall be provided everywhere within a period of 10 years from the promulgation of these Regulations.

"(2) If any Community has not undertaken the obtaining and preparation of playing-grounds within the time indicated, in spite of the need therefor existing and in spite of facilities being available, the Government will make the necessary arrangements on being requested so to do by a competent authority (administrative body, school or club) and will indicate a date by which a playing-ground must be prepared.

"(3) In the case of rural districts, such requests must be laid before the Government through the subordinate administrative organisation, which must give proper consideration to all requests based on sufficient grounds.

"(4) If a Community omits, without good reason, to procure and prepare a playing-ground within the stated period, it may be subjected to repeated penalties and the playing-ground may be obtained and prepared at the cost of the Community.

"(5) If complaints arise, the Landespraesidium has the decisive voice.

"Art. 2.

"(1) The minimum area of a playing-ground shall be one hectare (roughly 2⅓ acres) allowing for at least one playing-field of 65 x 130 metres with the necessary surrounding space. In special circumstances, a departure from this stipulation may be permitted by the Government. The playing-grounds shall be kept continually in good condition, and if possible prohibited from general public traffic.

"(2) The area served by any given playing-ground shall, as a general rule, not exceed a radius of 3 kilometres (less than 2 miles).

"(3) The surface of a playing-ground shall be as porous as possible, in order that it may dry quickly even after heavy downpours. Turf is to be preferred.

"(4) It is desirable that trees should be planted round the edges if space permits.

"(5) If the ground is adjacent to farm-land, it shall be properly enclosed.

"(6) As regards the fitting-out of playing-grounds with changing-rooms, lavatories, etc., the barest necessities may be installed as a beginning but the original plans should be designed with a view to subsequent improvements and extensions.

"Art. 3.

"(referring to No. 3 and No. 4 of the Law)

"(1) All proposals submitted by the Communities to the Government with regard to subsidies towards the cost of laying out and furnishing the playing-grounds shall be accompanied by sufficient facts and figures. These data must show clearly the sum required for each piece of work or construction and how it is proposed to employ the funds obtained.

"(2) A subsidy for procuring the land for the playing-ground can be granted only in quite exceptional circumstances. In such a case, incontrovertible proof must be given of the necessitous circumstances of the Community in question.

"(3) In Rural Districts, such proposals must be presented to the Government through the administrative body, which must in every case make enquiries into the circumstances, and, if necessary, endeavour to find a more practicable scheme, to reduce the costs, or to divide the burden of costs more to the advantage of the Community concerned, as the case may be.

"(4) The administrative body shall use its best endeavours to expedite the completion of the playing-grounds as far as possible, and to see that the arrangements are to the advantage of the whole district and fill the special requirements of its component parts.

"(5) If it is desired that several Communities shall join together to form a Playing-Ground Association, any such scheme is to be submitted to the administrative body, which shall first have considered the views of the Communities concerned.

"(6) The Playing-Ground Association shall be responsible for procuring and preparing the joint playing-ground. The Association shall manage and supervise the playing-ground as agent of the associated communities. Its regulations are to be considered as emanating from the Community.

"(7) The Playing-Ground Association shall consist of two representatives of each of the member Communities and of a Chairman, who shall be domiciled in the Community in which the playing-ground is situated and who shall be elected by a majority vote of the representatives.

"(8) When a Playing-Ground Association is formed, the share of the costs to be borne by the different associated communities shall be based on the population of said communities.

"Art. 4.

"Public bathing establishments in rivers or pools shall be considered as playing-grounds within the meaning of the Law.

"Art. 5.

"(1) The furnishing of playing-grounds shall be carried out as cheaply as possible. For this purpose, every use should be made of all resources available (such as gratuitous loans of horses and carts, free delivery of materials, etc.). Above all, the young people interested shall give extensive assistance by way of digging, fencing and such work, without special payment.

"(2) If the young people concerned refuse to co-operate in their own interests, the subsidy may be reduced or entirely withdrawn.

"Art. 6

"(1) The Playing-Ground Committee shall consist of one representative of each of the member organisations, or, in the case of a Playing-Ground Association, of one representative of each of the member Communities. The Playing-Ground Committee shall support the Local Authorities (Magistrate, and Local Government Board) or the Playing-Ground Association, as the case may be, in laying out and furnishing the playing-grounds. It shall, further, supervise the work undertaken by the young people of the district; and it shall, finally, assist the Local Authorities or the Playing-Ground Association in the management of the playing-ground and shall draw up the by-laws governing the use of the playing-ground.

"(2) Associated clubs which refuse to co-operate in the preparation of playing-grounds will be the last to be considered in allocating the use of the playing-grounds to its member associations.

"(3) The Communities shall be responsible for the formation of the Playing-Ground Committees.

"Art. 7.

"(referring to No. 5 of the Law)

"(1) The land required for the playing-ground shall be acquired by purchase whenever possible, unless it can be provided out of the property of the community or other public body.

"(2) If there is no possibility of purchase, a lease of several years' duration shall be arranged.

"(3) Should the Community not be in a position to buy or rent the required land by negotiation, it can (if a rural district) request the subordinate administrative body for a Requisition Order, or (if an urban district) it can make such requisition on its own authority, after considering the statements of both parties concerned. Complaints shall be referred to the Government, and a final appeal may be lodged with the Landespraesidium. The Settlement Office may also be called in to support the interests of a Community in carrying out a legal decision.

"(4) A landowner may be compelled to let land out on lease up to a duration of 30 years. Before such compulsion is effected, the Landespraesidium shall be consulted.

"(5) In order to acquire the necessary ground, several landowners may be dispossessed, in that one may be required to surrender the land required for the playing-ground, while part of the land of neighouring owners may be allotted to him in compensation. It is also permissible to evict landowners or tenants having less than 50 bushels of seed in the ground, but in such cases they should as a general rule, be compensated by allocation of land out of the estates of more important landowners in the neighbourhood. This can also be effected by compelling landowners to let out on lease.

"Detmold, 31st March, 1924,
"Lippe Landespraesidium."

Existing Open Space Legislation, Berlin.—The Berlin Building Regulation of November 9, 1925, provides that in residential districts only building fronting on the street is to be undertaken; the many rear-houses, wings, and courts will thus be avoided in future. The resulting unbroken area of free space within each square of buildings is to be used for gardens or playgrounds. Since the new construction is mostly in the hands of concerns interested in the promotion of the house-with-garden type of real estate development, it is expected that this regulation will be observed to good purpose, as these organisations have a special interest in laying out the spaces attractively. It must, however, be noted carefully that the regulation is that these courts are to be used "as gardens *or* playgrounds." This provision is obviously very flexible, and does not indicate any definite requirement that they shall be playgrounds. One doubts that these spaces will be employed to any extent as playgrounds in the formal sense. A considerable knowledge of Berlin apartments has yet to reveal to us a child at play in a court; the courts are usually arranged with flower beds or grass plots and hedges, and appear absolutely unsuitable for children.

This lack in Berlin of specific legislation requiring open spaces for exclusively recreational purposes does not mean that the city is notably lacking in such open spaces. Berlin in respect to its amount of playing-field space in relation to population probably would not suffer by comparison with almost any other large city in the world, and would undoubtedly prove to be notably superior to many other cities in playing-fields facilities. Particularly interesting and well-planned are the great parks containing playing grounds, etc., such as the Wuhlheide and the Jungfernheide, the lovely Tiergarten, etc. But the open-space provision perhaps most valuable in Berlin is that of numerous open squares, in all residential districts, which are like very pleasant miniature parks; here often simple facilities are provided for children's play—such as sand boxes, etc., although in the Tiergarten, except in a special playground area, children are not permitted on the grass. But on the whole, the city parks in Berlin are especially well provided as to playing grounds, Volkswiesen (which are rather like our picnic grounds), and outdoor theatre space for pageantry or folk-dancing. And of paramount importance in its possibilities for outdoor recreation is the great public forest, the Grunewald, where the River Havel and various notable lakes (the Wannsee, the Schlachtensee) provide opportunity for all manner of water sports.

Zentralkommission Fuer Sport und Koerperpflege *
(Central Commission for Sport and Physical Development).—This organisation, which is affiliated with the Deutsche Reichsausschuss fuer Leibesuebungen (National Board for Physical Training) has a membership of 600,000 adults. It is the head organisation of all (socialist) workers' sport federations. Its headquarters are in Leipzig, where its own school is situated; the Berlin office is the propaganda and political de-

* Social-Democratic.

partment. In its activities all conceivable sports are represented—handball, hockey, football, etc. It receives annually 50,000 Marks from the State; the school in Leipzig 30,000 Marks. Its influence is strongly against professionalism, and against records and the exploitation of individual proficiency; it is for "pure sport"; among its members, the slogan for their play ethic is "ritterlich," which is an expression of the English spirit of "playing the game."

"*A Department of Physical Training.*"—The above is the title of a draft signed by Frederick Wildung, Secretary of the Central Commission for Sport and Physical Training, Leipzig. It is another instance of the thoroughness of German thought on one aspect of the recreational problem; for its author specifically recognises physical training as a recreational activity. A part of the draft follows: "The after effects of the World War constitute a great danger for the German nation. It is essential that adolescents be guarded against the sapping of their moral and physical strength. It is no longer sufficient to leave this duty in the hands of private enterprise; *it must be organised and actively carried out by the Government and the individual communities, and the youth of the whole nation must be included in the scheme.* The German Reich, its component States and the Municipalities must recognise it as their task to arouse interest in the welfare of the young and to use private effort to the utmost, insofar as it is capable of providing what is necessary. The most urgent requirements are gymnasiums, playing-fields, light and air baths, hostels for young people, etc.

"Our opinion is that well organised gymnastics and athletic sports and games are incomparably the best training for youth. We argue that a healthy body, fit and willing to work, is bound to be the home of a healthy mind. All forms of physical exercise, if performed under proper direction and in appropriate surroundings, promote the 'joie de vivre' which should be youth's normal possession; further, they encourage the fighting spirit, exercise and sharpen the senses, and are an education in the team spirit and in willing submission to discipline. Their immediate result, however, is the promotion of physical strength and agility to a degree which cannot be attained by any other means.

"Although it used to be widely believed that the usual compulsory military service was quite enough physical training at least for the male youth of the nation—a view which we have never shared—this is now a thing of the past. In any case, this system did nothing for our young women, whose physical training was left to the care of gymnasium and sports clubs, for even the schools offered very few facilities of this sort. But before the war, social conditions were healthier than they are to-day, although even then they left much to be desired.

"Public organisations must support the private associations and clubs with their authority and with their financial means. For this purpose there ought to be a body composed on lines laid down by mixed deputations, so that the local authorities could confer with representatives of the gymnastic and athletic clubs of all kinds and with appropriate experts. A LOCAL OFFICE FOR PHYSICAL TRAINING ought to be set up in all the more important centres; in smaller districts the work could be carried on by recognised clubs. The best interests of the cause can be properly furthered only by such an institution."

The Commission has prepared suggestive legislation for the establishment of local physical training offices, requiring each municipality or district to establish such an office "for the purpose of promoting the physical well being of young people of both sexes." Each official organisation, with the advice of a committee or "deputation" consisting of representatives of the local official governing bodies, of the sport and athletic organisations and of educational and medical experts is to organise and supervise the construction and use of local facilities, both indoor and outdoor, to control the expenditure of public funds, to organise classes and the various games, gymnastic activities, swimming, etc., and to aid physical education in all possible ways, including educational propaganda.

"Sport and International Good Feeling."—The above is the title of an article which appeared in the "German Workmen's Sporting News," Berlin, July 12, 1927. We shall quote rather freely from the article as an example of the statement of a German "Left" agency opposed to militaristic motives and a narrowly nationalistic outlook in sport.

"If sport has any object, it is simply to make people better fitted for life. Very few athletes will content themselves with the idea of caring for their health; the usual ambition is rather towards physical prowess. That is only human; only an invalid thinks of regaining health; a man whose health is sound will often deliberately risk it in order to gain some special end. The motives which induce individuals to take up athletics are, however, unimportant. As soon as the problem touches society in general, the isolated individual is thrust into the background, and athletics become the affair of the nation, of society, which gives them the goal towards which they are to strive. The only object which society can have in encouraging sport, is the improvement of the nation's efficiency, and it is therefore the duty of State and Society to work towards this goal as directly as possible. Athletic clubs and associations are organs of the people and of society, and it is their duty to perform the task allotted to them by the community. They cannot fulfil their duty to society unless they are fully aware of their responsibility. The State is in a position to assist considerably in awakening this sense of responsibility by recognising the athletic unions as national organisms, as has been done to a certain extent in the German Reich. If the State expects the citizen to have a sense of responsibility, it must first confer on him a citizen's rights. If this is not done, the State is claiming the right to reap where it has not sown. The same is true in an even greater measure in the case of organisations whose object is the furthering of projects for the general good. The more the State recognises and treats these organisations as socially useful bodies, the better it will be serving the needs of the nation.

"Sport is obviously an international matter, for it reaches out far beyond national boundaries, influences international relations to a very great extent, and appears to be destined to direct international intercourse into quite new channels. The object of sport being to improve the efficiency of the human race, its international influence cannot be otherwise than pacific; otherwise it would have no meaning. This fact is apparently gradually being recognised even in nationalistic circles. Sport is pacifist in its very nature, for it replaces murderous conflicts by chivalrous combats with nature's weapons. We do not seek protection in strange weapons; those that nature gave us are our safeguard and our strength,—that line is taken from one of the oldest gymnasium songs. There is no doubt but that sport is one of the first and most efficacious means by which war may be stamped out, and it appears to be cast for a more important part in the future than was played in the past by the Church, which never shrank from actually taking the lead in warfare.

"These lofty aims can, however, never be gained while athletics touch only the surface of human nature, instead of exercising a definite influence on the mentality of the race. Mankind has to learn to think in a sportsmanlike manner, as the English have already learnt to do to a certain extent. A spirit of sportsmanship must govern the nations in their political and economic rivalry. . . . Political rivalry certainly wears a cloak of civilisation, but it always conceals the mailed fist of militarism, ready to strike at a moment's notice. But sport will draw the fangs even of this tyrant, once his true nature is realised and an effort is made by each nation to suppress him at home.

"At present we are still far from this point. In almost all countries, the athletic pursuits of the middle classes are inseparable from selfish national interest, although they are celebrated by pretentious Olympic games. In our country, the gymnasts have adopted a particularly nationalistic attitude, while the true followers of sport are much more cosmopolitan in their outlook. It is deplorable that in every country the middle classes are the prey of nationalism, although in war they stand to lose more in blood and in property than any other class. . . . Even in the world of sport, this class entrenches itself behind a barbed-wire entanglement of nationalism, and weaves around itself a web of warlike ideas, with which it obstructs the path of international goodwill."

This article proceeds with a statement that when, not long ago, a politician asked in the Düsseldorf newspaper, "Der Mittag," what was the attitude of the German middle-class sport-lovers towards sport and international goodwill, he received nothing but bellicose replies. Particularly characteristic was the answer sent by an official of a gymnastic club, who disposed of the question with the Latin quotation: "It is difficult not to write a satire." There is national shortsightedness of this middle-class athletic organisation. These bodies certainly aim at improving the efficiency of the nation, but only as a reluctant afterthought in comparison with the cult of the nationalistic spirit. Then follow statements which may be abbreviated as follows: Even now, the highest motto of this Club is "Be prepared," and this has not merely the old meaning of feeble self-protection, but has come to embody the idea of light-hearted aggression. This mental attitude is shared by middle-class associations in other continental countries, especially in France and Italy. It is true that a strong vein of romanticism runs through this conception, and nothing could be more foolish than to take these things too seriously; still, they remain definite obstacles in the way of a healthy state of affairs.

The German College of Physical Education.—The German official consciousness of the importance of recreation is nowhere better illustrated than in the attitude toward the German College of Physical Education and toward various other physical training projects. An idea of the German College of Physical Training may be gained from the following excerpts of an account of the College by Dr. Carl Diem. Dr. Diem writes: "Our College is the outcome of Germany's need, but also of its courage in the hour of need. The idea originated and the need for it was felt in the heart of the athletic movement, and it has been created by spontaneous effort. Probably there are few establishments of this kind which are founded so entirely on pure idealism and spontaneous sacrifice. Up to the present the voluntary co-operation of leaders of gymnastic and sport-centers and of scientists has been its greatest support.

"The idea of an independent physical training college arose as a result of the great loss of men in the World War. This war naturally found many victims among the leaders of gymnastic and sport associations. It is not to be wondered at that they stood and fell in the front ranks. The more one studies the groups of physically fit young men who belonged to the principal gymnastic and sports associations in 1914, the more apparent it becomes what tremendous losses were sustained by these circles. Not only did very few men return who had had peace-time experience in the organisation of gymnastics and sport, but moreover the almost complete breaking-off of the activities of the associations had interrupted the training of new leaders. The tradition was completely broken. There was a lack of leaders, which was all the more serious because the young people joined the associations in large numbers.

"This was the immediate occasion of the foundation of the College. The State institutions had up to that time not been able to pay much attention to the work of the associations; they were fully occupied with the training of gymnastic teachers for the schools.

"The true reason for its foundation, however, lay deeper. In Germany, then as now, the healthy life-forces were fighting the feverish nightmares of the war and their consequences.

"Gymnastics and sport had the necessary elements for re-creating enterprising, well-balanced, cheerful, industrious and hardy human beings. An inner desire among the people led to heightened interest in the value of physical training. New and better forms of physical training were sought. Well-organised sport became a matter of importance to the people; physical training was a method of reconstruction.

"These forces in the inner development of the people called for a training school which would at the same time recruit new forces. The new creed called for apostles. It also needed to forge its spiritual outfit; idealistic youth desired games not as a pastime but as part of a new culture. No mere gymnastic school could accomplish this task. An independent instructive, constructive and research institution was required; it was necessary to have a 'College.' How should this come into being? It was not a mere accident that the scientists of the Berlin Unversity co-operated with the mental leaders of the games-associations in this new enterprise. . . .

"It is true that physicians and educationalists, in fact, men in every walk in life, had uttered warnings against one-sided 'intellectualism.' But the tremendous upheaval caused by the war made it clear for the first time that the mysterious interdependence of body, mind and soul could not in the long run allow one part to predominate with impunity. This acknowledgment had to be made by science, and it was not the philosophers nor the pedagogues, but the physicians, who felt and admitted the necessity for a research institution in the field of physical training and who placed their laboratories and their time at its disposal.

"In this way the character of the new institution was determined. It was to be a 'free scientific research center' to investigate the manifold workings and problems of physical training and to revive the teaching of physical exercises in close co-operation between science and practice. . . .

"The aim of the college is the co-ordination of all forces working on a scientific basis; in this sense it is an academy which reaches out beyond the circle of its collaborators.

"The leaders of the four divisions, physical training, hygiene, education and administration, have always made every effort to secure harmonious working. In this way the college should avoid any rigidity of system by a constant interchange of scientific and practical knowledge. It hopes to discover and perfect a new German form of physical training and bring the body into its own through systematic training, and thus contribute sensibly not only to German science, but to future German culture."

The college is located in Berlin at the Berlin Stadium. The grounds contain 8½ hectares (about 20 acres), with an amphitheatre seating 60,000. There is adequate space for football, for games and track events, and for gymnastic exercises. There are also a cement cycle track outside the cinder track, a swimming pool 100 metres long by 22 metres with locker rooms, etc., adjoining cycle track, and a gymnasium hall with additional rooms for wrestling, boxing, fencing, etc. Resident students for both the regular winter and for special summer terms are received.

A noteworthy feature of the college has been the development of its extension programme. In 1924 there were 60 courses covering the most varied sports, with lectures and special features. Dr. Neukirch, director of the extension courses, states, "The extension courses for physical training are organised for everybody. Of course, neither religion, political views, nor the age of the person, makes any difference. The course, the exercises, the readings, and the lectures are held in the late afternoons, in the evenings, and on Sunday mornings, from which it follows that the courses are primarily intended for all who work in the daytime and who wish to devote to sport what time they may have free from their work. . . . Many of the participants are not clear as to what kind of sport they should choose to devote themselves to. In the extension courses they can, to a certain extent, experiment with all the various forms of sports, which makes it easier to choose later on. . . . These extension courses constitute a source of supply for the existing athletic and sports clubs which gain new members from the students. . . . They also have a social value. Suppose—and coincidences are more frequent than one imagines—a bank director happens to meet at the boxing course an employé who is better at boxing than he is himself, he will be likely to take notice of him and to take an interest in him, for where sport is concerned it is ability and not cash that counts."

The Frankfort Stadium.—At Frankfort-on-the-Main exists an enterprise that has been called "A People's Versailles." It is typical of developments in other German cities—for instance, Cologne. Apparently the men who planned this people's summer resort at Frankfort had the imperial play places of Louis XIV at Versailles and of Marie Theresa at Schoenbrunn in mind as they drew their lines across the former military training camp of the Kaiser, which the city of Frankfort bought from the Empire after the war. Only in this case the men who built the play place built it for themselves and their fellow citizens; the resort is planned for 500,000 people. The site is in the heart of the public forests which surround Frankfort on every side. It lies along one of the main residential thoroughfares of the city, scarcely fifteen minutes from the centre of the city by street car. Apparently neither citizens nor officials raise any protest against an invasion of this aristocratic centre by twenty thousand people on every Sunday and feast-day for six to eight months of the year.

The resort, with its stadium, is impressive. City planners, engineers and landscape gardeners aided in its planning and building. Every bit of natural scenery was preserved. The surrounding forests provided an excellent setting, isolating the spot from the outside world. The park is shaped like a triangle with the main entrance at the apex. Within the park are two principal axes converging at the entrance, each of which is about one-half mile in length. The base is a half mile wide. The main entrance opens into a broad parkway which brings one to a large two-story clubhouse, containing restaurants where food is provided at low cost. On the façade opposite to the entrance is a big open balcony where coffee, tea and drinks are served and where band concerts are held in the afternoons and evenings. Before this balcony is a sunken garden with fountains and sand pits for sunbaths where people may sit and lie in the open all day long. On either side are retiring rooms. Immediately beyond is a pool about four hundred feet square. Beyond this first pool is a swimming pool 350 feet long and 100 feet wide. There is a deep diving space at one end. The pool is elevated. On the tops are benches for spectators. The pool itself is lighted above and by incandescent lights in the bottom. Provision is made for heating the water so that the pool can be used in the spring and the autumn. On the sides are dressing rooms and shower-baths.

Still further on is a stadium. Designed especially for bicycle races and sports of various kinds, it will seat several thousand people. The centre can be flooded for skating in the winter. This whole section, as in fact the entire park, can be brilliantly lighted at night for contests, competitions, play.

There is also a play space for children, detached from the main thoroughfare and enclosed with trimmed shrubbery artistically fashioned. There is but one entrance, and hundreds of children can easily be supervised by a single person. Further in, beyond the excellent clubhouse, is another series of play places each planned in every detail for the widest possible use. The first is a close-cropped green lawn with raised terraces on the sides and possibly 800 feet in length, where the Turnvereins of the city can meet to exercise. Beyond this is another field of even greater length and width. It, too, is sunken with benches and seats on either side. There is provision for four football fields with another field for handball. At the end of this field is a huge indoor gymnasium elliptically formed and two stories high.

Although the whole enterprise is known in Frankfort as the Stadium, the stadium is actually one part of it. The stadium is colossal. On one side is a grandstand, on the other the administration building and tribune for judges. Here competitions of all kinds can be and are held, and it is in constant use during the summer.

In a magazine article (to which we are indebted) Frederick C. Howe has praised this Frankfort park as follows: "Few things have given me such an understanding of the attitude of the German city towards its people, of the intelligence of municipal officials, and the essential democracy of the life that seems to be finding expression in that country since the war."

Bremen.—Bremen was recommended to the investigators by the authorities in Berlin as an example of the German free city, and as a community where leisure is widely provided for by voluntary and official means. Here organisations of all kinds flourish; voluntary associations—clubs—of all kinds fill a place in "bourgeois life" similar to that taken among the workers by the typical workers' and socialist organisations. One out of every two families in Bremen has a garden allotment. (It was said by officials of the Arbeiterkammer that the type of worker who enjoys the cultivation of allotments is often unsocial and hard to interest in other activities. The same complaint is made in France.) The banks of the River Weser are lined with allotment-sites and with municipal bathing-beaches. There are some ten thousand in the youth-sport movement, representatives of all classes. Wandering is very popular; there are several Youth-shelters in the vicinity. At the time of the visit a large community centre within the city was under construction (under the auspices of the Arbeiterkammer) which was to contain a hall for moving pictures, over-night accommodations for young wandering visitors from other parts of the country, and the usual club facilities of the Jugendheim. It is interesting to note that there are more women than men in the gymnastic societies here. The working day is in general long; opportunities exist for the workers to follow evening courses which supplement the continuation courses, besides the usual vocational courses, lectures, etc. There is a workers' dramatic society, which during the preceding season had given eighteen performances. There are a great number of choral clubs of both men and women. Enthusiasm for the folk-dance exists only among the Socialist youth-groups. The sports most popular with the general public are swimming, hockey, ball, and gymnastics. Athletic grounds are provided by the city.

Labour Developments.—The various labour developments in Germany are mainly Social-Democratic in
politics, and are largely hostile to other initiative; they
are invariably characterised to a marked degree by the
class spirit—the workers' strong demarcation and self-
consciousness.   Many of the labour developments, of
course, in Germany as elsewhere, are concerned with
the question of workers' hours.

Length of Working-Day.—In all industrial undertakings the eight-hour day was introduced by order
of November 23, 1918.   Until the autumn of 1923 the
eight-hour day was strictly observed.   (According to
statement made at International Labour Conference,
1924, Germany at this time enforced the eight-hour day
more strictly than most other countries.)   Since 1923
the hours of the working-day have been prolonged by
collective agreements, the lengthening being necessitated
of course by the peculiar economic conditions.

Possible Activities of a German Workman.—It is
not unusual for a German workman to belong to a
trade union, a political society, a sport club and to
the Volksbuehne or a similar cultural society.   The
trade union requires his attendance one night a week;
if he is an officer (and one man out of every ten holds
some office), two nights a week.   The political society
requires his attendance one night a month and as many
as one or two nights a week if he is an official.   The
sport club usually requires one of his nights each week,
the Volksbuehne, one night a month unless he is an official; in that case, one a week.   It is therefore hardly
surprising to find in Germany some degree of feeling
that there are too many organisations which take the
workers out of their homes.

Christian Trade Unions.—The trade union movement in Germany has two principal divisions—the So-

cialist, and the Christian. (Allgemeiner Deutscher Gewerkschaftsbund, and Deutscher Gewerkschaftsbund.)
The socialist wing number probably five million; the
Christian, two million. Here, as elsewhere on the Continent, the non-socialist forces endeavour to oppose to
the influences of Socialism the influences of the life of
the family—the enjoyment and use of the home, and
the development of liberal and individualistic recreations. Dr. Rohr of the Christian Federation, a member of the National Economic Council, has a special
interest in all questions of leisure occupation. In his
opinion the damage to home life resulting from numerous present-day conditions constitutes one of the
chief factors of the German leisure problem. It may
be assumed that his opinions and recommendations indicate the policy or attitude of the Federation: he
believes that an improvement of the conditions of the
home, and so far as possible the ownership of homes,
will do much to counteract many current harmful and
artificial recreational influences. It is interesting to
note that it is the belief of Dr. Rohr that the American
influences which have found their way into the field
of recreation in Germany tend entirely to a use of
leisure *away from* the home. The passion for games
and watching games, which is largely post-war, was
said to be on the one hand a natural outlet for youthful energies formerly occupied by the military training, and on the other, a relief for nerves over-stimulated
and frayed by war. Too great an absorption in sport
is here regarded with keen disapproval.

Employer's Provision.—In general, according to size
and wealth of the industry, employers in Germany
provide for welfare and use of free-time. In many
cases athletic grounds, halls, etc., are placed at some
distance from the neighbourhood of the industry, in

recognition of a desire on the part of the workers to feel that their free-time is not being spent too much in the shadow of the work.

Siemenstadt.—This is an industrial community built up by the great electrical company of Siemens, and its welfare-recreational provision may be considered as a typical example of German employers' initiative. One of its noteworthy features is a sort of leisure-home for the children, where small ones are tended as in a day nursery, and where larger ones come for hand-craft (woodcarving, silhouettes, basketry, drawing,— each according to his fancy) and for supervised study of homework after school; the home contains a hall with a small stage where juvenile performances may be given. For the workers themselves there is a large athletic ground, with running track, tennis courts, etc. Boating is provided on a lake in the vicinity.

Much is done here in the way of "vacation homes"— a characteristic German welfare provision; Siemenstadt has a Home at the sea and one in the Harz, where workers and their children of all ages are aired and sunned and exercised at intervals. The company has made an excellent film of the various welfare activities, showing workers and children happily engaged in sports and play.

As to the attitude of German workers toward such paternalism in industry, it is said that they generally recognise the practical advantages of welfare provision and are willing to avail themselves of it.

Note on Workers' Education.—Vol. XIX, No. 12, "Industrial and Labour Information" (published by the International Labour Office at Geneva) contained an article called "Germany and Workers' Spare Time," in which occurred the following statements relating to workers' education:

"The promotion of workers' education is undertaken by the Federal Government, the State governments, and in particular the municipalities. One of the chief means of promoting workers' education is to be found in the people's libraries which exist in almost all towns, even very small ones, and also in the people's colleges which have been set up throughout Germany by local authorities, municipalities, and municipal unions. The Government contents itself with encouraging these efforts. It institutes and maintains official consultation offices which give help and advice in the establishment and upkeep of people's libraries and people's colleges. It also gives financial assistance to existing libraries and colleges.

"No Federal legislation dealing with popular education as a whole has as yet been adopted, and nothing of the kind is likely to be proposed, as the growth and development of the popular education movement in Germany, apart from the ordinary schools, has shown that free development with State encouragement is preferable to regulation by law. The work of popular education is undertaken partly by large associations covering the whole of Germany, and partly by smaller societies, local institutions, semi-official local bodies, and municipalities.

"Among the institutions which are of special importance for the workers and which devote special attention to instruction in labour law, are the Academy of Labour in Frankfort, the public Economic Colleges in Berlin and Düsseldorf, and the works council schools which are supported by grants from the Federal Government. The economic colleges give preparatory instruction to persons wishing to attend the Academy of Labour. The latter provides higher education on university lines. The Economic College of Düsseldorf has widened its sphere of activity by instituting a number of local courses in various large towns."

Gardens.—The Report of the Minister of Welfare in Prussia contains an interesting section on "Small Gardens and Allotments": "The encouragement of the cultivation of small gardens is, from political and economic grounds, one of the most important duties of domestic welfare work. Although the present allotment system has not made it possible always to have a garden attached to each house, measures must be taken to admit of such city-dwellers as wish for a garden plot of their own—and this demand exists in a daily increasing number of large towns—being able to rent a modest plot.

"The cultivation of small gardens showed a considerable increase in our towns during the war, on account of the increasing scarcity of food and the insufficient importation of foodstuffs. But even since the war, although the food difficulty has sunk into the background, the movement has continued and even expanded, which is sufficient proof that there are other than purely material motives for it. This movement is typical of the rebellion of the town-dweller against the unnatural way of life imposed on him, and of the growing desire felt by a large section of the population to live in closer touch with nature.

"The Central Government has sought to encourage this very healthy spirit by issuing a Small Holdings and Allotments Order, which places the allotment system on a definite footing. The gist of this Order is that now any one who wishes to own a small garden can claim the right to be given an opportunity of satisfying his wish; moreover, the Order affords legal protection to small holders with regard to their work and their efforts. The necessity for such legislation has gradually become evident. It was sometimes necessary to uphold the rights of small holders against the landowners, who often resisted strongly, and sometimes against the Local Authorities themselves; further, it was necessary to place a reasonable limit on the demands of the small holders and to promote the usefulness of their horticultural activities with the object of justifying in the eyes of the community the legal privileges bestowed on them. The Welfare Ministry took it upon itself to hold the balance between small holders and opposing interests in administering this Order."

The Youth Welfare Act, July 9, 1922.—The German Youth Welfare Law of 1922 has been called "the Magna Charta of youth." While it is concerned principally with questions of what in the American usage is broadly termed social welfare, it has also served in certain ways to develop the leisure-time activities in which we are interested. Among the provisions of the Act is one for the establishment of the Jugendamt or Youth Bureau. These, established throughout Germany, are interested chiefly in "social welfare work," in co-operation with the juvenile courts, etc. The local bureaus in Berlin and elsewhere have, however, encouraged and provided for all sorts of leisure occupation, particularly sports, wandering, etc. They have extensively co-operated with various organisations and groups interested in sports and physical training.

The Prussian Minister of Welfare explains "that in order to maintain close relation with all circles and individuals working in the cause of juvenile aid and the youth movement in general, including physical training, and in order to have the benefit of their advice in making important decisions," the national committee of juvenile aid and the youth movement, including physical training, was established with six working committees:

1. Committee on physical training of the young.

2. Committee on economic and social conditions prevailing among the young.

3. Committee on spiritual and moral education of the young.

4. Committee on the special requirements of young girls.

5. Committee on the special requirements of young country dwellers.

6. Committee on the special requirements of welfare workers, male and female.

It will be noted that the first of these committees has a direct bearing on recreation, since there is in Germany a growing tendency to regard sports and games as being an indispensable part of physical training, and that most of the others have distinct recreational implications.

The Minister recognises this in one of his reports: "The task of the district welfare workers is to keep in touch with all juvenile aid associations, to support them with advice and practical work, and to encourage them to combine in the organisation of sports and fêtes and in the establishing of such institutions as . . . recreation grounds, gymnasium halls, cinemas, libraries, etc., which are often beyond the resources of the individual associations. . . . The committees, too, have recognised the high importance of the work and have done their best to further it. They employ various methods to gain their objects. Meetings, readings and lectures, parlour games, folk song, lute or mandolin evenings, class singing and instrumental music classes, lantern lectures, theatrical performances, folk dancing

. . . classes for papier-mâché work, needle work, organising walks and physical exercises, are the best
known of these methods of education. . . . The weakening of family life in the big towns is growing ever
more apparent, and the consequent state of joyless-
ness and homelessness is creating a real need for the
organisation of a happy community life."

During the years 1919 to 1922 grants have been allocated from the central fund to the governing presidents for purposes including the following list: "Drill,
games, and recreation grounds—1,520 cases; gymnasiums—130 cases; shelters for juvenile and travellers'
shelters—101 cases; bath and swimming cases—111;
young people's clubs—13,026; gymnastic spaces and
game clubs—148,111. Often the sum allocated was
inconsiderable but always sufficient for the purpose, as
experience has shown that very little help from the
state is enough to encourage donations on the part of
the public."

This department in Prussia is also responsible for
physical training except where the schools are concerned, and has given much attention to gymnastics.
It administers also the national sports fund so far as
Prussia participates in that fund, and has established
various committees for technical advice to local groups,
and to establish helpful relationships between the municipality and the chief organisations and clubs.

The Youth Movement.—The Social Welfare Minister of Prussia, in his account of the administration
of the Youth Welfare Law, gives his attention to the
Youth Movement as follows:

"Although we have spoken chiefly of Juvenile Aid,
the Ministry has not neglected the Youth Movement,
which is not quite the same thing. As it is obvious
that forces are at work in the Youth Movement with

the object of inaugurating the improvement of the
race from within, the representatives of this movement
have also been granted the ear and the assistance of the
Ministry.   Though the Youth Movement refuses all
adult co-operation or influence and is strongly in-
sistent on retaining its independence and autonomy,
nevertheless the Leagues of Youth have more than
once applied to the Ministry, for instance for concessions of different kinds (reductions of railway fares,
grants for organised leisure, congresses, expeditions,
periodicals, etc.)   Whenever possible, their requests
have been complied with.   As this sometimes involved
the instrumentality of the District or Local Welfare
Workers, relations have been established between Juvenile Aid and the Youth Movement, the limits of which
are not at all clearly defined; and this can only tend
to be a useful factor.   The Leagues of Youth are
beginning to understand that a sharp differentiation
between Juvenile Aid and the Youth Movement is not
practicable, and, above all, that such differentiation
could in certain circumstances only be harmful to the
Youth Movement, and that, on the other hand, Juvenile
Aid has been encouraged by the Youth Movement."

What, then, is the Youth Movement?   Several volumes might be devoted to a complete answer of that
question; the ramifications of the Movement are so
varied and so numerous that a full account of them is
here out of the question.   We shall, therefore, not attempt to convey more than a general impression of the
scope and nature of the Youth Movement.

Historically, the Youth Movement tendency in Germany found its first notable expression in the rise of
the student-patriots * in the early nineteenth century.
The gymnastic societies inaugurated at this period by

* The Burschenschaften.

Jahn, later suffered division between Catholics and
Protestants. The first vocational Youth organizations
arose in 1870—associations of apprentices, etc. In
1897 the first "Wander-group" was formed, among
students. The development of this "Wander-bird"
(Wandervogel) movement was at first "bourgeois"; it
had particular strength about 1910; manifestations
of it still persist which will be discussed later. An interesting outcome of the Wandervogel movement was
the construction of many Jugendherbergen,—outdoor
shelters for wandering youth. Another aspect of the
Youth Movement was the development of the Path-
finder (or Scout) Movement; before the war this organisation was Christian-nationalist-conservative. The
Wandervogel Movement on the other hand was freer,
and tended to consideration of and agitation over
social problems, feminism, sex relations, etc.; it encountered strong opposition in some quarters. From
1910 to 1913 the Wandervoegel numbered only about
10,000, but were of intense enthusiasm. During these
years before the war the "Youth Movement" influenced
all organisations of young people toward interest in
folk music, primitive arts, simplicity in recreation and
life; "the old songs were introduced to the city."

It is probably necessary to distinguish here between
the psychological "Youth Movement,"—that is, the
dawning twentieth century revolt of German youth
against its environment,—and the history of youth
organisation in general, as given above. Thus we
might say that the already existing organisations of
youth which had grown up during the past century
made it possible for the psychological "Youth Movement," a definitely modern impulse, to take a form and
gain attention. It is important to remember, however,
that since the war the "Youth Movement" in its earliest

form has virtually ceased to exist; no longer represented by unified and powerful initiative, it has broken
up into numerous divisions, such as the Communist
group, the Socialist group, the Pacifist group, the
Catholic group, the Protestant group, etc.   What
were formerly its primary ideals have tended to become secondary to those of the numerous political or
religious groups of which it has become a part.   If
an analogy be needed to clarify a somewhat confusing
situation, one might say that a similar situation would
exist if, in the United States, a movement resembling
the German Youth Movement were in existence, and
certain members of the movement should decide to ally
themselves with the Y.M.C.A. and thereafter pursue
only such of their former "Youth" activities and ideals
as were compatible with Y.M.C.A. activities and ideals,
while at the same time other members of the same
movement should decide to ally themselves, say, with
the Rotary Club of America and henceforth continue
to act only on such of their "youth" principles as were
congenial to Rotarians.   If this analogy be kept in
mind, and if it be remembered that in Germany, instead of having split into merely two, the "Youth
Movement" has split into half a dozen or more main
divisions, a more definite idea will be had of the present
complexity and diversity of "youth" activities in Germany, and of why one is justified in concluding that
the "Youth Movement" of which Americans, interested in recreation, hear so much, no longer exists in
Germany as a definite and unified force.

The administration of the Juvenile Welfare Act
bears an intimate relation to certain aspects of the
Youth Movement. This interrelation no doubt results
from the fact that the Ministry of Social Welfare, in
order to facilitate its administration of the Juvenile

Welfare Act, instituted, throughout Germany, "Youth
Welfare" societies. Concerning this interrelation, the
Welfare Minister in his 1925 "Memorandum" on the
"Furtherance of Youth Welfare Work in Prussia,"
writes: "Although it must be admitted that the Youth
Movement itself is at present in a state of crisis in
which the question of leadership and older members
predominates, it must be accorded to it as a noteworthy triumph that the Youth Welfare societies have
borrowed a great deal from it, so that the difference
between Youth Welfare and the Youth Movement has
become negligible." It becomes obvious, then, that the
difference between them is one that can be of vital
concern only to specialists; throughout the remainder
of this report, therefore, the term Youth Movement
is to be understood as in many instances applying
equally to Youth Welfare societies. In the same
"Memorandum," concerning the Youth Movement itself,
the Welfare Minister writes: "It must not be overlooked that before 1911 a movement sprang from
Youth itself that aimed at a deepening consciousness
on the part of young people. A section of growing
Youth sought with a vague but compelling eagerness
for the right way. It was this section that came to
be known as the 'Youth Movement' (Jugendbewegung).
They had grown tired of accepting without examination
old ideas and habits of life, merely because their elders
told them to. They wanted, according to the formula
later enunciated, to build their lives 'out of the desires
in their own hearts, on their own responsibility, with
inward truth.' In the Wandervoegel this section of
Youth found its first and most adequate expression.
And in turning away from artificial people and things,
in returning to simplicity in clothing, food and mode
of living, avoiding the civilised poisons, alcohol and

nicotine, they found their way back to nature and love of the home and revived such ancient properties as folk songs, folk attire, folk dances and folk games. And if this young force often behaved absurdly it must not be forgotten that it carried on with determination and success a war against what was obsolete, unnatural, unhealthy and destructive.

"They were only a handful of high-minded young people with a community of ideas, but they formed a leaven to the whole of Youth. Nor could the societies for the welfare of youth avoid their influences, since their leaders actually came from the Youth Movement. They took something of the outward forms of the Youth Movement, and their inward order was in many respects similar: in particular, there was a new relation between leaders and the young. The leader, whose position before had been so often based on outward authority, became in innumerable Youth Associations the older and experienced friend of the younger members. So, in each of the circles referred to, the reaction from the materialist-intellectual mode of living, which had gained so much ground before the war, took shape. The soul of youth, which had been so long starved and unsettled by a mere culture of appearances, turned eagerly to all those who wished to raise it above the smallness and baseness of everyday. The Youth Movement and the movement for youth welfare, despite their differences in origin, entered into relationship. The result of this mutual inclination was that new life flowed into the work for Youth.

"All these activities found their practical fulfilment in the resurgence of the life of the Youth societies. The great gaps torn in the Youth societies by the war were quickly filled after it ended; both the profound

experiences of the war and the political situation arising out of the revolution moved the young to band
themselves together. For not a few of them, feeling
that the youthful slogans of 'freedom to live one's own
life' and 'right of self-determination' would be fatal
to many, desired association and leadership. They
thought to find these leaders in the ripened youths and
men who had returned from the battlefields. Thus innumerable new foundations of Youth societies were
registered that had their origin not least of all in the
prevailing political and philosophical disputes."

These numerous Youth Societies undertook many activities which were in the nature of social welfare and
which therefore need not be gone into here in any
detail; among these was the campaign "against alcohol, nicotine, venereal disease and obscenity"; other
instances of these welfare activities will be given later
in connection with our account of the Bellevue Youth
Exhibition; but since several of them have given rise
to specific remedial recreation and leisure provisions,
they deserve to be mentioned here. Thus the Welfare
Minister, in reference to a campaign "against alcohol,
nicotine, venereal disease and obscenity," writes: "The
most practical way of countering these evils is to accustom young people to gymnastics, games, sports,
walking-tours and edifying moral amusements (folk
songs, music, pictorial art, scientific lectures, folk
dances, and home-games among many others). The
Government was therefore anxious to support, by State
assistance, all associations working on these lines; and
especially by the creation of establishments designed
to lead young people away from bars and dance-
places. Thus it was necessary, above everything,
to further the building of Homes of Youth.* Who-

* The "Judgendheim" or community clubhouse for youth.

ever wishes to withhold Youth from the destroying
influence of the streets must provide it with some
place where it will find an agreeable home and desirable
companionship. The catastrophic shortage of homes
made this all the more necessary."

One of the most striking instances of official sympathetic understanding of the Youth Movement and
co-operation with it in one of the most notable of its
recreational developments is brought out by the Welfare Minister's paragraphs on "Walking-tours and
Shelters":

"The form of physical exercise least dependent on
rules and regulations or on any essential equipment,
and at the same time the one which affords the most
varied forms of bodily activity, is walking. The great
popularity of walking among Youth does not date from
the post-war period, nor is it to be attributed solely
to these arguments. As has already been pointed out
the Youth Movement began with the 'Wandervoegel,'
and found in them its most marked expression. It has
also been pointed out that this was a spiritual movement, having for its object the inner reform of the
young people. It was, however, fortunate that at the
same time it was a means of developing their physical
capacity in a high degree. The war, which took many
young people far afield, and a certain tendency to
romanticism which became very evident among the
young after the war, had the effect of awakening or
reviving the love of wandering in all circles. The
'Wandervoegel' themselves had many imitators. Hardly
any society of Youth could escape the overmastering
attractions of the walking-tour, and at the same time
the properly prepared and executed tour was a brilliant help to other activities. He who wanders gaily
with congenial companions becomes neat in dress and

other daily affairs, learns to keep house with the simplest means, adds to his knowledge of geography, nature-study and history, acquires understanding for the culture of his country, comes into contact with fellow countrymen who would otherwise be far removed from him, learns the love of nature and stands bowed with solemn awe before the wonders and mysteries that are revealed to him in sunlight or by the rays of the stars. He also acquires community sense and knows a real joy in life, as he wanders with his comrades, singing the old folk songs, or sits with them beside the camp-fire.

"So to-day, despite the hardness of the times, we see thousands and still more thousands of young people of both sexes striding with undaunted mien by field and wood and mountain and valley; the hope of a better future for our people.

"But this bright side of the picture is not without its shadows. The lack of restraint which has characterised many young people as a result of the war and the post-war period has also infected some of the young people of the walking societies with a tendency to exaggeration in clothing and behaviour and with lack of consideration for the public, private property and official regulations, which is to be condemned in the interests of a movement in itself at once so healthy and desirable. This development has been severely repressed by the authorities and the associations. And since, beside this, no small section of the young people themselves have earnestly striven to avoid such undesirable features of the walking-hours, it is to be hoped that the evil will gradually disappear.

"Closely connected with the question of walking-tours is the development of a system of Youth-shelters. It is evident that the walking-tour habit could not have

attained such extensive popularity if the arrangement
of resting places for the night had not to some extent
made equal progress. It is generally not possible for
the young people to afford the comparatively high expense of passing the night in inns; and, moreover, it is
altogether undesirable that they should do so, since
the inn presents altogether too many temptations in
the form of alcohol and nicotine and other so-called
pleasures.

"It is due to the Association for German Youth-
shelters that this question was early accorded the necessary attention. To its tireless activities is to be attributed the fact that to-day many Youth-shelters
are available. Besides the simple, small, provisionally
equipped shelters that have been made out of old
buildings no longer in use (barns, barracks, watch-
towers and the like), there are also shelters for several
hundred sleepers, some of which have been designed
especially for the purpose. Among these are a few
old castles and strongholds which have been converted
into Youth-shelters and are also used as meeting places
for Youth assemblies and courses of instruction.

"But despite the considerable numbers of these shelters already in existence they fall a long way below
the most urgent requirements. Steady and methodical
co-operation is necessary between State and Communal
authorities and the Association for German Youth-
shelters for the next few years in order so to extend the
net of these shelters that youthful wanderers shall find
everywhere an adequate number of resting places.

"The institution of Youth-shelter meetings and
Youth-shelter weeks has proved itself a good way of
raising means to carry on this work.

"The Ministry has encouraged by every means
within its power the development of these walking-

tours and of the shelter system. In 1923 it was possible to devote not inconsiderable sums to assist the excursions of school children and young people who had left school. The 'Rules for State subsidised Holiday-walking-tours' were drawn up for the tours subsidised in this way. Unfortunately in 1924 not sufficient means were available to carry on the work thus begun. It would be regrettable if it should not be possible to give such assistance in the future years.

"To assist the work a great many courses of instruction for the leaders of walking parties were held in different districts.

"The secretaries (Geschaeftsfuehrer: lit. business leaders) of the branch committees of the Association for German Youth-shelters receive compensation for their expenditure on actual costs out of the Youth Welfare Fund, and are invited to the district conferences of circle Youth Welfare Workers. At the session of the provincial council on November 19, 1924, the question of Youth-shelters was one of the most important on the agenda.

"Besides this, subsidies are granted for the building of Youth-shelters. Negotiations with the Minister of Agriculture, Fields and Forests has in various cases made it possible to buy wood at low prices from State properties; and it was also possible to persuade the Minister of Finance to part with former army equipment such as barracks, and in one case two ships, at reduced prices for conversion into Youth-shelters.

"Finally, it must be mentioned that the extensive reduction of railway-fares for the young (half-price in the 3rd class, and since 1921, in 4th class, for minimum party of ten and a leader) made as early as 1912 in conjunction with the Ministry, has been especially valuable in assisting the Youth walking-tours. This reduction was later granted to all Youth-associations affiliated to the local and circle committees for Youth Welfare work. After the railways were taken over by the federal system these privileges were further extended and otherwise regulated. The new order, after the setting-up of the federal administration, led to a good deal of confusion, which was largely responsible for the decrease, so regrettable from the point of view of young people, of the reduction privilege from one-half to one-third. The Prussian Government and other official bodies immediately and emphatically agitated for a return to the previous extent of the privilege. At the time of going to press the negotiations have not led to any result."

United Youth.—The "Principles of the National Committee of the German Leagues of Youth" officially adopted, include the following:

"No. 1. The fact of belonging to the National Committee in no way restricts the internal independence and external freedom of movement of the associated Leagues. This gives rise to the following highly important principles: that no League will be urged by the Committee to any particular decision or obliged to carry it out against its own wishes. Only unanimous decisions are valid in the National Committee.

"No. 2. The National Committee of the German Leagues of Youth does not represent the individual Leagues and does not seek to further their individual endeavours and aims, but to foster all that is recognised as the common good. The Committee is the representative of the whole of German youth and its interests, and not of individual Leagues or ways of thinking. It adopts no attitude towards individuals and holds no views as to their respective value.

"No. 3. The chief object of the National Committee is to attain by sincere and conscious endeavour, harmonious relations between all its members, not by persuading some and giving way to others, but on the basis of honest conviction and practical considerations. Its motto is, Not to insist on one's rights, but to find out what is right and truly public-spirited in the interests of the community.

"No. 4. The National Committee of the German Leagues of Youth does not wish to do away with heterogeneousness, nor to conceal divergent and contrasting elements in its different members. On the contrary, it considers that mutual understanding and honest respect can better be obtained by accentuating and recognising points of divergence, than by ignoring them for fear of disagreement; and it considers this the only honest way of attaining true and sincere mutual understanding.

"These principles were laid down by Carl Mosterts (deceased), first Chairman of the National Committee from 1921 to 1924."

The Cassel Congress.—The first concerted action of the various youth organisations in regard to leisure hours occurred at the Cassel Congress, held at Cassel under the title of "The Free Time of Youth," on October 6 and 7, 1925. At this Congress the whole problem of the free time of Youth was exhaustively discussed. The following Resolution was passed:

"The Board of German Leagues of Youth, meeting in open session, is strongly convinced that the demands made by the said Board in January and April, 1925, for legislation on the subject of working-hours and leisure periods for young wage-earners ought to be conceded by the legislature without delay, in order to avoid serious harm to the nation's health and to its mental and economic strength.

"The Board requests all organisations and authoritative bodies interested in youth and general social welfare to give their adherence to the carefully considered, unanimous demands of the 74 Leagues of Youth, and to co-operate in obtaining their speedy fulfilment.

"The Board is confident that those responsible for the economic prosperity of the country will recognise the importance to the nation of the demands made and that they will not place any obstacles in the way of their fulfilment."

The "demands" referred to were in substance, the following:

"1. Extension of the protective regulations for apprentices and young workers and employés from the age of 14 to the completed 18th years.

"2. Establishment of a working week of, at most, 48 hours (including trade instruction and the time which may be required for clearing up).

"3. Beginning of the Sunday break at Saturday, mid-day.

"4. Establishment of adequate breaks in working day.

"5. Prohibition of night work for young workers."

The spirit which motivated the Congress was eloquently reflected by its Chairman, Herr Mosterts, who observed in his preamble to the above-cited Resolution, "We see that man is his own enemy by the way in which he has let himself be mastered by economic forces. If we are not in a position to remedy this situation by degrees, we are nevertheless in a position to introduce a certain measure of equality. We cannot reinstate the harmony, the meaning and the object of work, but we can create a kind of rhythm between this crippling, soul-destroying toil and the leisure which recreates and elevates mankind. In my opinion, that is the most convincing reason for our demand for recognised daily, weekly, and yearly periods of leisure, that men need an opportunity to recover from the effects of grinding toil and become men again. It is really not much to ask for two or three weeks of annual holiday for young wage-earners, when we consider that secondary schoolchildren of the same age have 12 weeks' holiday in the year, and university students of the same age, five months. We do not merely wish to afford a breathing space for the wage-earners because we see them being killed off; we are fighting for periods of leisure, because we leaders of youth hold the following view,—young humanity is in our charge, they are our followers, and in Humanity we see Man, God's highest creation, and we wish to bring him back and make him a man again; this is the reason for our demand, and this is why we see ourselves obliged to request the economic powers not to hinder us from making men out of a mass of humanity. We wish to devote our own leisure to this purpose."

Socialist Union of Young Workers of Germany.— Any one desiring a detailed account of the activities of this important Youth organisation, one of the leading forces in the Cassel Congress, is referred to their "Report for 1924-1925," published by the Young Workers Press, Berlin. The report gives detailed accounts under such headings as "Educational Work," "Amusement, Companionship, Holidays," "Young People's Libraries," "Rambling, Outdoor Games," "Hostels for Young People," "Foreign Travel," etc. This organisation, as one would expect, is one of the most zealous of all the Youth groups in its advocacy of social welfare and free-time legislation and provision for young people. It has a staggering strength of numbers, and engages largely in the study of political questions and political theories; the aim here is to "move young people to think" (from a Social-democratic standpoint, naturally).

Youth in Frankfort-am-Main.—In Frankfort-am-Main there is a keen movement toward a spirit of understanding and co-operation among the numerous and varied youth groups. Here a great Day of Youth has been celebrated—the uniting in athletics and various exercises of all the organisations of youth, Catholic, Socialist, Jewish, etc. A mutual purpose does much to unite the young people; they are working for the establishment of a great central community House of Youth, which is to serve as headquarters and recreation and meeting place for all the youth of Frankfort. The spirit here seemed, therefore, one of the healthiest and pleasantest encountered throughout Germany. The Jugendamt (Youth Bureau) of Frankfort is mainly concerned with welfare work. The affairs of the stadium and all matters pertaining to athletics and sports are under the direction of the Town Office for Athletics, Sports and Baths (Stadtamt fuer Turn-Sport-und-Badewesen).

The 1927 Youth Exposition.—Perhaps the most adequate idea both of the Youth Movement and of its relation to official provision may be conveyed by an account of the Youth Exposition or Exhibition held August-September, 1927, at the Schloss Bellevue, Berlin. On the occasion of its opening, several Ministers of the Federal Government and of Prussia, and various individuals prominent in education, hygiene, and youth welfare work, were present. The exhibition was

financed by the federal Ministry of the Interior and
by the governments of the different states, by private organisations, by the Youth associations themselves, etc. The exhibition had three divisions, whose
purpose was to demonstrate the needs of the youth,
the provisions already existing for youth welfare, and
the actual tendencies and accomplishment of the youth
movement itself. The divisions comprised the following
subjects:

1. Population problem
   Professional problems
   Social standard
   Hygiene and health
2. The problem of young workers' leisure—setting
   forth data as to measures taken by authorities,
   organisations, industrials, youth organisations,, etc
3. The cultural movement of German youth.

As the subjects in the first division concern chiefly
social welfare, we shall not go into them further; to
the subject of the second and third divisions we shall
now give some attention.

The purpose of the exposition was stated as being
one of public education, to set forth hitherto unclear
or neglected facts and statistics informing the public
of the actual problems and tendencies of the youth
of the nation, and especially in this manner to bring
public attention upon the conditions affecting the leisure of young workers.

The stress of the cultural aspect of the German
youth-movement created one of the most interesting
sections of the exhibition. The exhibit of primitive
arts was particuarly good. Excellent examples of
weaving, metal work, cabinet work, design, etc., were
displayed, and there were exhibits indicating the in-

terest and achievement of the young people in music, painting, and folk dancing. Perhaps a few random quotations from the prospectus of the exhibition will best serve to convey an impression of the spirit motivating the cultural activities of the youth movement. Thus, under the heading "Dancing, Music, Literature, Amateur Theatricals," appears the following: "It would have been an impossible undertaking to attempt to illustrate this phase of juvenile life by means of pictures and literature, as this side of life, and the impulse of youth towards a new form of culture, do not lend themselves to pictorial illustration. Let me explain by giving an example: The new movement that has arisen in music cannot be shown to visitors to the exhibition by means of books and pictures, however beautiful; it can only be done by means of the living music itself. For this reason, the important features of this division are performances by troupes of juvenile musicians, dancers, and actors, and, last but not least, the evening lectures which are designed to supplement the exhibits in this room. We therefore recommend all visitors to take advantage of this rare opportunity and to see the best young German dancers, musicians and actors, thus obtaining a vivid idea of the spirit of culture which is obviously now informing the youth of Germany.

"I should like to make a few remarks about the literature displayed in this room. The library of a leader of youth is so constituted that it forms a nucleus containing all the works most essential for all leaders of youth. By means of collaboration between the representatives of Leagues of various sects or classes, this nucleus is supplemented by the books necessary to a leader of youth in his own particular branch, *i.e.*, Evangelical, Catholic, National or Socialist. In the same way, leaders of youth have collaborated to add a collection of light literature (top shelf), which contains books likely to be popular with young readers or especially suitable for reading aloud.

"In this connection, mention should be made of the works exhibited by the publishers connected with the Youth Movement. The German Leagues of Youth have a total of 42 publishing organisations of their own, in addition to which there are a number of publishing houses which were founded in close connection with the League of Youth. . . . The periodicals of the Leagues of Youth are more than mere journals of the activities and interests of the Leagues; they are highly important vehicles of expression of the inner life and organisation of the Leagues of Youth. . . . As newspaper cuttings and pictures show, all branches of cultural and social life are treated in the Youth periodicals. Another exhibit well worth noticing is that showing the development of these periodicals. This historical comparison between the periodicals of yesterday and of to-day reflects most clearly the desire of youth for reform in cultural and in social conditions."

And under the heading "Pictorial Art and Artistic Handicrafts": "In comparison with the movement started by Youth for a renewal and deepening of music, the artistic activities of Youth appear to the outsider much less important. Nevertheless, the whole Youth Movement is so closely bound up with artistic endeavour and activity that it would be an injustice to take the efforts of youth in pictorial and applied art less seriously than its other activities.

"On account of the limited space available in the exhibition, our workers in the domain of pictorial and applied art thought it best to show only modern forms as pursued by youth. In every branch of fine or applied art, really good craftsmanship and technical knowledge were required, in order that the exhibits might have a real educational value.

"Our exhibition of fine and applied art only comprises a small proportion of the artistic work of the rising generation, but still it gives an idea of their keenness in the matter of arts and crafts. The young artists and craftsmen whose work is on show are nearly all at the beginning of their artistic development, but we trust that this modest exhibit of artistic works and handicrafts is sufficient proof that the Youth Movement has already borne good fruit in this direction."

Youth Labour Problems at the Schloss Bellevue Exhibition.—The second of the three divisions of the Schloss Bellevue exhibition devoted to the problems of young workers' leisure set forth data as to existing conditions, measures advocated, and measures taken by authorities, organisations, industrials, youth organisations, etc. Concerning these measures and conditions sufficient indications, for the purpose of this report, have already been given in our account of the Cassel Congress. As to the spirit behind this section of the Exhibition, it was probably best expressed by the words of the Bulletin: "The second part of the Exhibition is concerned with the importance of leisure and shows how the young themselves have organised it. This division is interesting not only in connection with the demands of the Leagues of Youth for the protection of the young, but also because of the important fact that the present tendency towards efficiency methods and mechanical processes in industry is making it more and more urgently necessary to see that young people's leisure is used for good purposes. The exhibition gives an idea of what has been accomplished in the way of protective work by the Leagues of Youth, the Churches, the schools, industry, the self-government associations, the German States and the Central Government. It is the endeavour of the exhibition to indicate that the various work that is now already being done in the way of organising young people's leisure is a safeguard for the judicious employment of extended leisure, since the young people themselves evince a strong inclination to work seriously for their own improvement and to prepare themselves for the multifarious duties that face every one to-day in public or professional life. This division of the exhibition also indicates what further measures should be taken for juvenile welfare, in order to make youth's efforts at self-education still more efficacious."

Its spirit and purpose were further expressed when, referring to a certain room, the Bulletin stated: "Here again we have a striking example of the needs of youth as regards leisure hours. The central exhibit recalls to mind the statistics as to working conditions among juveniles, and points out that without leisure there is no means of instilling culture into the young."

The Report of the German Youth Exhibit brings out the fact that in the year 1926 the Ministry expended half a million marks for Youth Welfare, and a million marks for athletic and sport activities and "Youth-wandering"; we have quoted at some length an instance of the far-sighted official attitude in regard to this latter.

Music, Folk-Dancing, and Other Cultural Activities Encouraged by Youth Movement.—Folk dancing, folk music, primitive crafts, and various other cultural activities, including amateur theatricals, are encouraged by all the divisions of the youth movement. A sort of birds'-eye view of the progress of the youth movement in this direction may be had from the following brief extract from the aforementioned Report of the Ministry of Welfare on Youth Welfare Work in Prussia:

"The vulgar street song and doubtful comic opera hit must be counteracted by the encouragement of good German folk songs. And here, too, good progress has recently been made. The 'Wandervoegel,' who not only encourage walking tours, but also strive towards cultural rejuvenation and who have accomplished valuable work in some of the spheres mentioned, have brought the folk song again into being. In recent years a movement has come into being to develop a new mode of life on the basis of the revival of the old folk songs, and is endeavouring to further this idea by the institution of singing-weeks. Here, too, district and circle Youth Workers are taking the lead.

"In order to develop a feeling for good music, folk concerts for the young, at low prices, and nowadays with the assistance of youthful orchestras, have been inaugurated. Not a few local committees for Youth Welfare have developed successful activities in this sphere.

"What applies to music can also be said of folk dances. The modern jazz negro dances, so beloved of the young, have found a formidable competitor in the revived folk dances. For these the old-time dresses are used, which compare so favourably in cut and gaiety of colour with the products of the modern factory and are at the same time so much more suitable. And with the old rounds and dances good old dramatic games have been remembered that come down from the Middle Ages and the days of Hans Sachs and others. The attempt to awaken them to new life has shown that even in our time they have lost no attraction and that by their means one can do away with the unrepeatable jests and not unobjectionable pranks which formerly dominated community life. The old home sagas are also recalled; they are dramatised and enacted in the open-air or on the spots where they actually took place—for instance, in the ruins of a castle. How eagerly the young people take part in the preparations, and how enthusiastic they are at the performances! Classical pieces have also been successfully given by the Youth associations, and occasionally by professional players in special performances for the young.

"All these activities should provide Youth with desirable moral amusements, give them back their homeland, and bind them to house and home, country and countrymen, customs and habits, history, culture and the thought of their native land.

"These efforts have been furthered by district, circle and locality committees, by district and circle Youth welfare workers, by conferences, courses of instruction, exhibitions, the holding of competitions and festivals in connection with the societies."

A completer idea of the Youth movement in its relation to music is given in an article by Walter Ulrich Schmidt called "The Youth Movement and Music," which appeared in "Young Germany" in September, 1926; excerpts follow:

"I attempt to give as accurate a picture as possible of what the Youth Movement has done in the way of music during the past year. . . .

"In this study we will mention only one of the paths it discovered—the one which led to music. Once more it was unerring instinct which led to the rediscovery of the folk song,—not the romantic folk songs of recent periods, but the songs of by-gone ages that flowed spontaneously from the springs of the human heart. Who has not heard the marvellously simple airs of the olden time, who has not realized the indescribable, the almost brutal directness and yet the sweetness of the old original words? These songs contained what was being sought,—unity between the people and their music, for only a nation which was truly at one in its culture could have given voice to these melodies. Still, let us examine the real motives which led the Youth Movement to the rediscovery of the folk-song, and we shall find that it was not in reality a matter of *musical* perception. What was originally, and quite consciously, being aimed at, was to establish unity between people and music and to counterbalance the rubbish turned out by the manufacturers of music-hall successes and the cabaret idealists. Take the example of the wandering fiddler, the chief product of the 'Wandervoegel,' and observe how real pearls of mediæval melody are mixed up with worthless songs of a later period. From this it is easily seen that it was enough, in the first place, to make these tunes popular in the true sense of the word, without making any selection according to their musical value. There is only one thing that prevents this new collection of folk songs from sinking again into oblivion, and that is that they have the support of the youth of the nation, which sings these songs and sings them with enthusiasm. It is true that there have been various editions of folk songs for scientific purposes, some of which are gently accumulating dust on the shelves devoted to the theses of candidates for musical degrees, and many fat books of this kind are to be found. But now they have been given new life, arranged in accordance with the laws of music, and made to re-echo through the country.

"At first—and this is significant—these songs were sung only in unison. On pleasure trips, in the leisure moments of countryfolk, in the evenings round the village pump, or around the family hearth. They began to develop and to spin threads between man and man. Recognised by the older people, dimly apprehended by the younger ones, the moment began to dawn when music should become a real force in community life. Quite without any such intention, music in this way helped in promoting the community sense; it became an indispensable factor in the formation and consolidation of groups. For the original idea of the Youth Movement was, of course, spiritual, world-embracing, educational, but not musical, just as Nature was not the goal of the movement, but a path, a bridge, a school for the humanity of the future. In extreme cases, a point was reached where all gaps in a somewhat empty evening were filled up with singing. Fortunately, however, these were rare cases, though such things always occur, just as it is a phase of adolescence to develop the kind of voice suitable for singing sentimental seconds. . . ."

Then follows praise of the lute and guitar, and, to a lesser degree, of the flute and violin, instead of the piano, organ or harmonium, as an accompaniment to song; and the history of the development of better technic and taste.

"This brings us to the present day. What is now being aimed at in the important Guilds of Music and Song Clubs, is the continuation and development of what has been described above. Choirs and orchestras of young people (and here I would like to emphasise the point that I speak of youth of the spirit, not merely of years) are exercising their influence throughout Germany. Any one who doubts whether this work is justified and worth while, should convince himself, if he has a sufficiently objective mind, by considering the Musical Congresses and Festivals."

Music and Drama.—In general one may say that conditions in Germany as regards music and drama,— apart from the special instances and developments to be considered shortly,—are not markedly different from those in other central European countries. That is to say, music is in all forms generally popular. As to the theatre, its trend, outside the subsidised theatres and the Volksbuehne (People's Stage Societies), seems about the same as elsewhere; repertory has in numerous instances declined, giving place to the long-run system; and the usual proportion of public interest inclines toward the trivial and tawdry.

Subsidy System for State Theatres, Operas and Orchestras.—Of the three opera houses in Berlin two belong to the Prussian State, one to the city of Berlin. The Prussian State owns furthermore in Berlin two playhouses (the Schauspielhaus and the Schiller Theatre).

These theatres do not get a subsidy in the strict sense of the word. In the budget of the Prussian State there is one item for the estimated revenues and expenditures of all these theatres. In every case, of course, the expenditures are, by far, greater than the revenues. The deficit is made up by the Prussian State. For the budget year of 1926, for instance, a deficit for these state-owned theatres in Berlin was estimated at 3,500,000 Reichmarks; of this amount 70 per cent or nearly two and a half million marks are the deficit of the two opera houses.

The city of Berlin owns, as mentioned above, one of the opera houses in the city. This is run in the form of a joint stock company. Nearly all stocks—around 95 per cent—are owned by the city of Berlin. Of course, this opera house also has a deficit always; in 1926 it was estimated at one million marks. This deficit was made up by the city. The source of this money, whether it comes from the state or the city, is always public taxation. There are no private funds available to make up these deficits.

The Philharmonic Orchestra of Berlin is an entirely private orchestra. They also are not self-supporting; therefore the city pays them an annual subsidy, which in 1926 ran up to 60,000 marks.

Music and Drama in the Schools.—At the State Bureau of Educational Information (in Berlin) the matter of encouragement and instruction in music and drama in the free schools was discussed. The present dearth of activities is forced by the strained condition of public finances; the wisdom of such encouragement is fully realised by German educators.

The Volksbuehne (People's Stage Societies).—"The Guiding Principles of the People's Stage Society" are given in the "People's Stage Programme" which was drawn up in Jena in 1925 at the great People's State Congress. These principles clearly indicate the path mapped out for the adherents of the movement, the scheme of work they are to follow and the object for which they are to strive. The programme reads as follows: "The People's Stage is intended for all in this country who recognise the value of the artistic, and especially the dramatic expression of human greatness, and who therefore object to all political or commercial interference with such expression; who regard the theatre as a powerful instrument for the further development of human society in the form of fresh, free general culture; and who therefore desire to place the theatre within the reach of all their compatriots. . . .

"The next task of this Society will be to replace the present aimless and obviously commercial system of management prevailing in the theatre, by setting up a theatre whose existence the Society will guarantee, and whose object will be the encouragement of artistic creation. Further, the Society will foster and encourage all other forms of art. Its final aim is to co-operate actively in the building up of a true community life."

In order to give a fuller idea of this important cultural and leisure-time movement in Germany, we shall now quote various sections of a publication of the League of German People's State Societies, by Dr. S. Nestriepke, Business Manager of the League of German People's Stage Societies; the publication is called "The Nature, Formation, and Effects of a People's Stage Society."

Dr. Nestriepke's statement of "The Nature of the People's Stage" is as follows: "A theatre which aspires to the right to call itself the 'People's Stage' must be second to none in what it has to offer. Groups of stage-struck amateurs, eager to show their talents on the stage, are much too fond of adopting this appellation, to which they are by no means entitled. The living representation of a poetic work nowadays requires a measure of ability possessed only by the gifted few, besides training and practice which are generally possible only to professional actors. It is pure presumption when the name 'People's Stage' is adopted by entirely commercial managements, who wish to present to a naïve public a lot of trashy so-called 'People's Plays,' full of clap-trap sentiment and cheap effect. A 'People's Stage' worthy of the name must be artistically faultless as regards both production and performance.

"Further, the name 'People's Stage' implies an obligation on the part of the management to consult public taste. It is not enough to fix cheap prices and produce popular plays. The true 'People's Theatre' must be much more deeply in accord with the spirit of the people. It should not be an undertaking that gives performances *for* the people; it must be managed and supported by an association of representatives of the people and must express the culture and tastes of the people.

"The object of the modern 'People's Stage Movement' is, therefore, in the first place to form associations of this kind, ready and able to lay the foundations of a new intellectual theatre. It appeals to artistic circles everywhere, and particularly among the working classes, to join together in forming 'People's Stage Societies.' Every member has to guarantee a fixed amount in contributions to the Society every year. For every contribution a member is compensated by means of a ticket for a theatrical performance got up by the Society or reserved by the Society in an ordinary theatre. Every member has to submit to a certain discipline: for instance, he is obliged to attend the performances of the Society for which he has received a pass, and he must accept those plays selected by the management of the Society, but that does not give him a season ticket to the theatre. The Society gives its members a certain voice in the selection of plays, as they are allowed to speak at the meetings of the Society, and they can bring forward those whom they trust on the occasion of the election of the management. The management then makes the selection of what plays are to be produced, naturally in agreement with those responsible for the production side of the undertaking, decides what plays shall be performed on what days, etc."

According to Dr. Nestriepke, the formation of stage societies of this character is a step toward the following aims: (1) a reduction in the price of theatre seats; (2) the levelling of class distinctions in the

theatre audiences and the development of the community spirit in the public; (3) greater interest in the
theatre and more respect for works of artistic value;
(4) financial security for the theatrical business; (5)
the possibility of running a theatre on really artistic
lines and at the same time making it the expression of
the cultural taste of the people; (6) a revival of artistic creation.   Dr. Nestriepke gives convincing ex-
planations under each of the six, as to how each would
accomplish what he claims for it.   We have not space
here to quote all six, but shall quote the fifth and sixth
as being of especial interest from the point of view of
this survey.

Concerning the possibility of running a theatre on
really artistic lines, and at the same time making it
the expression of the cultural taste of the people, Dr.
Nestriepke writes: "No doubt, there is a wider public
for amusing and sensational shows than there is for
productions offering artistic enjoyment.   A theatrical
management whose chief interest is the box office re-
ceipts, and which therefore wants to attract the largest
possible audiences, will have the greatest success with
frivolous or sensational entertainment.   The most expensive seats will then 'go off,' for the 'new rich' do not
care about Goethe or Hauptmann, but are much more
attracted by dance reviews and sugary tunes.   But the
'People's Stage' with its organised public, need not
cater for this class of audience.   Even the producer of
'People's Stage' performances is not wholly free.   He
has to consider his organised audience.   But he has to
deal with a community which was formed because all
its members felt the same longing for art and the same
wish for culture.   This wish for culture will be the
guiding principle of the theatre and will at the same

time afford the opportunity for the true cultivation of art."

As to "a revival of artistic creation," he writes: "If the formation of 'People's Stage Societies' means new respect for any study of artistic works, this must be to the advantage of the actor's art. When an audience is extremely varied and therefore uncritical, it is a strong temptation for an actor to focus attention on himself by ranting and other cheap stage tricks. When, on the contrary, an audience is united and deeply absorbed, it is easier for an actor to sink his own ego in the assumed personality and to give a sincere and thoughtful performance. And if a poet to-day, wishing to forsake the well-trodden paths of convention and to make new experiments of his own, fails to find any community in which the heart of the people beats, which yearns for the expression of its secret, inner aspirations—his listening ear will soon hear new sounds emanating from the 'People's Stage Societies,' which will encourage him to new creative efforts.

"The formation of 'People's Stage Societies' in large numbers *is the only way in which the theatre can be saved* from the serious crisis through which it is now passing, and the only way to the salvation of the cultural theatre and, simultaneously, to the cultural theatre's being taken to the heart of the great mass of the people."

An idea as to the origin and development of the "People's Stage Societies" may be obtained from Dr. Nestriepke's account, under the heading, "League of the German People's Stage Societies and Theatrical Union": "The People's Stage Movement arose from the endeavours of the Labour Movement to ensure a share of culture to the proletariat. In 1890 the 'Free People's Stage' in Berlin, the first of its kind, was founded by Socialists. But there was no intention of using this new organisation as a party tool. And it became more and more evident that the 'People's Stage Movement,' which gradually grew up out of this Berlin foundation and which resulted in the formation of many kindred societies outside Berlin, especially after the revolution of 1918, was of the greatest importance in helping the proletariat to culture, and further, that, leaving aside all party or class considerations, it must make it its object to unite all those who wished to co-operate in the building up of a new cultural community, and who wished to see in the place of the commercial theatre, a theatre run on Socialist lines, *i.e.*, one that caters for the needs of the general public. The Societies that had been formed according to the pattern of the 'Berlin People's Stage,' banded together in 1920 under the title 'League of the German People's Stage Societies.' The Statutes of the League set forth as its purpose:—To arouse public interest in the idea of the 'People's Stage,' to represent the organisations, and to make the 'People's Stage Movement' into an active force in realising all endeavours directed towards the communal encouragement of art, and above all towards getting theatrical management into the hands of the public. The following 'Associations of a publicly useful character' are eligible for admission to the League:—

"(1) Those which aim at securing the lowest possible uniform seat prices at artistic performances, especially theatrical performances by professionals, for their members, without making a remunerative business of the undertaking:

"(2) Those which are based on the right of their members to make their own decisions, and which try to reach all classes of the population irrespective of politics or creed, desirous of attaining a new national culture.

"The League of the German People's Stage Societies expanded extremely rapidly. It was largely due to its influence that the number of People's Stage Societies became greater daily. By the end of 1923, more than a hundred People's Stage Societies, with a membership of over 400,000, belonged to the League. The League had meanwhile set up several District Secretariats, had taken over as the organ of the League the periodical entitled 'People's Stage' started by the Berlin People's Stage Society, had initiated a 'People's Stage Correspondence" to give regular news to the Press, had inaugurated a Dramaturgical Bureau, had started the 'Dramaturgical News' which was published for the purpose of supplying intelligence to all the member Societies, and, finally, had organised a special publishing house for the People's Stage Societies, which issued acting editions of stage plays, and also an exchange for approved films of real artistic value. The work of the League contributed sensibly to the popularisation of the idea of a People's Stage and heightened the respect of the public for the movement. The League was a tower of strength to the theatrical societies among its members, as it was always at pains to help them by word and deed; moreover, it worked successfully in their interests by asking for concessions from the authorities as to reduction of railway fares, obtaining of theatres and so on; it further gave financial assistance from its own funds, supplied valuable properties and artistic accessories—for instance, in 1923 the production of the 'Maskenwagen' by the Holtorf Troupe was made possible by the assistance of the League, which wished to offer its member Societies the best possible productions in the most favourable circumstances—and, finally, it obtained subsidies to the movement in general, as well as to individual Societies, from public funds.

"When quite a number of People's Stage Societies on the model of the original Berlin Society had come into being, the 'Theatrical Union' was founded in Frankfurt-am-Main, with the object of linking up these 'Free People's Theatres' everywhere with theatrical societies based on the 'German Christian spirit.' The considerable means at the disposal of this Union made it possible for a widespread agitation to be set on foot, with the result that quite a number of Societies on this plan were formed in various centres. The Theatrical Union also set up local Secretariats, a publishing house and an acting edition of plays. But the Union never became as important as the Leagues. Its member bodies nowhere reached the proportions even of the original Berlin People's Stage Society."

Although as we have seen the People's Stage Society began in Berlin about 1890, the provincial development did not begin until 1918. The membership throughout Germany is 550,000—260 groups; there are 130,000 members in Berlin.

There are two companies in Berlin; and Berlin has organised three road companies—one for Brandenburg, one for Pommern, and one for Schlesia.

No account of the People's Stage Society would be complete without mention of the great and justly famous Volksbuehne Theatre in Berlin. For the excellence of its stage in the way of dimensions, lighting facilities, and all conceivable mechanical equipment, it is hardly equalled,—certainly it is not surpassed,— by any other theatre in the world.

In Berlin, besides the regular performances of the two Volksbuehne companies, members are enabled at intervals to attend certain performances in the opera houses at special rates. As an example of the system of a provincial Volksbuehne organisation, we may take the city of Koenigsberg. Performances in the municipal theatre are given over to the Volksbuehne once or twice a month throughout the season. For these occasions the seats are classified A, B and C, and the members are alternately assigned seats in each of these classes. The cost of tickets for opera performances is two marks, and for drama one mark fifty.

Absence of Widespread Amateur Movement in Germany.—It will probably have been noted that there is not in Germany anything like the English or American Little Theatre Movement, which is distinctly an amateur development based on active participation of the people themselves in the production of plays. It would seem that the German interest in the theatre is largely passive,—an attitude resulting probably from the tendency to regard the theatre seriously, as a primarily educational agency.

ENGLAND

GENERAL OBSERVATIONS

Recreation in England is a particularly difficult matter to investigate. This difficulty is not caused, as in France, by a general indifference to the more obvious recreational problems, or by absence of the various types of recreational provision, but by a lack of centralisation and co-ordination, as well as by a marked disparity of motives, on the part of the numerous agencies engaged in fostering and furthering leisure time provision in one or another of its various forms— Adult Education, Playing Fields, Playgrounds for Children, Industrial Welfare, and the like. It is of importance to remember that insofar as a formal recreation movement, or any manifestation of such a movement, exists in England, it is almost entirely dependent upon private initiative and subsidy.

Furthermore, in the absence of any unifying State influence in the varied fields of leisure activity, there has not been developed any adequate general perception of the centripetal implications of the many varying approaches to the whole problem of the use of leisure. When specific needs become sufficiently urgent, concrete efforts are usually undertaken to fill them, but without much attention to underlying social problems and usually without a very clear realisation of the potential importance of such effort in the development of a well-integrated system of provided recreation. A report of this nature is hardly the place for an analysis of the forces and influences which result in the lack of centralisation and co-ordination, and in disparate motives, in the English recreation movement, but it may be advisable to indicate some of the more important factors which have contributed to establish the situation.

In little more than a century England has changed from an agricultural country, in many respects still feudal, into one of the principal industrial nations of the world. It is hardly strange, therefore, to find something of the feudal attitude persisting under modern conditions, even in recreational matters. This attitude manifests itself in a strong tendency on the part of the less fortunate to imitate as far as possible the manners and pursuits of the more fortunate, so that the English tradition of sports, which emanated from the privileged classes, is doubtless responsible for the general hold of sport on the English public. A further persistence of the feudal influence may be seen in the feeling of responsibility of the English upper class toward the poor, at present evidenced in volunteer social work.

Nevertheless, the individual independence of the English, in all matters relating to what they consider the conduct of their private lives, must not be underestimated: it is the principal cause of their lack of centralisation and co-operation in matters affecting the use of leisure. Feudal benevolence concerned itself with supervision of the material conditions of its dependents, but for the most part adopted toward them a policy of non-interference in matters relating to their purely personal happiness. It might readily be considered an imposition, perhaps equally insufferable to both parties, for the upper classes to sponsor propaganda intended to instruct and direct the masses in their general use of leisure. Moreover, the English governing classes, who have always had "play," cannot see the point of taking it seriously as a "movement," or as a field for evangelism and propaganda. The English public is temperamentally disinclined to join widely in movements of any kind. The Englishman is apt to regard as infringement upon his personal liberty anything which may be interpreted as an interference with the manner of leisure occupation to which he has been accustomed, and anything appearing as an attempt to "improve" him is offensive to his native pride and self-esteem.

In the English there seems to operate, simultaneously with the gregarious instinct, a tendency to selectiveness and localism in social intercourse. It has been said that "if ten Englishmen were set on a desert island they would form three clubs." Throughout England there exist numerous recreational clubs of all sorts, but very little wide co-operative organisation. Similarly, there is very little general provision for recreation by religious bodies; the interest of the churches in England in the use of leisure does not approach that of the churches of America and the Continent.

The historical origin of sport is to be sought in early contests intended to develop prowess in war. The evolution of the contest, however, has varied in its different habitats: in Scandinavian and Teutonic countries the emphasis in one stage fell upon gymnastics, in Latin countries directly upon military preparedness, and in England, which is generally looked upon as the mother country of sport, upon the game, with the ultimate development of the idea of the game for play's sake. With the growth of the game as opposed to the military contest came the necessity for an artificial social concept which would keep rancour out of the heart (or the conduct) of the vanquished; out of this need there grew up in England the convention of "good sportsmanship." It is probable that this ideal of sportsmanship has influenced much of the English approach to leisure provision.

Whatever its origin, the fact remains that in England, as in Germany and the United States, and in marked contrast to France, a strong ethical motivation is expressed in the leisure time movement, with a strong appeal to social consciousness. For example, in a pamphlet entitled "The National Playing Fields Movement" issued in the interests of securing more playing fields for England, the "cause" is described as being "for the regeneration of the British people . . . it is the cause of Humanity and Justice." Most of the organisations dealing with recreation for young people appeal directly or indirectly to some ethical ideal: "Sportsmanship," "good citizenship," "raising the standards of the people," and the like. However, they do recognise the importance of play for its own sake, and strive to make provision for it. It is, accordingly, perhaps inadvisable to lay too much stress upon this ethical aspect of the English recreation movement, since propaganda appealing to the social consciousness is universally necessary to secure playing fields, and it is unlikely that the actual players will ever consciously play for the purpose of improving character.

It is interesting to observe that where individual opinion in England has attained a high degree of intelligence in appreciation of the question of the use of leisure, it is invariably regarded as a problem requiring an educational solution. A means to this solution has been furnished by the admirable work of the Adult Education authorities, the only official agency concerned in a broad sense with general questions of leisure occupation.*

One of the London daily papers recently carried an editorial taking to task the English youth for their passion for games and sport, which it considered dangerous to intellectual development and to the forming of more cultural tastes and interests. The writer even went so far as to classify sport as a menace to education: particularly he contended that the youth of the Continent, less addicted to sports, were intellectually superior to the game-infatuated Britons, and that if England was to hold her own in the international future, there must be a strong reaction from the present tendency to overemphasise and overdevelop the sporting interests of her young people. At about the same time, a Dutch journalist issued a note of warning to the British to the effect that, if they wished to hold their

* The important and interesting work of Miners' Welfare can hardly be classified as "official" in the sense in which the term is used in this report.

international position, they must cease to employ in play so many hours which were being used by their competitors for work. To all such criticism, British public opinion answers, in effect: We are more, not less, efficient because of our play.

Playing Fields Societies.—One highly important aspect of English recreation is represented in the activities of the many bodies, such as the London Playing Fields, the Manchester Playing Fields, the Commons and Footpaths Preservation Societies, the Metropolitan Public Gardens Association, and the like; all of whom, in their own areas and on behalf of those whose interests they watch, have given an immense stimulus to improving matters in regard to recreation, especially in the way of providing the people with adequate recreation grounds.

Of such bodies the London Playing Fields Society is largely typical. In its "Thirty-Sixth Annual Report," published in 1925, the London Playing Fields Society stated that "the objects of the Society as set out in the Royal Charter are: (1) To encourage and develop the playing of cricket, football, and other like games, by the clerks and working men and boys of London, with a view to the physical and moral welfare of the population; (2) to ascertain, organise, and represent the requirements and wishes of cricket and football players of those classes, particularly in negotiating with the public authorities in regard to the playing of games in the parks, commons, and other open spaces, and with railway companies in regard to reduction of fares and facility of access; (3) to increase the existing supply of public and private playing fields, within or adjoining the administrative County of London, by acquiring land and letting pitches for the season to clubs, which, though not able to give the high rents demanded by persons who let for profit, can yet pay a moderate charge, and thus reduce the competition for the limited space available in the parks and public open spaces, and leave them free for the poorest players; (4) the collection of sports gear and the distribution thereof to elementary schools and other institutions in poor neighbourhoods; and (5) the provision of miniature rifle ranges or other facilities for military purposes with a view to National Defence."

The 1925 report of the London Playing Field Society shows that the Society has made available to the London people 187 cricket pitches, 104 football grounds, 5 hockey grounds, and 145 lawn tennis courts, covering a total of 286 acres. This means play space for 4,200 cricket players, 2,900 tennis players, 2,300 football players, and 100 hockey players. These facilities are rented to various clubs for regular use.

Additional playing facilities are made available by the London County Council. Their report for 1923 shows 205 football grounds, 316 cricket pitches, and 725 tennis courts in London or in parks controlled by the London County Council, some of which may be partly outside of the city and county. In addition, other public authorities, such as the Metropolitan Borough Councils, the National Government, or the City Corporation, maintain parks and open space, some few of which are used for active recreational purposes.

These facilities are inadequate. Requests received by the authorities controlling the use of these available grounds have shown a need for an additional 900 acres, just to take care of the existing current demand.

National Playing Fields Association.—The National Playing Fields Association was organised in 1925 for the purpose of doing for all England what these other bodies have been doing for smaller areas. In its pamphlet, "More Playing Fields for the People," the Association pays tribute to these others and makes clear that it does not wish to trespass in any way on any of their functions, but at the same time ventures to suggest that "in some cases, they have failed to achieve their purpose through lack of funds and also owing . . . to the want of a central organisation to back up and support their praiseworthy efforts." Thus, at the outset, we meet with an instance, within one separate field of recreational endeavour, of that lack of centralisation characteristic of the recreation movement throughout all England. The pamphlet goes on to add, "We sincerely hope that these many bodies will now take a further step and combine with others who are equally interested and prepared to devote their time to this matter, in order to create the central organisation which, in our opinion, must be formed if a satisfactory solution of the problem is to be reached." Another pamphlet, entitled "The National Playing Fields Movement," contains further explanation of the movement's purpose and of the conditions which called it into being. "Calculations have been made," the pamphlet states, "which show that our British Public Schools * have, on the average, one acre of playground to every thirty boys. The Schools have, in fact, very much more ground than this—areas, that is to say, which are not used. But they find in practice that about one acre of playground, actually in use, is required for the healthy exercise of their boys. And there

* British Public Schools are the equivalent of American "private" schools.

are boroughs in London which have less than one acre
of open space for each 25,000 of the population. . . .
And this is not a matter which concerns only the most
congested London Boroughs. In small towns, and even
villages, the situation is often little better. It is no use,
and it would be unjust, to blame our forefathers, for
allowing the present conditions to arise. The rapid
industrialisation of the country and the enormous
growth of urban population took them unawares.
But we of this generation have no excuse for shirking.
We are no longer blind. Of the candidates for admission to the army during the last year 63 per cent
were rejected on medical examination as physically unfit for service. And this is only half the story. Besides
this 63 per cent, another large proportion, estimated
at between 10 and 15 per cent, never reached the doc-
tors for examination, but were rejected by the recruit-
ing sergeants as too obviously unfit to be worth
considering. These figures show a very pitiable state
of affairs, and the conditions, it must be borne in mind,
weigh equally heavily on both sexes. Unless they are
checked, the deterioration of the people will go on and
the standard of the British people will fall lower and
lower." Then follows an eloquent appeal for "associated effort on a national scale" to cope with the emer-
gency.

Mr. A. N. Hutt, secretary of the National Playing
Fields Association, furnished the following statement in
June, 1926, from statistics received from local authori-
ties:

"Thirty-five towns in Cornwall, Devonshire, Durham,
Essex, Lancashire, Gloucestershire, Northumberland,
Norfolk, Somerset, Sussex and Staffordshire, with a
total combined population of 1,535,730, have supplied
statistics of their public recreation grounds and pub-

lic playgrounds. The figures disclosed are somewhat
startling. They show that in these 35 towns (which include Stoke-on-Trent, Plymouth, Gateshead, South
Shields, Norwich, Southend, Barking, Chelmsford, Jar-
row and other smaller places) there is—

one public football ground	for every	14,219	persons
one public cricket ground	for every	25,595	persons
one public hockey ground	for every	127,977	persons
one public grass tennis court	for every	6,765	persons
one public hard tennis court	for every	16,000	persons
one public bowling green	for every	26,478	persons
one public putting green	for every	49,538	persons
one public playground	for every	29,533	persons

"The above figures take no account of the playgrounds attached to each School, which are reserved
exclusively for the use of school children attending each
School.

"The figures from Manchester, which are not included above, are worth recording in detail because they
show how much can be done in a great city with an
enlightened Parks Committee and a sympathetic and
progressive Council. Manchester, with a population of
758,000, has 1,615 acres of Public Open Space, of which
800 acres—an unusually high proportion—are devoted
to recreation. These 800 acres comprise 156 public
football grounds, 88 cricket pitches, 23 hockey
grounds, 115 grass tennis courts, 303 hard tennis
courts, 71 bowling greens, 9 putting greens and 44
playgrounds for children. These figures reflect great
credit on Alderman Tom Fox and the other members
of the Manchester Parks Committee who have been
preaching the 'gospel of games' for years.

"In addition to 800 acres of public Playing Fields
and Playgrounds, Manchester has approximately 800
acres of private Sports Grounds, thanks largely to the

efforts of the Manchester Playing Fields Society, and
to the energy and enthusiasm of Councillor W. Mel-
land, J.P., who founded it and who now represents
Manchester on the Council of the N. P. F. A.

"It will be noted, however, that in spite of this fine
record of achievement, Manchester has still a lot of lee-
way to make up before it can attain the standard which
the N. P. F. A. considers a reasonable ideal to aim at,
namely FIVE acres of Open Space per 1,000 of the
population, of which FOUR acres should be set aside for
recreation."

The Open Space Standard, which is the aim of the
National Association, reads as follows:

"After mature consideration of every need and difficulty, the Association has decided to urge all Local
Authorities to aim at a minimum standard of five acres
of Public Open Space for every 1,000 persons, of which
four acres should be set aside for team games (*i.e.*,
cricket, football, hockey, tennis, netball, bowls, etc.).

"An analysis of the recreational needs of the average
population will show that four acres of playing fields
is the barest minimum provision, if facilities are to be
found for all who want to play.

"According to the 1921 Census, every 1,000 persons
in England and Wales include 180 children under 10,
and 320 adults over 40; so that 500—exactly half the
population—are between the ages of 10 and 40, when
active games are mostly played; 189 of these 500 are
between 10 and 20 years old.

"Of the 500 persons between 10 and 40 years of age
it may be assumed:

"(I) That 150 (at the most) do not desire to play
games or are prevented by physical infirmity from
doing so;

"(II) That 150 are attending schools or colleges which have playing fields of their own, or are members of private sports clubs, or employes of firms which provide recreation grounds for their own people. This leaves 200 per 1,000 of the population who are neither too old nor too young to play games, who for financial or other reasons do not belong to any private sports club and who may therefore be assumed to be entirely dependent on the public pitches and courts provided by their Local Authority.

"In view of the fact that a football or hockey pitch requires at least $1\frac{1}{4}$ acres, that an acre will only provide five netball pitches or five tennis courts and that additional space is required for playgrounds for small children under 10, it will be found that at least four acres of playing pitches and playgrounds are required per 1,000 of the population.

"The Association therefore appeals to all Local Authorities and Town Planning Officers, when calculating the amount of public open space and playing fields required for their respective populations, to work to this minimum standard."

The public schools of England are, of course, famous for their interest and support of games and sports. In the public schools, which it should be remembered are what Americans call "private" schools, and also in the day schools corresponding to our public schools, games in addition to regular gymnastic exercise are recognised as an important part of the curriculum. Some day-school children are taken during school time to various play fields and to swimming and bathing places. Teachers show a genuine interest in this and are often willing to sacrifice some of their own time to make some of this play possible. Here, all of the efforts of physical education are carried on not only with the idea of physical improvement but also as a conscious means of developing character.

The Board of Education has drawn up a series of building regulations for secondary schools, comprising the principles to be observed in planning and fitting up new buildings in England. In these regulations appear the following:

"7. In every school there must be a playground suitable to the size of the school, which should provide a clear space of 50 square feet per head, but in no case must the playground contain less than 750 square yards. Special consideration will be given to the case of schools in large towns.

"8. In schools for Boys and Girls there should be separate playgrounds for the two sexes.

"9. (a) The playground should be given a warm, sunny aspect, and provided with seats. (b) The buildings should be so planned that the effective playground space will not be unduly diminished by projecting wings or buttresses.

"10. (a) The playgrounds should be properly levelled, drained, and provided with a suitable surface. Cinders, large stones, grass, and loose gravel are to be avoided. (b) The drainage should be so arranged that man-holes, gulleys, etc., are not placed in the central parts of the playground. (c) Some portion at least of the surface should be so paved as to provide sufficient space for exercise in wet weather. (d) The playground must be effectively enclosed.

"11. Bicycle sheds should be provided.

"12. Playing fields must in all cases be provided. Wherever possible, the playing fields should be adjacent to the school, and every effort should be made to secure a site which will admit of this arrangement. If this cannot be obtained, the proximity of, and ease of access to, playing fields should be taken into consideration in the choice of a site for the school.

"13. The minimum effective area for a playing field may be taken as two acres. This will usually suffice for a school of 100 pupils, but the area will require to be increased in proportion to the number of pupils and the extent to which games enter into the organisation of the school. Boys, as a rule, require more playing space than girls."

The report of Howard J. Savage, staff member of the Carnegie Foundation for the Advancement of Teaching, on games and sports in British schools and universities, contains an excellent statement of the English university and school situation in this matter of games and sports. One or two quotations may be made here:

"Naturally, public school playing fields vary widely in size. One school may have two or three rugby grounds, three or four cricket pitches, and a few fives or tennis courts. Another possesses grounds extensive enough to accommodate twenty football fifteens and nearly as many cricket elevens, twenty courts for fives, a dozen tennis courts, both grass and hard, squash and 'real' tennis courts, a cinder running track, and extensive housing for as many as two hundred boats of all sorts and sizes, to say nothing of a gymnasium— from our point of view rather slenderly equipped— where fencing, boxing, jiu-jitsu, and the like are carried on. No public school of whatever poverty would long exist without accommodations for games sufficient to allow every qualified boy to take part in at least one, or even two, contests a week. . . .

"On almost every week-day afternoon in term time, be the weather what it may, games are indulged in by some or all of the boys at an English public school. A few of the wealthier or smaller schools are said to be able to accommodate at the same time all of the boys who play, but for the most part time-tables have to be so adjusted as to release the boys for their games in sections."

The situation in day schools is thus described:

"By and large, matters concerning fields, personal equipment, coaching, schedules, and finance offer fewer contrasts with those of public schools mainly for boarders than might be anticipated.

"At a great many day schools, the real need, natural and unstimulated, for athletic grounds and fields is acute. Most day schools, having grown up in populous areas, have found themselves possessed of very little land nearby that could be devoted to games. Accordingly, in order to accommodate sports, recourse has been had to the purchase of rental of ground at some distance from the school site. For example, King Edward's School is situated in New Street, Birmingham, while its playing fields adjoin Bristol Road, Edgbaston. Merchant Taylors' School, in Charterhouse Square, has a ground at Bellingham. St. Olave's and St. Saviour's field is at Dulwich. The Manchester Grammar School has two fields, one at Cliff, Lower Broughton, the other adjoining the Manchester Athletic Ground at Fallowfield, near the grounds used for sports by Manchester University. Nottingham High School plays at Mapperly Park. The extensive playing fields of King Edward VI School, Southampton, lie about a mile and a half from the school, while those of Queen Mary's Grammar School, Walsall, some twenty-two acres in extent outside the town, constitute 'one of the finest playing fields in the Midlands.' Comparatively few municipal aided or secondary schools have athletic grounds of any large acreage in the vicinity of the school, although most have a meagre and, it must be confessed, unattractive playground adjoining, where stand cricket nets and a few melancholy pieces of stationary athletic apparatus. This condition may, however, in time be changed by the results of the Playground Movement to provide suitable playing space for people of all ages and especially of school age.

"School playing fields vary in size, and few are the schools that possess all the area that they could desire. Grounds range from as few as five acres in area to as many as fifteen, and in some instances more. . . . In the case of London County Council schools, one writer implies that if 'the playing fields will accommodate fifteen per cent of the pupils at a time,' this is 'after all a very reasonable proportion in the eyes of the (competent) authority.' This statement, being interpreted, means approximately that every boy in the school gets one organised game a week, about the minimum that is considered permissible."

Compulsory Play—Rewards—Leadership.—In spite of its obvious virtues, criticism is by no means lacking in England of the compulsory games-system of the public schools. In an interview, Commander B. T. Coote, Adviser to the Miners' Welfare Committee, and one of the best informed and most far-seeing men in the recreation field in England, deplored the system of compelling pupils in the public schools to play athletic games, such as cricket, football and hockey. "I have been attacked in the Press," he said, "for stating that the effect of compulsion in regard to recreation is bound to react in making boys lethargic about recreation when once they leave their Public School. I am also convinced that the methods adopted by Public School authorities in regard to rewarding only those who are born to excel is pernicious; when they leave school these boys desire to take part only in those forms of recreation in which they have been encouraged to excel by reason of the prize awarded them at school."

On the question of leadership, Commander Coote further stated that "there certainly is a lack of centralisation in England in recreational matters. In my opinion we shall continue to ignore many of the real recreation problems unless we have some National College for the training of leadership."

Holiday Play Centres.—According to a director of the play centre of the Mary Ward Settlement (from which the holiday play-centre idea radiates), mothers do not know how to play with their children and very little is being done to teach them. Asked if the parents' observation of play-centre activities stimulated them to similar efforts, she replied that the usual comment of visiting parents was simply, "Well I never; I don't see how you have the patience." In the play centres many activities are made possible—various group games, singing games, some handcraft, etc., and the children choose whatever they prefer to do. There is supervision but no direction on the part of the leaders; the desire is to keep absolutely away from any suggestion of the school atmosphere. The children go simply to amuse themselves; and they go in swarms.

Holiday Play Centre, Shadwell.—At the Holiday Play Centre of the Broad Street School, Shadwell, in the poorest sort of district, some perhaps interesting facts were observed. There was no direction of the boys; they were engaged in cricket. The grounds were large, paved, and walled; there was no equipment but swings under a shelter-roof, and materials necessary for drawing, tracing, and undirected needlework. The children did entirely as they pleased. There were some individual toys—hoops, tops, small hobby-horses, and the like. The girls seemed to enjoy an hour of singing games, and old nursery rhymes pleasantly set to music were rather well and spiritedly sung. The total impression given was one of activity without gaiety.

Evening Play Centres.—In London there has been a rather extensive development of the Evening Play Centres movement, founded by the late Mrs. Humphry Ward. Such play centres mean the loan for the evening from five to seven o'clock of a school building with its playgrounds, to the Evening Play Centres Committee, which is responsible for the organisation of the centres and for the raising of the necessary funds. The London County Council and the Board of Education show their confidence in this work by contributing between them about 75 per cent of the cost.

There are at present 33 play centres scattered all over London. They take in over 12,000 children every evening for games, dancing, handicraft, painting, gymnastics, and similar occupations. Each centre is under the direction of a paid superintendent who is responsible to the Play Centres committee.

London Federation of Working Boys' Clubs.—The London Federation of Working Boys' Clubs deserves mention, since these clubs represent one of the few attempts being made to meet the problem of the boy who goes to work at the age of fourteen, and, feeling himself already an adult, tends to regard such organisations as the Scouts as childish. It is significant, in relation to these Boys' Clubs, to note that "it has been observed that delinquents are almost never members of a club." In their games and athletics these clubs make a point of competition for the honour rather than for prizes.

The Federation of London Working Boys' Clubs was founded in 1887. There are similar federations in

Liverpool, Manchester, Chester, Eastbourne, Glasgow, and other British cities. The London Federation has 104 Boys' Clubs affiliated with a total boy membership of 7,672, indicating the preponderance of small clubs. In fact, there are only 26 clubs reporting a membership of over 100, and the largest club in the Federation has only about 400 members. The Federation conducts a camp for its member clubs not able to run a camp of their own. In Manchester are one Boys' Club with some 2,600 boys enrolled, and two with over 1,000.

Scout Leaders' Training Camp.—A visit was made to the Scout Leaders' Training Camp at Epping Forest. The seriousness as to Scout ideals was impressive; again an emphasis on ethical purpose was in evidence; as nearly always in England, the play factor was seen as subservient to the development of character. Notable was the loveliness of the camp-grounds, with council meadow equipped with a great fire-place and grass platform for special ceremonies and Morris dancing. Notable, too, were some good wood-carving and symbolic design on camp implements. Adjacent to the main camp-ground was an open one where boys, singly or in small groups, could come and sleep out and cook their own food with the advantages of proximity to the main camp, but with relative freedom from supervision.

The Duke of York's Camp.—Perhaps the most interesting of all the various camps for boys is the Duke of York's Camp, as described by Commander B. T. Coote. The camp is held at Romney each summer during the first week of August; it was carried out as an experiment for the first five years, 1920 to 1925, and now exists as a permanent activity. Funds provided by "an anonymous gentleman" made possible the development of the idea. A football team composed of steel workers from Cardiff, South Wales, had been anxious to come to London. In order to justify the trip they wanted to play some football. A game was arranged with Westminster, at which the "anonymous gentleman" was present. The novel aspects of the contest intrigued him so greatly that he handed a sum of money to the Duke of York to be used in trying an experiment which would bring public-school boys and boys in industry into contact. This sum of money he was willing to equal annually for five years, and if at the end of that time the scheme had proved successful, he would undertake to endow it permanently.

Four hundred boys are selected each year. One hundred of the public schools—and it should again be remembered that the English "public" school corresponds to the American private school—send two boys each, and two hundred boys are sent from a hundred industries. (Boys are not sent a second season by the same industry, or school). An opening dinner is served at the Royal Buckingham Palace. The first evening and the following day are extremely quiet; as yet the boys having nothing in common to talk about. On the first evening, by way of "breaking ice," an entertainment is provided. Sunday begins with a later breakfast than usual, a service in the morning, dinner; and in the afternoon comes the task of marking out the grounds for the week's games. The sections are combined into groups. Each group has a colour—red, green, blue, yellow, white. The section of ground for which each group is responsible is marked off with flags of the group colour. The camp unit is a section numbering twenty boys, with ten public-school boys and ten industrial boys in each section, and a secton-leader; in the matter of leaders, a delightfully wide range of professions and interests is represented. The games to be played are most of them invented for the occasion, and are new to all the boys, in order to prevent the unfairness of bringing into competition boys who have had much practice in a given game and boys who have had none. Throughout the week the games are progressive, the interest developing from the group competition, which is very keen. A record is kept which shows the position of each group in the games of the various days; a group one day scoring very high may not be able to maintain the position. The boys swim four times each day. The final event is the mile and a half cross-country run on the last day of the camp. This is a real test for the boys who have never done any running in their lives; a tradition has been established whereby every boy enters and finishes "all-out."

The boys learn to cheer the losers; the ideal is that everybody shall take part to the best of his ability in each game and in each event.

The last evening is celebrated with a great bonfire, and then the boys listen to a brief talk as to what it has all been about, and there is singing of Auld Lang Syne and the national anthem.

The idea which is perhaps most strongly encouraged throughout the week is that "the one who tries and achieves little, which because of lack of training and fitness is a lot for him, deserves applause; and that applause must never be reserved only for the successful few." Competition for mere "prizes" and record-breaking are frowned upon.

Question of Importing Foreign Movements.—Interesting in relation to the question of importing recreation movements from other countries was an interview arranged through the kindness of "The New Era," "an international review of new education." The official interviewed, commenting on the attempt of "a few rare spirits" to transplant the Youth Movement from

Germany, said that in England the Movement is artificial and forced.   In Germany the Movement was initially motivated by a spirit of revolt, but in England "there is nothing sufficiently definite to revolt against." The return to the simple life implies the possibility of appearing ridiculous, and in general, English people, even English young people, "could never walk through the streets of London in eccentric clothes, singing." Such attempts at importing the Youth Movement as have taken root are motivated, it was said, by "a vague desire to make the world better."

Industrial Welfare.—Industrial welfare in England is, in general, of the most comprehensive "feudal" type. The employer adopts a paternalistic attitude toward his employés, feels responsible for their health and welfare, and consequently makes every effort to give them, to an unstinted and often elaborate degree, every possible recreational means.   This is not to say that the employer is unaware of the material advantages, to himself, of having contented workers.   It is simply to say that his fundamental approach to the problem of a fuller and better utilisation of leisure on the part of his workers has in it, almost always, a very large element of the paternalistic attitude which we have already described as being characteristic of the English upper class traditions; indeed, one cannot long observe many aspects of English life without being impressed by the conspicuous extent to which this traditional attitude still survives.

If, however, due allowance is made for this fundamental difference of approach, it will be recognised that, in respect to means if not always in respect to ends, what is being done in the best examples of English industrial welfare is fairly similar to what is being done in the best examples of American industrial welfare.

Bournville.—A case in point is the work at Bournville, the industrial community of the Cadbury Brothers, as recorded in their 1926 "Annual," titled "Work and Play." The following statement occurs in the introduction: "It is not proposed here to embark on an exhaustive discussion as to how far welfare work is an assumption by employers of responsibilities that are morally theirs, or, on the other hand, how far it is a business proposition." In order to "interest the worker in his occupation and the purpose of the industry in which he is engaged," many and various means are employed at Bournville. Among these are an initiation school; lecture courses concerned with the industry; the invitation to the worker to contribute his thought to the business side through suggestion; the freest opportunities of training "for promotion to higher functions"; constant participation in the factory social life, through games on the playing fields, or association with fellow-workers in the pursuit of arts like music or the drama, or working together at some hobby or craft; in short, an amazing variety and range of welfare schemes through which it is felt the workers "are being helped to utilise better than might otherwise be possible the larger leisure that has come with shorter working hours." It is interesting to note that the question, whether such complete recreational provisions in a small community may not destroy home-life, asked when Bournville was visited, was answered: "It was destroyed already: the war took the people out of their homes, and sent them back imbued with restlessness. It remains to provide the best possible substitutes."

Miners' Welfare.—There is, however, one form of industrial welfare in England which is public and independent of the attitude of employers, whether that attitude be paternalistic or otherwise,—Miners' Welfare. Under the Mining Industry Acts, 1920 and 1925, and the Mining Industry Act of 1926, the welfare of miners was assured by national legislation. By the terms of these Acts, annual allocations for Miners' Welfare—analogous to taxes—are made from mines throughout the country on a basis of total output. Voluntary district welfare committees, set up for the purpose in each district, decide within certain general principles what particular type of welfare is to be recommended for assistance, choose suitable schemes for the selected type, and recommend the amount of the allocation to be made from a district fund in each case. The ultimate responsibility in these matters falls, of course, to the central statutory body—the Committee appointed by the Board of Trade to allocate the Miner's Welfare Fund.

Distribution of Available Funds.—It has been found that there is considerable variation between districts as regards both the type of scheme supported and the manner in which the available funds have been proportionately distributed—largely according to decisions of district welfare committees—among approved applicants. Heading the most important of the welfare schemes as Recreation, Health, Education, and Expenses, the 1926 (fifth) Report entitled "Miners' Welfare Fund," issued by the "Committee appointed by the Board of Trade to Allocate the Fund," shows that, of the District schemes, Recreation accounts for approximately 85 per cent of the schemes and two-thirds of the money; Health for approximately 13 per cent of the schemes and one-third of the money; while Education has been practically ignored in most dist.icts and is in fact credited with rather less than Expenses. But there are some districts which have devoted all their attention to Recreation, and others which have dealt only with Health.

Recreation.—Funds allocated for Recreation are put to a variety of uses. In some cases they go to the carrying out of lay-outs for outdoor recreation; the Report comments on the often injudicious variation of a comprehensive playground-plan, and gives example of the method followed in costing a comprehensive plan for partial development. In other cases the funds are used for children's activities, such as Evening Play Centres and Children's Playgrounds.

Health.—Funds allocated for Health go chiefly to Convalescent Homes such as that of South Wales and that of Lancashire and Cheshire.

Education.—The allocations, from the Central Fund, for Education are used for expenses of building; for senior and advanced instruction in mining, such as that given by the Coal-treatment Laboratory of Birmington University, by the Senior Centre, Pontllanfraith, Monmouthshire, by the Mining School, Buckhaven, Fifeshire; and also, for the Miners' Welfare National Scholarship Endowment Fund, the latter held under a simple declaration of trust which requires the trustees to apply its income "in or towards defraying the expenses of and incidental to the provision of University Scholarships . . . for workers in or about coal mines in Great Britain and their sons and daughters in accordance with the recommendations of the Selection Committee appointed by the trustees." The qualifications for an award are not "tied too strictly to a scholastic basis. . . . The object of the scheme is to afford an opportunity for working miners and their sons or daughters to enjoy the full advantages of university life, for the purpose not only of attaining educational distinction, but also of benefiting from social intercourse in the laboratory, the lecture room and the playing fields, and from the general atmosphere of residence at a university." In order that this object may be attained, the awards are based on such a scale "as to afford relief from embarrassment which might otherwise arise from a scholar's inability to associate on equal terms with his fellow students."

Aim and Spirit.—The aim and spirit of the various Miners' Welfare recreational developments, and the type of leadership given to the local committees by the general committee and its advisers, are shown in a series of pamphlets by Commander B. F. Coote, Adviser to the Miners' Welfare Committee. These pamphlets compile and make available to local and district committees experience which the fund is having, and are available in general answer to the many questions addressed to the Adviser about various projects. The office of the Adviser is always ready to give counsel to the local committee.

"Outdoor Recreation for Children."—In "Outdoor Recreation for Children," Commander Coote writes: "I have met hundreds of mining welfare committees in every part of the country, and have never failed to argue the cause of children and young people, and I have still to meet a member who can argue against the plea, yet I know that up to date the bulk of the money has been allocated in the proportion of 4 to Specialists, *e.g.*, footballers, cricketers, and athletes, and 1 to the cause of the children. I ask again, Why?"

"The answer, I think, is as follows: This great sporting country of ours is slowly but surely allowing its sport to be commercialised; our Press finds a readier sale for news of the 'latest results' to-day than in 1914; we are out of proportion in our value of recreation; we reward those who are born to excel and seldom, if ever, encourage the majority who are not so gifted. Who will deny that the fellow who does his best and comes in last in a race is as worthy of applause as the winner? Does he get it? . . . Can you blame people for being lethargic or apathetic when we only cater for the energetic minority? . . . I refuse to put adult recreation first. We must reconstruct our ideas if we are going to improve matters, start at the bottom and lay a sound foundation with regard to the children. Give them a happier time, make them realise the value of organised play and the harm of loafing, and year by year lead them on to want healthy leisure occupation in ever increasing numbers until the time will come when, as adults, recreation will be to them far more real and valuable than at present, when people are more ready to exercise the turnstiles than themselves."

Similar in its implications is a paragraph in the "Miners' Welfare Fund Report": "We view with some apprehension what appears to be the fairly common practice of letting to a local club the football or cricket ground provided in connection with a welfare scheme. We also feel some doubt whether the heavy expenditure which has been incurred in providing facilities for other experts, such as those who excel at tennis and bowls, is altogether justified if those who are not so well fitted by nature to excel in those games are overlooked. . . . We fear that the introduction of challenge cup competitions in certain districts will tend more to discourage those who will never be more than mediocre at games. It should be the object of welfare committees to cater for all, and especially for the great body of mediocrities, rather than to confine themselves to the favoured few who form the teams."

"Outdoor Recreation for Boys and Girls."—In "Outdoor Recreation for Boys and Girls" who are "too old for the children's Playgrounds and too young for the Adult Section," Commander Coote writes: "The leisure hours of boys and girls from 10 to 16 are those which must be seriously considered from every point of view, moral, physical, and mental. Lack of occupation leads to sex dissipation, gambling, drinking, oversmoking, etc. . . . The first point to consider is the value of giving boys and girls an opportunity to play together under healthy conditions, so that they may learn to be courteous and considerate each to the other, and have their characters so moulded as to be able to appreciate fair play. I want to see organised games provided for these boys and girls which cannot be ruined by commercialism, and where only one rule is needed, viz., PLAY THE GAME. In order that this may be appreciated, I should like to see every boy and girl who joins the Recreation Club presented with a Membership Card on which is printed the following:

"One Rule Only.
PLAY THE GAME
which means:—
Don't Play Foul.
Don't Give In.
Go all-out to Win.
Don't Play for Yourself, but think of others."

"Outdoor Recreation for Adults."—In "Outdoor Recreation for Adults," Commander Coote contends that "If recreation is to be for the majority of adults in mining districts, it must be so conceived and organ-

ised that it will provide for *active* instead of *passive* participation. . . . If we estimate those born to excel at 10 per cent of any community, what of the remaining 90 per cent?" As an instance in point, Commander Coote points out that "a bad bowler or poor tennis player is soon made to feel unwelcome by those who are more skilled, and the game is gradually monopolised by those who develop more rapidly into experts by reason of possessing a natural gift for games, and the unfortunate '90 per center' finds it very difficult to get a chance to play."

"Our methods of dealing with games, even in schools, teach us to admire the 10 per cent type. Hero-worship is an asset up to a point, but I am convinced that the nation in general, and the mining industry in particular, will benefit by a little more consideration of the 90 per cent type. . . . If every one is to be given an opportunity of taking an active part in recreation, the first step must be that of SIMPLICITY."

Commander Coote then goes on to mention examples of these simpler games, such as putting, croquet lawn skittles, clock golf, etc. It is interesting to note that he takes for granted the advisability of charging for these games in order to provide for the maintenance and upkeep of the recreation scheme as a whole. Of putting, for instance, he writes: "The more undulating the ground, the more attractive the game. It is, incidentally, a great source of income. On an area of 200 square yards, a nine-hole course has been the means of raising over 1,000 pounds in one year, the charge for play being 2d a round, which charge included the use of a club and ball."

On the subject of Control, he observes: "We obviously cannot leave the adult section to run itself, but must have some form of organisation which makes

clude some provision for children to play, and very often, especially in the more recent developments, the children's playground is the first activity to be considered. . . . For every 300 children there should be at least one acre of ground. . . . A playground of the plainer sort is not expensive. It can be amply equipped at a capital cost of one pound per child, and when it is remembered that many local welfare committees will cheerfully spend 4,000 or 5,000 pounds on a four-acre cricket or football ground on which only 22 players play perhaps once a week, it should not be difficult for such committees to find 1,200 pounds for a children's playground of similar size which will provide hours of enjoyment for 1,200 children every day."

Lord Chelmsford also urgently recommends co-operation between the Miners' Welfare Committees and the local school authorities for indoor accommodations for children, similar to those provided in the evening Play Centre movement in London. In planning for the young people's recreation the experience of the Committee, as recorded by Lord Chelmsford, recommends play fields, camps, and buildings for indoor activities commonly known as institutes. These buildings should and do frequently provide a reading room and library, a room for parlour games, rooms for committee meetings and evening classes, a swimming pool, a room for billiard or bagatelle, and a buffet for light refreshments. All these facilities are "common to both sexes, but there would be separate work shops or hobby rooms, such as cobbling or basketball for the boys, and dressmaking, laundry work, or cooking for the girls. In such an establishment it is not difficult to supplement the weekly subscriptions by organised concerts, dances, lectures, plays, exhibitions, etc., or even by the sale of the properties of the hobby rooms, but success is entirely dependent on the right kind of leadership." An ideal building for this type of service, serving both the boys and girls, erected at Mantznoll is described as costing about 5,000 pounds.

"There are now nearly one thousand separate recreational schemes for adults, most of which provide some form of outdoor development, while over half of them include substantial buildings for indoor activities."

These allocations have helped to furnish athletic fields for various popular sports, outdoor swimming pools, pavilions and club houses in connection with the sport centres, and buildings for indoor recreation consisting of institutes, halls, indoor swimming pools, club rooms, reading rooms, library, game rooms, hobby rooms. The past five years have seen the erection of a great variety of buildings, varying in cost between 150 and 25,000 pounds.

In general the allowances for outdoor recreation have been smaller than those for indoor recreation. The allocation during the year 1926 for indoor recreation, including institutes, halls, clubs, libraries, swimming pools, etc., was 1,399,482 pounds, and for outdoor recreation, including recreation and sports grounds, playing fields, swimming pools, colliery bands, etc., 965,841 pounds.

The whole plan of providing for Miners' Welfare recreation out of funds derived from the industry as a whole, on what amounts to a tax basis, constitutes an exceptionally interesting experience for contemplation by those American industries, such as lumber, coal and iron mining, oil production, etc., which employ large numbers of workers at points remote from natural provision of recreational facilities either as a part of the community recreation programme of a city or as a commercial investment.

Industrial Welfare Conclusion.—In conclusion, it may perhaps be enough to record a point brought out in an interview arranged through the Teachers' Registration Commission. The person interviewed suggested that in England "class and trade distinctions are too settled and economic conditions not flexible enough for the hope of individual material progress to lend any colour to the monotonies of mass production in the imagination of the working class." Industrial recreational provision, therefore, he said, "is generally designed to keep the workers amused and to forestall too much organising of the workers among themselves." In support of this contention, he pointed out the significance of the recommendation, by a member of the Royal Family, of fifty thousand pounds for recreation activities and facilities for civil service workers, as contrasted with the Royal unconcern for the gamins in the London slums.

Adult Education.—The authorities state that twenty years ago the term Adult Education would have meant little to the majority of the people; to-day news of the various forms of the movement is to be found in newspapers and books with ever-increasing frequency, together with references to its social and political significance. At the General Elections, the addresses of leaders of both Conservative and Liberal Parties have contained references to provision for adult education. It is to be understood, of course, that the term does not cover technical or vocational instruction. The Adult Education Authorities define it as "*the pursuit by men and women in their leisure hours of those liberal and non-vocational studies by means of which a man may understand himself and his world, determine the personal and social values that shall govern his thought and action, and learn to serve his generation in what-*

ever way seems to him most vital." The range of
studies includes economics, industrial history and theory
of politics, modern history, geography, literature, science, psychology, and philosophy. Art, architecture,
music and drama, folk-dancing and "rhythmic" dancing, are not neglected. It has been proved impossible
that the cost of systematic and continuous education
of this kind should be met out of the fees that adult
students can afford; state aid is necessary. The Fisher
Act of 1918 made local Education Authorities responsible for providing or aiding all forms of education
within their areas; this of course includes adult education. The Board of Education has announced the
purpose of making its grants to voluntary organisations for Adult Education through local Education
Authorities rather than making them direct, in order
to foster closer relationship between them. The autonomy of the voluntary organisations—some of which
we shall presently describe and discuss—is always re-
spected.

Probably the most interesting aspect of the movement is the liberal attitude of the authorities in recognising that "to be real and potent, education need
not necessarily be formal and academic," and in considering amateur music and drama as equal in value with
the conventional tutorial class or extension course.
The Adult Education Committee has prepared for presentation to the Board of Education a report on British
music, and a report on the drama, considered as factors in Adult Education; later we shall give attention
to some of the findings of these reports. We shall also
touch on the work of the Women's Institutes, which is
likewise taken into account by the authorities as possessing a definite educational significance.

The war period, although destructive in some degree

to various adult education agencies of pre-war development, proved rather unexpectedly a time of fruitful experiment, through the activities of the organisations concerned with providing recreation of a more or less educational nature for the troops in training and in active service.   At this time, too, primarily in connection with the problem of food production, the first Women's Institutes were established.   In 1921 a committee was appointed to advise the Board of Education on the Liberal Education of Adults, and in 1924 the Board issued a new and separate body of regulations for the supervision and financial assistance of liberal education among adults, in the drafting of which the Adult Education Committee acted in an advisory capacity.

After the war, in spite of the losses among the members of all related organisations, there appeared a redoubled enthusiasm.   New experiences had apparently widened interests and sharpened minds; a spirit of social criticism became evident; there were increasing demands for opportunities for study, discussion, and experiment in the arts.   Certain voluntary organisations which before the war had been predominantly social, political, or religious in character, began to encourage their members to take up directly educational activities, generally along informal lines.   And an immense development in amateur music and drama took place.   The educational movement in labour groups widened greatly; new "Educational Settlements" arose; the Women's Institutes spread throughout the country; the British Broadcasting Company developed an educational programme, with the advice of the Adult Education Committee and the British Institute of Adult Education, with the result that in the main the radio programmes in England, controlled by a single company, have been uncommonly good; the performers were paid from the first.

In organised labour occurred a notable development. The Workers' Educational Association and the Labour Colleges, representing divergent views of working-class education, both appealed for support to the Trade Unions, which in many instances assisted both. The Trades Union Congress has now concluded an agreement with both bodies. Enthusiasm has not been restricted only to the pursuit of the more or less political and social subjects: according to the Handbook and Directory of Adult Education, 1926-1927, compiled under the auspices of the British Institute of Adult Education, the Independent Labour Party has lately created "a vigorous new movement for the practice of the drama, of music, and of folk dancing."

Other Adult Education Associations.—There are many other voluntary associations comprising the adult recreation movement listed in the Handbook and Directory of Adult Education. Any detailed account of them would require a volume. With the list is given a clear indication of the bodies, their scope and function. The reader who wishes detailed information is referred to the handbook.

The principal Associations are: The Trades Union Congress General Council; The Workers' Educational Association, previously mentioned in its relation to Adult Education in Rural Areas; Workers' Educational Trade Union Committee; National Council of Labour Colleges; Young Men's Christian Association; Young Women's Christian Association; Catholic Social Guild; The National Council of Social Service; National Federation of Women's Institutes, also previously mentioned; the British Drama League, The English Folk Dance Society, The British Music Society, and the British Federation of Musical Competition Festivals. The Arts League of Service, an important body, well known for its Travelling Theatre and Travelling Exhibitions of Contemporary Art; Seafarers' Education Service; and the World Association for Adult Education, which includes among its present activities a Bureau of Information relating to all countries; introductions and itineraries for travelling educators; research into Adult Education throughout the world; publications of quarterly Bulletins containing results of research; inquiry into the Drama throughout the world as an educational force. In addition it announces, as pending, "a World Conference on Adult Education."

English Folk Dance Society.—A Voluntary Adult Education body having obvious recreational significance is the English Folk Dance Society. It was founded in 1911 by the late Mr. Cecil Sharp (Honorary Director until his death in 1924) to disseminate and popularise the Folk Dances and Music of England, and at the same time, by providing a directing agency, to "retain and uphold the standard created by tradition." Since the death of Cecil Sharp the Society has made certain modifications in its constitution. It is administered by a Central Executive elected by Members and Branches, and there is, in addition, a General Council (advisory) composed of representatives from every local Branch and certain persons of distinction who represent kindred interests outside the Society. Each Branch is organised as an independent unit and administered by a local committee on which the different districts and centres of the Branch are represented. It is only on artistic matters that the parent Society exercises any prerogative, and the Central Executive

Committee has appointed a Board of Artistic Control for the purpose.

The parent Society and the Branches depend to a considerable extent on the subscriptions of Members for their financial resources, but the expenses of all classes organised, with the exception of those in and for rural areas, are met by the fees of the students attending. During the past three years the Carnegie United Kingdom Trustees have made a grant to assist the giving of instruction in rural districts. Every opportunity is taken to co-operate with educational and other organisations, and these are to a certain extent represented on Branch Committees. The Local Education Authorities in many cases give assistance by lending or hiring class rooms for a nominal charge, and also by making grants to their teachers to enable them to attend Vacation Schools.

The present Secretary of the Society believes that folk dances are being taken up in England because of racial background. "The people," he said, "are fond of the folk dance music." He remarked that although English folk music is lacking in colour, it nevertheless has a definite appeal to the modern English: since the folk dance and folk music are both authentic expressions of the English race-spirit, they should not fail to arouse some response even when presented under modern conditions; and, seeing it as a racial expression, he doubts that the folk dance movement could have similar success among a less homogeneous people. The London County Council and the Education Authorities have some folk dance enthusiasts among them, and folk dancing is taught in the elementary London County Council Schools. Grants are given teachers in some cases to attend training courses. (A training course was held at Cambridge last summer). Here, according to the Secretary, the problem is to present the dancing as part of the play of the child rather than as a "school" subject. Obviously, much depends on the approach of the teacher. When the dances are presented to the children rather as musical games, they are tremendously liked, and he believes that this enthusiasm will carry over into older years.

Educational Settlements.—The Educational Settlements in their activities are both rural and urban. An Educational Settlement—to quote from "Educational Settlements in England," which is Bulletin XXVII of The World Association for Adult Education—is in essence "a company of adult students, made up of groups with diverse desires and purposes, who agree to make their home together in premises that contain not only classrooms and library, lecture hall, and if possible, a little theatre, but also a Common Room where all can meet for friendly intercourse." A warden is appointed whose business it is to teach, if he is qualified, but above all "to be guide, philosopher, and friend to all the individuals and groups in the Settlement." He arranges all activities and is in fact always approachable on any subject. The lines on which an Educational Settlement should be organised are clearly drawn in a book published in 1924 by the British Institute of Adult Education under the title "The Guildhouse: A Co-operative Centre of Adult Education." There are now affiliated to the Educational Settlement Association fifteen Settlements together with four full-time colleges for adults. These colleges, according to "Educational Settlements in England," are in two instances intended "To give an opportunity for a year's general study, without any particular bias, to people who have previously taken leisure-time courses and classes." The Educational Settlements Association is a federation created by the Settlements and Colleges in this group for the purpose of mutual counsel and assistance. The Educational Settlements Association has now been recognised by the Board of Education as an "Approved Association," under the Board's new regulations for Adult Education. In all cases the Adult Schools, in most the Workers' Educational Association, in many the University Extra-Mural Authority, co-operate with the Settlement. Also, other bodies such as Trade Unions, Women's Institutes, Dramatic and Musical Societies, and other educational organisations co-operate with the Settlements in certain instances.

Workers' Educational Association.—The Workers' Educational Association is one of the most important of the societies serving adult education. According to a pamphlet titled "The Workers' Educational Association," "The W. E. A. is an association of working-class and educational bodies together with people interested in education. Its objects are (a) to stimulate and to satisfy the demand of workers for education; (b) to work for a national system of education which shall provide for all children, adolescents, and adults full opportunities for complete individual and social development. The Association is non-partisan in politics and non-sectarian in religion. . . . Within the space of twenty-one years it has created the largest voluntary movement for workers' education in the world. . . . More than 40,000 students yearly secure educational facilities through the W. E. A." Its programme serves both urban and rural populations. The Association depends entirely upon voluntary subscriptions to meet the costs of organisations, administration, and propaganda.

Development in Rural Areas.—One of the most significant aspects of the movement has been its development in rural areas. In defining "rural areas," the Adult Education Committee, in a paper called "The Development of Adult Education in Rural Areas"—which may be referred to for more detailed information than can be given here—explains: "We have taken into consideration only those areas which are definitely dependent on agricultural interests, and owing to distance or deficiency of transport, are little influenced by urban life. Such areas comprise market towns, villages, and farmsteads. The problems to be met in each case are much the same, for although the conditions of a small town are naturally more favourable to education than those of a remote farm, both are at present alike in their general deficiency of those means to a fuller life which it is the main purpose of adult education to provide." Here we see an interesting instance of the fact that whenever in England any grasp at all is shown of the leisure problem, it is almost invariably considered one for educational solution. Fortunately, as already indicated, the definition of education is broad. The paper goes on to state that "it is a commonplace that the success of certain voluntary organisations has been due not only to their command of educational resources but also to the co-operative spirit which they have instilled. But it is this which the countryside has lacked. It is not therefore a matter of surprise that . . . rural education can show a long record of failure." Part of this record may be accounted for by the fact that "There is practically no provision by Local Education Authorities of non-vocational subjects for adults in rural areas." In spite of these discouragements, however, the paper expresses a faith "that the descendants of those who created our national dances and music, and of the craftsmen who built our churches, can re-create a rural culture no less great." The paper then goes on to discuss the work of the National Federation of Women's Institutes, the Village Clubs Association, and other organisations confined to rural areas. It stresses the urgent necessity, in all rural adult education and social work, of the provision of a village hall or institute. In summarising its conclusions the paper suggests, "That in each county there should be a Rural Community Council." Because Rural Community Councils are the principal centralising agency for voluntary organisations, we shall later give attention to them in general and to one of them in detail. Other conclusions of the Adult Education Committee are: that "a nucleus of teachers, whether provided by a University or Settlement or other body of full-time teachers, is essential"; that "any subject of instruction forms a suitable method of approach if the teacher has the necessary gifts"; that "dramatic production is a most effective means of education"; and that "the necessity in adult education of proceeding from the informal to the formal applies with particular force to the countryman."

Essence of the Country Problem.—Let us consider briefly a few of the voluntary organisations of which the Rural Community Councils are the centralising agencies. In the words of an article in the International Labour Review, titled "Spare Time in the Country," agriculture "remains the largest and most vital industry of many countries, and agriculture is even more than an industry, it is a way of life." The importance of the agricultural population is therefore self-evident. In recent years there has been a quickened movement for better living in the country, and from the outset those most vitally concerned have believed that "the essence of the country problem is to find means to enable countrymen and women to help themselves."

National Federation of Women's Institutes.—Prominent among organisations having that vision of the country problem is the aforementioned National Federation of Women's Institutes, of which the fullest account is to be found in "The Story of the Women's Institutes," by J. W. Robertson Scott, published in 1925. It relates that in the ten preceding years four thousand Women's Institutes with over 150,000 members had sprung up in the United Kingdom, and it explains that a Women's Institute is the village unit of a very human, democratic, non-party, non-sectarian organisation, which prides itself on the fact that every member, from cottage to throne, pays an annual fee of two shillings, no more and no less. The movement had its origin in Canada in 1897, through the interest and enthusiasm of Mrs. John Hoodless. Its first name was "The Women's Department of the Farmers Institute of South Wentworth"; Mrs. Alfred Mott brought the idea from Canada into England, where the first English Institute was started thirteen months after the outbreak of the war, with the purpose of providing for the rural life of the nation. At the end of 1916 there were forty Institutes in England. Inevitably their most important activity and interest at this time was to meet the emergencies created by the war. Nevertheless in the spring of 1919 the objects of the Women's Institutes were set forth, and the statement contains no reference to war activities, but simply the following: (1) Study of home economics; (2) provision of centres for educational and social intercourse and all other local activities; (3) the encouragement of home and local industries; (4) development of co-operative enterprises; (5) the stimulation of interest in agricultural industry. On October 16, 1917, representatives of sixty Institutes (there were one hundred and thirty-seven existing at this time) met with certain other members of the movement at the Central Hall, Westminster, to approve the severance of the Institutes from the Agricultural Organisation Society, and to accept the guardianship of the Board of Agriculture. The Institutes were to be regarded as self-governing and self-supporting bodies. They were to be affiliated to a National Federation of Women's Institutes, which was to function through County Federations. The National Federation was to be directed by an elected Central Committee. This scheme of organisation they have thereafter followed.

A visit made to the Women's Institute at Loose, Kent, brought out interesting information as to its origin and development. Its first meetings were held in a barn; it has now been in existence more than four years. The women have earned enough to provide their own hall; they have also bought a piano, whist tables, and folding chairs. The meetings are so much enjoyed that an eagerness has been expressed to have them each week instead of only once a month. Whist drives are very popular; likewise fancy dress dances. Classes in certain handcrafts are offered—basketmaking, leatherwork, glove-making. A certain proportion of the meetings are educational. The particular "fête" visited took place in the garden of the Loose president. Various simple quiet games were carried on; tea was served under the trees; there was an exhibition of the various kinds of handcraft. Dancing and "duologues" furnished the entertainment in the late afternoon.

Of the many activities of the Institutes, one of their chief functions according to "Spare Time in the Country," "is to accustom women to the forms of public business and to endeavour so to train them to act in co-operation as to enable the local groups to take the initiative in obtaining such improvements in village life as they themselves desire." In some communities where children have played on dangerous roads, the Institutes have established playgrounds; these are the only rural playgrounds existing.

Village Clubs.—It has been thought advisable to give the following description of the Village Clubs Association, which is still in existence but has ceased to function actively, the probable reason being that the objects of the Association are being in some measure carried on upon the wider basis of Rural Community Councils.

The Village Clubs Association had its origin in June, 1918. According to "Spare Time in the Country," the stated purpose of the Association's founders was to provide opportunity for reasonable recreation, for social intercourse, and for mutual development to the rural workers, men and women alike. The watchword was, then as now, that "the foundation of all schemes must be reliance on the communal spirit." The aim of the Association is to establish or assist in the development of village clubs each of which must conform to the following principles: (a) that it shall be established as a centre of all social activities, and all forms of physical and mental recreation (b) that it shall be conducted on self-supporting lines and be free from the element of patronage; (c) that all inhabitants of the village or rural district or community, without distinction of class or opinion, and, when practicable, of both sexes, should be eligible for membership; (d) that the entire control should be vested in a committee elected either by the members or by the members and all persons who would be eligible for membership. Three-fifths of the clubs affiliated to the Association— there were 529 of them in May, 1924—have a library, and nearly four-fifths have billiard tables. About one-third have cricket and football clubs attached to them. Since the termination of the war a certain number of village clubs unconnected with the Association have also been started under the auspices of the Y.M.C.A., which was in the happy position of possessing huts in which to house them, and often had equipment as well. As with the Association Clubs, membership is open to all men and "where suitable arrangements can be made, to women also." That in every case the Y.M.C.A. Club "has been a valuable asset to the social life of the village where it has been established is the recorded opinion of the Department of Education of Nottingham University, which in 1923, at the request of the North Midland Y.M.C.A., conducted a special inquiry in four counties which present an unusually difficult problem from the point of view of educational or social work."

Other Important Rural Activities.—Other important rural leisure activities include those fostered by the Village Drama societies, the Musical Competition Festivals, and the English Folk Dance societies. However, since none of these is concerned solely with rural activities, we shall simply mention them now, and give them more detailed consideration in connection with other voluntary associations.

Public Library Service.—It only remains to mention, before going on to a discussion of the methodical attempts to co-ordinate the various rural activities, one example of co-operation—the Public Library Service—that had signally proved its value over a period of years even before the co-ordination movement had gathered momentum. The Public Library Service is a living thing even in remote villages of purely agricultural counties.

Rural Community Councils.—The increase of clubs and institutes such as are described above has undoubtedly been among the causes resulting in the development of a social spirit in many out-of-the-way country places; but the chief cause—to quote again from "Spare Time in the Country"—"is the result of democratic thinking on the part of the rural populations"; a kind of thinking which "commonly expresses itself at the outset in the formation of some sort of village council or committee. The village committee, under various names, and generally more or less informally, assumes the task of co-ordinating the activities which have been hitherto carried on in the village in more or less haphazard fashion. . . . The next step has been the formation of County Rural Community Councils or Committees on lines suggested by the National Council of Social Service. . . . The suggestions for county organisation were based on the experience of the County of Oxford, where such a council had successfully been at work for two years before the National Council of Social Service made their proposals, but the co-ordination schemes of the Rural Community Councils have made great strides in the years which have elapsed since Oxfordshire led the way in 1920. Some form of these councils exists now (1924) in eleven counties, and the question of their formation is being considered in others. No two are formed on exactly the same lines, or are developing in exactly the same way. . . . The same principle, however, underlies them all: they are consultative committees which include representatives of both voluntary and statutory authorities in the area. . . . Active organisation is already widening the opportunities of the English rural worker to an extent which was undreamed of before the movement for shorter working hours and above all the general demand for a weekly half-holiday had begun to take effect throughout the country. . . . Nevertheless, it should be emphasised that the Rural Community Councils have only, as yet, made a beginning, and there remain thousands of villages where clubs and institutes, educational and recreative agencies of all kinds, cannot get a footing, simply because there exists no meeting-place for their activities other than the public house. And when ground is needed for games, unless a village green or a common still exists, usually the cricket teams have to wait until the hay has been cut before any matches can be played, and football has to cease early in the spring in order that the field may be laid down for hay. While open spaces are maintained for the recreation of the town dweller, too often the countryman is unable to secure even the few square yards necessary for games." In conclusion the article states: "It is above all the creation and cultivation of the community spirit which is the keynote of the rural scheme outlined above, and so far as it has attained its end it is now on the way to prove that co-ordination is the only lasting solution of the rural problem, since success in isolated villages depends too much on the human factor, and when local leadership fails the whole structure which enthusiasm and devotion have set up is bound to go to pieces. But when public authorities work in conjunction with voluntary committees there seems good ground for hope that the movement will survive and expand."

Kent Rural Community Council.—Although no two of the Community Councils are exactly alike, all have

certain important things in common. Perhaps one
of the most typical is the Kent Rural Community
Council, as revealed in its "Annual Report of 1925-
1926." In this Report we learn that the Council's
office is being increasingly used by the villages as a
general information bureau. "Advice is sought on such
varied questions as the design and tenure of a village
hall; the lay-out of a playing field; the arrangement
of the season's lecture fixtures; the initial programme
of events for a new club; what authorities or organisations should be approached for particular purposes."

In dealing with such inquiries, the Council's effort
is to bring the villages into touch with existing organisations or with other neighbouring villages which
have successfully dealt with similar problems. The
growing volume of information and experience at the
Council's disposal is making this advisory work of increasing usefulness.

The bodies represented in the Council include: (a)
the Agricultural, Education, and Public Health Committees of the County Council and the Kent Insurance
Committee; (b) Organisations representing landowners, farmers, and agricultural workers; (c) a large
number of voluntary organisations interested in nearly
every aspect of country life.

The underlying purpose of the Council is "to call
together, at regular intervals, the representatives of
these bodies in order to bring their united efforts to
bear on the needs of the community and thereby to
encourage and foster pioneer work, and supplement
the public services which need the support of voluntary
effort, and generally to provide a means for concerted
action where this is needed and generally desired. In
many directions the Council acts as a consultative and
advisory body, but it undertakes specific functions

where the organisations and interests concerned consider that this course would be of general benefit."

The Report records a year of steady and very encouraging development, and goes on to show in just what way this development has operated beneficially in such varied needs and activities as playing fields, village concerts, folk dancing, the Kent Musical Competitive Festival, drama, lectures, juvenile welfare, camps, Young Farmers' Clubs, public health agricultural training and apprenticeship, apprenticeship charities, farm work competitions, handicrafts town planning.

In January, 1926, the Kent Rural Community Council also issued its "Lecture List," together with a summary of Educational Facilities available in Kent. These lectures cover a delightfully wide range of subjects, and many of the lectures are free. The headings are: Archeology; Architecture; Housing and Town Planning; Arts and Crafts; Biography; Boy Life; Brotherhood Movement; The Child; Civics and Sociology; Domestic Crafts; Domestic Animals; Economics; Education; Empire; Folk Dance and Folk Music; Foreign Life and Travel; Geography; Girl Life; Health, Food and Recreation; History; The Home Country; Journalism; Kent; Literature and Drama; Local Government; Music; National Savings and Thrift; Natural History and Science; Philosophy and Ethics; Political Science; Psychology; Temperance; Village Life. Various specific aspects of these subjects are listed under the general headings, and the lectures are usually on one or another of a given subject's specific aspects.

In addition to separate lectures, there are also lecture courses. The booklet explains that "a lecture course can usually be arranged when a sufficient num-

ber of villagers desire it. . . . The length of the course
varies: it may be three or six lectures, or it may be a
more serious course of study extending over a term,
a year or longer. The lectures are usually given once
a week or once a fortnight. Sometimes a single pioneer
lecture will arouse a demand for a course of further
lectures. The courses are conducted by specialists in
the particular subject chosen, and are based on an informal friendly relationship between lecturer and students."

The following list indicates some typical subjects on
which lecture courses have been held: Arts and Crafts,
e.g., drawing and design, modelling, embroidery, iron or
woodwork; Domestic and Commercial subjects; Drama;
Economics; Engineering; Folk Music, Song and Dance;
Health and Food; History—Rural, Industrial, European, etc.; Literature; Local Government; Musical Appreciation; Natural History; Practical Agriculture
and Horticulture; Psychology; Science.

Summary, Rural Areas.—Having given a summary
of the activities, educational and recreational, provided, fostered, or co-ordinated by the Kent Rural
Community Council, we have probably at the same
time given a fair idea of similar activities in their relation to other Community Councils. Likewise, in
explaining the work of Rural Community Councils in
general, and the nature and work of the various organisations which are seeking a solution of the country problem and are usually centralised by Community Councils, we have probably given a fairly adequate
survey of Adult Education in Rural Areas. We have
devoted considerable space to this aspect of adult
education for the simple reason that the importance
of the agricultural population of any nation, and of

that population's educational and recreational problems, cannot be overstressed.

Organisations Promoting Musical Education.— There are several organisations promoting Musical Education. The most important of these are the British Music Society, the British Federation of Music Competition Festivals, the Community Singers' Association. Our sources of information on British Music have been threefold: pamphlets issued by the various organisations, interviews with officers of those organisations, and a booklet called "British Music, a Report by the Adult Education Committee on the Development of Adult Education through Music."

The British Music Society.—The British Music Society exists, according to "British Music," to promote the organisation and development of music in the British Empire, to build up a body of musical opinion capable of making itself felt "whenever and wherever the interests of music and music-lovers are at stake," and to spread the knowledge of British music of all periods at home and abroad. It encourages its members, wherever they may be situated, to work towards this end by cultivating every kind of musical activity, and not least by making music themselves, believing that "thus the love and knowledge of music are chiefly stimulated and strengthened." The Society is not intended to supplant or compete with any existing organisation; it desires rather to co-ordinate scattered musical activities for the prevention of waste and overlapping. It enrolls not only practicing musicians, professional and amateur, but all who are conscious of "the importance of music as an element in national culture."

Community Singers' Association.—Another organisation fostering music and promoting Musical Education is the Community Singers' Association. An officer of that organisation criticised the American choice of songs for community singing as limited to the trivial, the cheap, and above all the sentimental. He believes that there is a fundamental response in England to community singing but that the British self-consciousness must be overcome before headway can be made. As to overcoming it, he believes that "if you can make an Englishman laugh, you can make him sing." The people invariably like whatever is familiar, he said; of the two, given equal familiarity, they tire sooner of the trivial.

A Community song session at St. Martin's Church, London, was illuminating. Crowds of people watched outside. A good number came to sing—some representatives of almost every conceivable class and age, obviously accustomed to regular attendance, and with an appearance of interest and enthusiasm. To a certain degree the criticism, often met with in England, that community singing is artificial and a forced "movement," would seem to be justified. It may be concluded that there is at least a limited desire for community singing, here as everywhere, and that the response is largely dependent upon the skill of the leaders.

Commander Coote, adviser for the Miners' Welfare Fund, has had experience also with community singing. He has said that the miners "are such simple-minded folk that even when one tries to get at them by this means, very different methods must be used. I don't give books because they are too shy to look at them and if one had a book of music he would be almost ashamed to look at it because it would give away the fact that he was going to sing. When it comes to that you have to think of simpler ideas, so we try turning out the lights so that no one will know who is singing, and if we have lantern screens with well known choruses, some might think it was worth while joining in. Always in a mining community before I start a lecture I find it useful to have singing on all occasions."

British Federation of Musical Competition Festivals.—The British Federation of Musical Competition Festivals is concerned with choruses and, in a few instances, orchestras; its main object is to encourage the singing of fine choral music and to eliminate the second-rate There has been for years in England a growing conviction that the most ready method by which people may learn to make good music is through choral singing; that people too often in the past have been content to be listeners. Moreover, the history of choral singing shows how great a gift the British people possesses for this form of music. The national Eisteddfod of Wales claims a record of 1,200 years, and other of the smaller Eisteddfodau make similar claims. In England the Three Choir Festivals at Gloucester, Worcester, and Hereford date back to 1724. The Competition Festivals date back 40 years. Folk tune is the basis of music, and all the subsequent development of symphony, sonata, opera, and oratorio can be traced back to folk song, folk dance, and miracle and mystery plays. English and Welsh folk song ranks among the finest in the world; and, states "British Music," "no account of British Music could omit to pay tribute to Mr. Cecil Sharp and the Engish Folk Dance Society for their magnificent work in restoring to our possession these song and dance tunes which are so instinct with the national genius." They may now be heard at the Competition Festivals; and country dancing is also a feature of the Festivals. Where the setting is appropriate and the traditional roots not too long obscured, folk dancing may perhaps take hold of public taste and prove a means of amusement and group-expression, and incidentally revivify public response to folk music.

The British Federation of Musical Competition Festivals is the incorporation, completed in November, 1921, of all the festival centres into one federation. In general, choruses are composed of villagers of all ages; in one instance the entire adult population of the village takes part, including the greybeards. The Choirs attempt the most ambitious material, and they seem to have a special liking for Bach. It is reported that they do not show any self-consciousness in approaching "good music"; their liking for it grows with familiarity and they seem to take pride in mastering scores in proportion to their difficulty.

The number of individual competitors range from 150 in the very small village festivals to 12,000 in the largest town centres, the average being 1,700. Children are admitted to the competitions; at one festival the number was 6,731 in 161 choirs. In 1906 when the movement came of age the number of festivals in England exceeded 60. The number now in existence probably reaches 150, excluding those organised entirely for the benefit of Girls', Boys', and other Clubs, Women's Institutes and Sunday School Unions.

Many festivals include orchestral as well as choral competitions. No village is too small to produce a choir. One quite admirable Choral Society is drawn from a village of 98 inhabitants.

The singing provides an outlet for animal spirits—the primitive satisfaction of making a loud noise in a crowd—plus a genuine pleasure in the music when it has been well learned. It "takes them out of themselves." There is a great devotion in attendance at rehearsals, which usually occur once weekly, and are often the sole diversion of the community. On the occasion of a competition festival, the spirit is one of excitement and enthusiasm. According to one competent observer, "The choirs don't care so much which one wins; they are getting a vast amount of fun out of the occasion, and are thrilled by the music."

Music—General Notes.—The musical situation is peculiar in England in that most of the financial backing is provided by commercial enterprises. The Queen's Hall Concerts, the Covent Garden season, The London Symphony, and the London Concerts (the "ballad concerts" of former days) are all sustained in this way—the first three by the music house of Chappell, and the last by that of Boosey. The commercial control has its unfortunate features. The wealthy citizen, rarely needing advertisement (and perhaps hardly musically inclined, fundamentally), confines his good offices to backing "special interests" in musical comedies. The two principal private benefactors have been Thomas Beecham and Sir Edgar Speyer.

It is said that the "cheap ballad," once so firmly entrenched in the heart of Britain, has given way entirely to jazz. It is thought, however, that the radio has made no appreciable difference in concert attendance or in public taste. Here as in the United States there is the complaint that no one is satisfied with being an amateur. . . .

The characteristic of the national musical life is the affection for choral singing and the tradition of oratorio. It has been said that "a festival without the Messiah and the Elijah would cause the entire elder rural population to die of shock." Since, in America, one hears that the old choral tradition is weakening in England, and oratorio dying, it was interesting to hear the lapse of certain festivals attributed entirely to post-war conditions. A mark of the sincerity of the popular interest in oratorio is the flourishing of a well-established class of unspectacular oratorio singers : the appearance of a "star soloist" or opera singer is not necessary to tempt the festival audiences. For purposes of comparison with the United States, it may be noted that the English are temperamentally apathetic toward opera.

The Drama in England.—There remains one other highly important activity to be considered—The Drama.—We must refer the reader to "The Drama in Adult Education," another report by the Adult Education Committee, for a detailed account on the matter. Just as the Little Theatre Movement in the United States is almost infinite in the variations and ramifications of its activities, so it is with activities of the amateur dramatic societies in England ; to attempt a full account of them would in itself require a volume.

The British Drama League.—No account of the Drama in England can omit the British Drama League. Its expressed aim is to assist the development of the Art of the Theatre, and "to promote a right relation between Drama and the Life of the Community." Since its foundation in 1919 the League has succeeded in founding or affiliating over six hundred independent societies, many of them in villages and in industrial districts, others attached to Educational Bodies, Schools, and Universities. The League's register includes, besides the bodies above indicated, such large organisations as the Manchester Playgoers, The Liverpool Repertory Theatre, The Royal Academy of Dramatic Art, The Village Drama Society, The Arts League of

Service Dramatic Section, etc., etc. The League undertakes many pieces of work for the theatre which, but for its existence, might be left undone. It has, for example, deputised the Board of Education, with the result that dramatic performances are now recognised and even officially recommended in Training Colleges and Schools throughout the country; it has financed or been otherwise responsible for the International Theatre Exhibit at South Kensington in 1921, the Historical Theatre Exhibition at Wembley in 1924, and the Exhibition of Modern Theatre Design at Wembley, 1925; the League has also done several important pieces of propaganda for a National Theatre, notably by organising the recent Competition for Architectural Designs for a National Theatre. The work of the British Drama League has also an international aspect, as may be evidenced by the fact that in the past two years a company of English amateur players has, each year, under the League's auspices taken part in the Annual Little Theatre Tournament in New York; and on one occasion, England, represented by the Welwyn Garden City Players, won the coveted David Belasco Cup.

Perhaps the greatest service which the League has rendered has been the establishment of a dramatic library which, through the generosity of the Carnegie Trust, is now housed, together with the offices of the League, in excellent premises. This library has been fortunate in obtaining a number of valuable gifts. Recently, for instance, the library of the late Mr. William Archer was entrusted to the League, greatly adding to the resources of the library as regards books of a reference character and foreign plays.

It may be claimed, finally, in the words of the League's prospectus, that "the League, which itself takes no part in the production of plays, is the only body capable of dealing in a disinterested manner with every side of the theatrical problem; of affording an open platform for the discussion of difficulties; of bringing isolated experiments in touch with one another; and of giving to pioneer work the encouragement of criticism and recognition."

Arts League of Service.—One of the most interesting of the bodies included in the League's register is the Dramatic Section of the Arts League of Service. This is a travelling "little theatre"; its prices are arranged according to the resources of the community to be visited. Help is given by the Carnegie Trust. In their work they stress the element of colour, the expressionist type of setting; and some of their most interesting drops and curtains have been designed by a young miner. They give mostly one-act plays. A project is impending for a caravan company of theirs which will visit the very smallest places. The interest stimulated often leads to attempts at community drama in the places they visit. One of their purposes is to show the people by their manner of presentation how much can be done with very simple properties, curtains and clever lighting effects. It is particularly interesting to note their experience that the finest things go best in the most remote communities where cheap forms of amusement have not penetrated to influence taste. Particularly in the northern mining district they find that there is great response to the colourful and romantic.

The Village Drama Society.—The Village Drama Society, too, has a great influence in the countryside; according to the account of it given in "The Drama in Adult Education," it endeavours to eliminate "the feeble little farce" and to set a high standard in the choice of plays. A lending library is one of its assets, intended first for the help of village producers and local playwrights, and the books are collected mainly for those purposes. The Society also possesses a Costume Cupboard, which provides the Society's various branches, at an extremely low rate, with correct and good costumes, in beautiful colours and in materials that hang in good folds. A Reading Committee of the Society is kept busy criticising plays by amateur playwrights, which it does at present free; on the Committee's recommendation plays are published from time to time; eight plays of different types have now been brought out. Generally speaking, the Society finds that the following types of drama make most appeal in the villages; short comedies, preferably of village life, for few characters; religious drama, (the first step toward serious drama of any sort), especially the Nativity plays, which are acted all over the country; long story plays, in demand particularly in villages of the north; these story plays, and costume plays, are preferred everywhere above any others; but symbolic outdoor plays, dealing with such subjects as Harvest, the Earth, the Seasons, etc., also find a response, as do operettas in the musical parts of the country. As for tragedy, the report states that "as a rule the village prefers to get out of its own life, and to use drama only in comedy; rural tragedies are not in demand at all."

Church Use of Drama.—A very remarkable element in the present dramatic revival has been the interest taken in it by the English churches. Indeed, the drama would seem to be one of the few aspects of Adult Education in which the churches are showing any active or vital interest. Nativity, Mystery, and Morality plays such as "The Mystery of the Rose," "The Story of the Nativity," and "Everyman," are constantly being used by churches of almost all denominations. In the Middle Ages, of course, the Church was the protagonist of the drama, and used it as a means of religious education. It appears that this situation may be arising again to-day.

Development in Schools.—An account of the widespread development, in recent years, of drama as an educational activity in elementary, secondary, and other schools would not be strictly in place in any survey of Adult Education as the term has been defined. One piece of evidence, however, may legitimately be included here, since it primarily concerns the audience. Mr. Sharwood Smith, of Newbury Grammar School, said: "Practically every year we give a performance of Shakespeare, and a Greek play in the summer term, usually one of the beautiful translations of Euripides by Gilbert Murray. I have found the Greek play very valuable in correcting the oversentimentality so common to-day. There is something in the austerity, the statuesqueness of the Greek play, and its beautiful convention of the chorus, that carries an extraordinary appeal not only to the boys but to the people who come to see us do it. Our audience is drawn from all sorts and conditions of people. The poor people in the neighbourhood, for instance, would not miss a Greek play for worlds." Mr. Smith supported this assertion by the story of a cook who was "unable to take up her duties on a Wednesday because she was going to the 'Bacchæ.' "

Drama in the Universities.—It is true that a consideration of drama in the universities has no immediate bearing on Adult Education, in the special meaning of the term; it has, however, a decided indirect bearing because of the profound influence which university dramatics wherever used have been observed to have on the amateur theatrical developments of the particular country; a case in point is the indisputably salu-

tary influence of Professor G. P. Baker's pioneering at
Harvard on the Little Theatre movement in the United
States. But while in schools throughout England
drama is regarded in an educational light and holds,
often, an honoured place in the curriculum, yet in the
universities, with one or two notable exceptions such
as the universities of London and Liverpool, the drama
holds no such place. Apparently it will be a long time
before the place of drama in the universities of England will be what it is in the United States, where practically every university has its Dramatic Department
and experimental theatre. There is, however, in response to the notable efforts of Mr. Granville Barker
and others, gradually arising in England a general tendency to recognise the understanding, knowledge, and
appreciation of drama as an important part in Education; in the course of years this tendency will probably
result in the instituting of a Department of Drama in
the more important of the English universities; after
that, university theatres will doubtless follow as a
matter of course. Even now there are at most of the
universities Amateur Dramatic Clubs that are doing
good work. It must be noted, however, that there is in
England, on the part of those most vitally interested
in the drama, a feeling that their country is many years
behind the United States in the matter of recognising
the importance of drama in higher education.

PART III

NOTES ON BELGIUM, DENMARK, CZECHO-
SLOVAKIA, AUSTRIA AND ITALY

PART III

NOTES ON BELGIUM, DENMARK, CZECHO-SLOVAKIA, AUSTRIA AND ITALY

VARIOUS other European countries were visited and studied besides England, France and Germany, and some of the outstanding items of interest in each of these should be presented. No attempt will be made to give a complete picture of the leisure time situation in Belgium, Denmark, Czecho-Slovakia, Austria and Italy, all of which were visited, and in all of which were found many facts of general interest. In this chapter, however, will be recorded only those especially significant or characteristic phases of the leisure time movement which seem to merit, either because of their importance or interest, special description and comment.

BELGIUM

Belgium is outstanding among the smaller countries of Europe as regards *official* provision for leisure. Idealistic though its system of "Loisirs des Ouvriers" (Workers' Leisure) committees may be, it is at the same time admirably planned. Evidences of realisation of the importance of the leisure problem are revealed by practically every Belgian organisation. The strength of the Roman Catholic recreation programme in the schools is an instance. Also, there is an appreciation of American recreation innovations by the people generally. And the playground movement is widely fostered, especially by the large towns.

Loisirs des Ouvriers (Workers' Leisure) Committees.—Soon after the war and long before the eight-hour day became a legal fact, the movement to provide for the free time of the workers was under way. The question was taken up not only by individuals, associations, and certain firms, but also by the public authorities of the three most highly industrialised provinces, Liége, Brabant and Hainault. Directly after the first discussions in the House of Representatives on the eight-hour day law, the Standing Committee of the Provincial Council of Hainault (1919) appointed a committee "to consider immediately what the worker will do with his eight hours' spare time, and to discover wholesome forms of recreation for him, and the means of providing them." This example was followed by the Province of Brabant in December, 1919, when a Committee on Workers' Leisure was set up by the Standing Committee at the request of the Provincial Council. In 1920 the Province of Liége also established a Special Leisure Committee.

A summary follows of the activities of the committees in each of the three provinces.

Liége.—Here, even before the Special Committee had been set up, a preliminary inquiry, in the shape of a questionnaire sent to the various communes, had been conducted on the problems involved. The response to this questionnaire indicated the need of the proposed institution. The Committee (the Special Committee on Workers' Leisure) appeared in the provincial budget for the first time in 1921. In March of that year the first Leisure Institute (Maison des Loisirs) was opened at Seraing. This institute is the chief and central work of the Liége Committee. Its activities include moving picture entertainments several times a week, with special performances for children; exhibitions of model furnishings for workers' dwellings; poultry shows; dances on public holidays; a games-room and a reading-room in constant use; short lectures and practical talks on subjects of general interest; a series of definitely educational lectures; a public library.

On the whole the work of the Committee is decentralised; it is carried out through local committees set up by communal authorities within the province; these comprise delegates of the various political parties represented on the municipal council and delegates of the workers' organisations. Their activities are generally confined to the winter season; lecturers and musicians and dramatic companies have been sent to each locality by the Provincial Committee. The audiences have been appreciative. One local committee organised a Mozart festival. In keeping with the Act of October 17th, 1921, whereby every commune in Belgium must devote twenty-five centimes yearly per head of population to the creation or development of public libraries, the Provincial Committee has organised a travelling library. Also, it supplies local committees with material for lantern lectures; encourages classes in dramatic art; conducts festivals of the Provincial Federation of Choral Societies; fosters gardening, poultry-raising, and domestic training.

Brabant.—Here the Committee on Workers' Leisure maintains that every worker should consult his own interest as well as that of the community by using his spare time for rest and recreation, and for intellectual, æsthetic and moral education. It stresses activities which foster and strengthen family life as the most desirable use of spare time from the point of view of the community: "The worker ought to spend by far the greater part of his spare time in his home, for it is impossible to offer him outside recreation every day, and he should be able to find wholesome recreation in his own home." With this in view the Committee organises exhibitions, lectures, and classes very extensively in furnishing the home, reproductions of good pictures, housekeeping, market-gardening, horticulture, and small stock-raising. In manner of organisation, as in Liége, the Provincial Committee works through Local Leisure Committees which include equal numbers of representatives of employers and workers; these local committees present annual financial estimates and programmes and receive grants from the Province. On request the Provincial Committee appoints one of its members a special delegate to act as educational adviser to individuals or associations which wish to provide facilities for the use of the workers in their spare time. A special sum is allotted in the provincial budget for the provision of such educational advisers. It is interesting to note that the Committee considers the cinema a powerful aid to education and recreation and believes that the advantages of educational films easily balance the effects of undesirable ones.

The provincial budget provides subsidies to gymnastic, games and sports societies concerned with the physical education of the worker. These subsidies are available for acquiring necessary facilities for games and sports—gymnastic apparatus, expense of prizes, manuals, payment of instructors, grounds, private balls, boating facilities, equipment, and entrance to swimming baths. To be eligible for subsidy, societies must state their purpose, what sports and games are included in their programme, actual sports practised, number of members, etc.; also they must have a governing committee and directing and instructing personnel, and must state the salaries allowed them.

For communities and groups organising concerts and

dramatic performances, subsidies are also available.
For theatrical groups, the requirements are an organisation of at least thirty members, six executives, and a
regisseur; to be eligible, they must have presented performances in halls with a capacity of two hundred and
fifty, and they must have given in the preceding season
at least three performances of which two must have
been of three acts, or more, and they must present reports on activities and a prospectus. The subsidy is
allotted according to the number of performances
played in the course of the year, and is doubled for
each play by a Belgian author. The rules for musical
societies are similar to those for drama.

Other of the numerous allotments include subsidies
to organisations encouraging folk music (the Committee believes that folk music is more readily *learned* by
the people than any other), provision for model garden
competitions, stock raising, assistance to decoration of
the home, to music and drama groups organising popular classes, and to the formation of a collection of educational moving pictures.

Hainault.—The Committee of Hainault is the oldest
of the three Workers' Leisure Committees, and its work
is the most extensive of the three. When established
the Committee had one hundred and twelve members,
all of whom gave their services. It was possible to form
seven sub-committees: housing; gardens and allotments;
small stock-raising; education; physical training; artistic training; intellectual and moral training. Two
years (1919-1921) were devoted to collection of information, theoretical study, and discussion of reports, the
whole problem being considered in its various aspects.

As to housing, the Workers' Leisure Committees com-
prehend the true relation of housing to the leisure
problem; they have left housing problems entirely to

the National Society for Cheap Housing, and have devoted themselves to beautifying the worker's home. The first programme of the housing section included: furniture; equipment; hygiene; heating; decoration of working-class houses and districts. Excellent work has been done in forming taste in furniture; simplicity is the standard, and all furniture is required to be economical and, as far as possible, "built in"; competitions and exhibitions have been arranged; the committees have approved designs on hand for reference; these are characterised by standard sizes and general style, leaving opportunity for individual taste in certain details of design and decoration. The Committee has also made arrangements by which it furnishes good reproductions of pictures and sculpture, and sells prints, china, pottery, etc. There is a provincial magazine on art and decoration, "Savoir et Beauté." Prizes are offered for harmonious houses—which are defined as practical and convenient houses where every possible labour-saving device is utilised, and where anything which holds dust or requires meticulous cleaning is banned.

As to gardens and allotments, there is a National Allotments League which during the war did much to promote the spread of workers' gardens and allotments; the Committee devotes itself in this sphere to financial and general assistance to this League. Besides encouragement of the allotments, the Committee encourages the cultivation of trees and flowers in and about workers' homes and gardens. Competitions are held in several communes.

Another sub-committee has charge of matters pertaining to small stock-raising. The stock-raising centre has been established at Mariemont. There is agricultural and horticultural training here; it is a kind of unusual agricultural college. The centre is open to the public and short classes and lectures are held, besides the more formal courses of one to three years, leading to certificates. The provincial interest is stimulated by various competitions, shows, etc.

The educational programme for Hainault includes: (a) domestic education for women; (b) industrial education; (c) vocational training, temporary classes, and continuation classes; (d) elementary education classes for adults, etc.

As to physical training, the plans include educational gymnastics for children and adults, establishment of playing fields and athletic grounds, training of instructors, general propaganda. The principal factor in this programme is the training of instructors. There are provincial training courses of which the object is to provide schools and athletic, gymnastic and military training societies with qualified teachers, who are to be "not simply physical training instructors but health educators." In addition to this expenditure the Committee gives financial support to the establishment of playing fields and athletic grounds by the communes.

In the matter of artistic training, effort is concentrated on music and drama. Provincial music festivals are arranged; folk music is encouraged a collection of folk songs has been published. In the field of amateur drama an inquiry was made (in 1922) before any plan was undertaken; it was learned that some five hundred dramatic societies were in existence, of which one hundred and sixty were in full operation. The Committee has directed its efforts to encouraging and improving these societies. To this end, classes in stage production have been held in various towns; dramatic festivals have taken place. Prizes are awarded for original plays, in which the use of dialect is encouraged.

As to intellectual and social education, the original recommendations advised the organisation of libraries, a model public library, educational cinema, domestic education, workers' institutes, tours and excursions. Much of this programme was immediately put into practice, by organisation and subsidy. Special training courses for librarians, advisory inspection of libraries, encouragement of educational lectures, educational moving pictures, and encouragement of educational excursions with lecturer-guides have resulted.

The spirit behind this whole Workers' Leisure movement in Belgium was expressed as follows by the Minister of Science and Art: "We can offer the workers a sample deck, but they must choose the cards for themselves." In other words, the necessity for leaving the workmen free to do as they please with their leisure is fully recognised. According to the report of the Hainault Committee, "Encouragement and guidance to the workers in the use of their free time are essential, but only when they reach the full development of all their faculties and of their personality will they find the real use and the real meaning of leisure."

Trazegnies—La Maison de Tous (*The House of All*).—The Community Council of Trazegnies have realised a centralisation of their different community services in the institution which has been named "La Maison de Tous." "It is the house of which all citizens of the community, and even strangers, may avail themselves freely. It is the house of the social life, the civil home where we have concentrated all the agencies destined to preserve, to conserve, and to develop the race, and destined also to co-ordinate, inspire, and ornament existence. It is the temple of work, activity, instruction, education, and of beauty." Its provisions include a lecture hall, which serves regularly for Sunday-evening concerts, amateur drama performances, dances, and lectures. Entrance fees are exacted toward the maintenance costs. Emphasis is laid upon instruction of girls in household economics, and it is stated that the purpose of the domestic training is "not only to make good housewives, but women capable of bringing into the home joy, gaiety, and beauty." A large hall communicating with the classrooms serves for dancing classes, etc. There are rooms for manual training for boys and for classes in design, and accommodations for exhibitions of the work of the students. Physical exercise is especially encouraged, but perhaps rather more from the health than from the recreational standpoint. The gymnasium and shower baths are open both to boys and to girls, and to the community. A large portion of the institution is devoted to projects for "intellectual, artistic, and moral education." Here are comprised a hall for educational moving pictures, a hall for family meetings; and the beginnings of a community music school. There is evident on the part of the directors of the enterprise a rather unusual appreciation of the civilising influences of the study and practice of music. Educational films, shown usually at weekly family meetings, are made palatable by entertainment in one form or another of music, or by amateur theatricals.

Workers' Use of Leisure.—In the light of the exceptionally extensive leisure provision existing in Liége, Brabant, and Hainault, it may be interesting to consider the recent findings of a Belgian commission appointed by the International Labour Bureau to examine the results of the law instituting the eight-hour day and the forty-eight-hour week. The commission divided into three sub-committees, of which the third was concerned with the influence of the eight-hour day on the physical, intellectual and moral life of the working population. The two investigators were Dr. Gilbert, general inspector of the medical service of labour at Cortenberg, and M. Gerard, general associate director of the central industrial committee of Belgium. The conclusions of the commission were published in an article in "Informations Sociales"—Vol. XXII, No. 8,* published by the International Labour Bureau. On the subject of the use of leisure in Belgium, the report is as follows:

"It seems that one of the effects of the law requiring the reduction of the duration of work should have been a greater development of family life; however, according to the employers, the influence of the law toward the development of family life has been, with few exceptions, nil. According to M. Gerard, the great majority of replies of employers are marked with strong pessimism as to the use made by the workers of the leisure assured them by the eight-hour day 'for their intellectual and physical development.' The employers estimate that in general the workers use their free time to go to the theatre, to the cabaret, and to dancing places. Certain employers, however, declare that the serious workers devote their leisure hours to various useful or remunerative undertakings. The young unmarried workers prefer pleasure and sport. On the other hand, the replies of the workers contradict those of the employers: with very rare exceptions these replies affirm that the workers make use of their new leisure not for remunerative work, but with a view to their intellectual and physical development and the elevating of their moral level. Among the workers' replies, a large number state that the workers devote their leisure to gardening, small farming, or small stock-raising; that they read to a considerable extent

* French edition of "Industrial and Labour Information."

and frequent the libraries, or that they follow professional courses or adult-education courses. Almost all the workers' replies indicate—sometimes with supporting statistics—the increase in the number of workers frequenting the libraries and professional courses, or affiliated with musical, dramatic, or sport societies. Eight of these replies, however, are unfavourable to the workers. Employers and workers recognise the interest of professional instruction; the trade union organisation claims to contribute to it to the full extent of its resources and influence, while the majority of employers' replies tend to show efforts made by the heads of industries to popularise technical instruction among the workers."

"Report of Playground Work in Belgium, April 15th-June 30th, 1922."—The above is the title of a report of the American Junior Red Cross from which an idea of the playground situation in Belgium may be obtained. It sums up as follows the significance of American playgrounds and playground methods in Belgium:

"The sport tradition in Belgium is limited to the tremendous enthusiasm for two games, one called the 'jeu de balle' and the other being an adaptation of archery. The former is played with a small, hard ball and large gloves. Matches are held on all public squares, the game is played mostly by professionals, and attracts immense audiences. Since the war, the presence of English troops in Belgium in the post-Armistice period has inculcated also a great taste for Association football. But the knowledge of a variety of sports sufficient to constitute a complete programme of physical education is lacking.

"To install one or several playgrounds which should combine the results of America's 30 years of experience in playground installation, to organise these playgrounds as centres of propaganda and instruction, to aid communities and schools to make the best use of their available spaces as playgrounds, thus to influence the education of all Belgian youth, is the work which invited the attention and energies of American school-children through the Junior Red Cross."

The first steps of the Junior Red Cross in Belgium comprised the opening of the playground at the Parc de la Garenne in Charleroi in October, 1921, and the organisation of the first training course for playground directors and directresses in April, 1922. There were at that time in Charleroi five communal schools for girls and five for boys. Each of these schools came to the playground in a body one half-day per week, according to a schedule pepared by the superintendent of schools; thus from one hundred and fifty to two hundred and fifty children arrived at one time for game instruction. This instruction was given them by the personnel of the aforementioned training course. Later, in response to demands, demonstrations of the Charleroi programme of games were given at various schools in the vicinity of Charleroi. The plan of the demonstrations was to have six or seven of the games, the principal ones on the Charleroi programme, played by two teams of boys from Charleroi, and then to issue an invitation to the boys and girls who were present as spectators to join in and play the same games under the direction of moni-trices who accompanied the demonstration group. The plan was very successful in interesting spectators in basketball, volley ball, and baseball, which have had a rapid and intense development in Belgium.

From such beginnings the Junior Red Cross play-ground-work around Charleroi gradually spread throughout Belgium. In general, the Charleroi playground has served as the model for playgrounds that have since been constructed. Furthermore, in many instances, simple game installations have been given the schools themselves; in 1922, twenty-five schools had received installation.

The Red Cross report continues:

"Not only is it true that great need exists, but its existence is appreciated by the Belgian people. For in social thinking and in the application of remedies for social ills, Belgium is very well advanced. It is recognised in Belgium, for example, that education should be a practical preparation for useful adult life. It is realised that the educational scheme should fit the conditions of the locality where each school is situated. Thus the great development of industrial and commercial schools in Belgium, such as the admirable University of Labour in Charleroi. It is realised that all efficient citizenship is based on the possession of a normal, properly functioning body; that, thus, physical education must be the basis of all education. It is realised, further, that the responsibility of the State does not cease with forming a citizen, but that it should maintain him in a state of health and efficiency and afford him opportunities for continued progress. So there have been instituted in all parts of Belgium evening courses for workmen. In the province of Hainault there exists a Commission for the Workmen's Leisure Time, which has more far-reaching powers than the Recreation Departments of any American city known to the writer. There is also being created in Belgium a National Commission for the Workmen's Leisure Time, which is attracting the attention of all European governments. And for a long time the Socialist party throughout Belgium has shown its appreciation of the importance of the Leisure time problem by creating its Maisons du Peuple which contain all of the opportunities for recreation and self-improvement found in our own Community Centres."

It was interesting to observe during the visit to Belgium that the playgrounds established by the Junior Red Cross have been well kept up, and that, in marked contrast to conditions in France, in the years since their establishment, public and official interest in them and appreciation of their value have strengthened and increased. A law providing for the establishment and maintenance of playgrounds in all communes above a certain population, is now before the Belgian Parliament (1927).

DENMARK

The main concern of our discussion of Denmark, will be that characteristic Danish phenomenon—the people's educational movement, of which the People's High Schools are the most notable development. This movement in Denmark, like the Sokol Movement in Czecho-Slovakia, may be considered of prime importance to a study of leisure utilisation, since both are racial manifestations which have aroused decided interest and admiration throughout other countries.

The explanation of the present nature and tendencies of the Danish people is doubtless to be found in their marked social and mental homogeneity. It must be remembered that in Denmark even the people of the city are usually no more than two generations removed from the land. Thus the home life, as in all largely agricultural societies, is wholesome and relatively strong.

It may be said, too, that Denmark has a conscious leisure movement, and that this movement is primarily

educational in tendency. A few characteristic manifestations will be mentioned.

Workers' Leisure.—It will be remembered that the
eight-hour day prevails in all the more important industries of Denmark. A large number of private and
state-subsidised institutions for the utilisation of
leisure exist there. The institutions in question are
closely connected with one another, especially those
which deal with workers' education by means of lectures, etc.

As to industrial provision, the workers tend to resent any suggestion of paternalism on the part of the
employers. It is said that the class-consciousness of
the workers is "pathologically intense." The tendency
of the State is to avoid much provision for industrial
workers in order to prevent any strengthening of the
demarcation. There is a good pension system; provision
for the unemployed is well-handled. As for the employers, we were informed that the more social legislation exacts of them, the more they tend to shirk any
direct responsibility.

It is generally felt that the location in the city of
the principal industries makes pronounced special provision for leisure unnecessary, since the worker has all
the recreational possibilities of the city at his command.* The excellent public library system was mentioned in this connection, and the availability of various
types of evening courses. However, an attempt has
been made to approximate the rural People's High
Schools in "Workers' High Schools" which provide
purely cultural curricula; there are four or five of these

* While in Norway and Sweden, where industries have been
developed throughout the countryside and workers live in communities of purely industrial origin and with corresponding limitations, it has been found necessary for the employers to provide various recreational facilities.

in Copenhagen. Also at Esbjerg a residence workers'
school exists which is similar to the Peoples' High
Schools.

Garden Colonies.—The colony-gardens are a very
old activity; one tiny villa pointed out in Copenhagen
had been built forty years ago by the present caretaker.
The gardeners are members of a national organisation
whose membership is 26,000. Ninety per cent of the
land is state-owned and rented by the organisation at
six oere per meter. There is great variety and ingenu-
ity in the design of the villas and in the arrangement
of the cultivated spaces. The colonies are conveniently
located as to transportation; it is usual for whole families to go out after the working-day, eating dinners at
the "villas." The gardens are sometimes used for week-
end and over-night camping.

At first largely a workers' organisation, the garden
colonies have become a recreation for all classes, so
that now one may see a manual worker's garden adjoining that of a Cabinet Minister.

Sports, Games, and Other Outdoor Recreation.—
There are over 200,000 bicycles in Copenhagen; over
a million in the entire country. These are used for play
and excursions as well as for practical purposes. On
week-ends in fair weather the roads swarm with cyclists
going into the country, often *en famille* with the young-
est members cradled in baskets.

Also, there is a great deal of picnicking, often in
family groups. The Danish people turn instinctively to
the outdoors in their free time. And the great extent
of seacoast, relatively accessible to a large part of the
population, is an important factor in their recreation.
The shore is lined with villas of every type—modern
houses which usually very wisely follow ancient architectural influences, and many reconditioned centuries-

old fishers' cottages, each with its strip of private beach. The people now regret that in the considerable distance from Copenhagen to Helsingör no land has been preserved for public bathing-beaches. The numerous accessible waterways also conduce to much boating of all sorts; yachting is very popular.

Among games, tennis is probably the one best liked by the people of Copenhagen; there are some municipal courts and many private tennis clubs. On the whole, however, it is still difficult to make the Danes regard sports as different from gymnastics. The "Anglo-Saxon play spirit" does not seem to have caught on to any extent in Denmark, although the values of the team game are appreciated by educators and leaders of the various athletic and outdoor movements. The Anglo-Saxon enthusiasm for the team-game is thus far foreign to the Danish temperament. Nevertheless, such an interest is definitely in process of development.

The People's High Schools.—First-hand knowledge of the People's High Schools was obtained through a visit to the typical People's High School at Frederiksborg, presided over by one of the men who was a leader in the earlier days of the movement. A long interview with his son, Frederick Begtrup, also a faculty member, yielded information as to the singular nature of the actual instruction given in these People's High Schools.

In considering the movement, it is necessary to take into account its religious origin. This religious spirit has persisted and is said to take its present form in a pedagogic method designed to develop in the young people a perception of and regard for "the spiritual elements of life." Therefore, the necessary qualification of the teaching staff is one of character (which means perhaps temperament) rather than academic attainment. The stated purpose of the movement is "to enrich the life of the people." It is believed that this end may be achieved by implanting a respect for certain virtues, and stimulating a desire to emulate them. Therefore the High Schools foster the study of history and literature, "biographically considered," that the pupils may perceive what courage, integrity, faith or imagination inspired certain historical figures and contributed to certain events. The national idea is ever foremost; nevertheless Mr. Begtrup declared that he could not be made to say that the People's High Schools are trying "to do a service to the Danish Community." It was suggested that the increasing of the ordinary man's self-respect, national consciousness, and faith in life might perhaps pardonably be regarded as a consummate service to the community, no matter how involuntary.

At any rate, faith in God, or at least (Mr. Begtrup was a little loathe to *name* their spiritual source) in a Transcendant Power, would seem to be essential for the teachers and the students. The students are to be made "to realise that it is fine and valuable to be a human being"; this, however, is said not to indicate the narrow limitations of humanism, but to extend into what is perhaps a sort of mysticism: the conception that a human being can be considered as having a conscious relation to "that Reality which ultimately disdains all forms."

The High Schools are unique *in that they do not qualify any one for anything.* Thus there are no examinations; the students need give no proof that they have absorbed anything in the classes. That is the secondary consideration, the primary being that some spiritual contagion be effected between teacher and students. The desired result would seem to be a quality of personality—a mood for meeting life. It is stated that there is no attempt made at any time or in any way to make the students *believe* anything, or to mould their attitudes toward anything. There is a daily service of prayer, but the students are entirely at liberty to stay away if they so desire. Matters of opinion make no differences in the attitude of the faculty toward the students.

At Frederiksborg simplicity of decoration prevails in the High School, with emphasis (by means of mural paintings and portraits) on national history and legend. There is an admirable room which reproduces the ancient main room of the Danish farm house—long benches, interesting panelling, certain examples of wood-carving in wall cupboards, some old pottery and brasses, and mural paintings representing the exploits of King Knud and certain other heroes. There is a good gymnasium which is used also for an assembly hall; there is a formal garden; and there are playing fields.

It seems essential, for the purposes of this study, to emphasise a distinction neglected by many outsiders who are enthusiastic about the Danish High School movement because of its liberal method and because it would seem an admirable way of supplying some cultural furnishings to people who have not attended higher schools. This latter proposed achievement would seem to relate the movement directly to the leisure problem. It is important to realise that the Danish High School must, however, be considered as a school for character, in much of its motivation, and, furthermore, that the chief value of the Danish High Schools is said to depend upon their being residence schools; the students are kept throughout the duration of the term in the same atmosphere, a thing that would be impossible in the case of evening courses in the city.

Question of Transplanting Such a Movement.—A little examination into the nature and origin of such a movement would seem to indicate that it cannot be successfully transplanted. It is simple enough to copy the form of any such movement; but the spirit is the factor determining its popular success. In the case of the Danish People's High Schools, it is surely clear, from the comments that have already been made, that an exactly similar phenomenon would hardly be possible among a less homogeneous and one-minded people. Furthermore, the curious mystical purpose involved indicates the extent of the religious influences in its origins, and its present purpose is obviously something more than the widening of the information and interests of the farming population. There is, of course, in the movement a genuine cultural aspect; however, the cultural influence is, according to their own statements, a secondary concern in the minds of the leaders. The whole intention and spirit of the Danish High Schools is nationalistic—which, of course, includes, in a country where there is a State Church as in Denmark, the implications of more or less conventional religion. In short, the success of the High Schools in Denmark is not proof that such a movement would flourish by virtue of its humanising or cultural effects alone, if transplanted to a place where it would be without strong sustaining nationalistic and religious motives.

From the point of view of the American investigator, the admission is regrettable, for the movement has certain extremely good features. The very fact that the students learn practically nothing, and that the High Schools "prepare no one for anything" is, it seems to us, worthy of the most ardent admiration. Surely there is nothing which human society in general, and particularly the American people, could so much profit by as some influence which would make of them amateurs of learning. This, to an appreciable degree and to a large extent—one-third of the Danish adult population are said to have attended the folk colleges—this Danish movement has accomplished.

CZECHO-SLOVAKIA

Just as Belgium provides a marked example of the *official* type of free time provision among the smaller countries of Europe, so Czecho-Slovakia may be studied as a country exhibiting a highly developed voluntary racial activity, a widespread recreational and leisure movement having its roots in the character of the people themselves. We refer, of course, to the Czech Sokols.

Czecho-Slovakia has all the political and religious divisions usual in European countries, and, in addition, certain peculiar racial differences and antagonisms which further divide some of its public movements. The northern section is peopled by Germans, the middle by Czechs, and the south by Slovaks. The Germans, some few million of the country's population, present a strong demarcation, and life among them differs in no-wise from that of the Germans of Saxony; they have their "wandering," their Turnvereins, their cycling, their camping, etc.; there are German organisations for every possible sort of leisure occupation. The Czechs on the other hand have especially and above all their Sokols; the Slovaks seem not to have developed any outstanding leisure characteristics.

Workers' Leisure.—Our general information on workers' leisure in Czecho-Slovakia is taken from a report published in the "International Labour Review," Vol. IX, No. 6, June, 1924. According to it, when the eight-hour law was enacted in December, 1919, the majority of the more important organisations and institutions for rational use of leisure were already in existence. As in other European countries, trade union activities and political interests receive their due share of the workers' time and attention. A certain tendency to political division may be noted in the fact that workers belonging to the National Socialist Party tend generally to join the Sokols. The Sokols will be discussed later; though their membership is derived from all classes, it is probable that about thirty per cent may be considered as "workers," as distinguished from tradesmen, manufacturers, members of professions, salaried employés, and agricultural workers, all of whom are represented. But keen interest in physical exercise has brought about the development of numerous sports and gymnastic associations other than the Sokols. Thus the Workers' Gymnastic Societies, having a membership largely drawn from the Social-Democratic party, were founded in 1895, with the special purpose of advancing the physical education of the working classes. In 1921, the workers belonging to the Communist party left the Union of Workers' Gymnastic Societies and set up their own Federation of Gymnastic Societies. In addition, the German working population has its Federation of Workers' Gymnastic and Sports Societies. All these societies organise large fêtes at intervals. Besides these general physical training and sports organisations, many clubs have been formed among the workers for the pursuit of special activities; these include cycling, camping, and tourist clubs. Football has great popularity, and there are amateur football associations. The state contributes indirectly by the granting of subsidies, and school gymnasia are lent to gymnastic societies. Employers have encouraged the physical education movement by providing sports grounds and by financial assistance.

The Union of Workers' Gymnastic Societies comprises also musical clubs, choral societies, dramatic societies, and arranges collective reductions for theatre attendance. The amateur drama and music societies give many public performances, and several hundred local branches own their own stages and properties. Courses of a vocational or general-information nature, lectures, etc., characterised by socialist indoctrination, are carried on under the auspices of the Union. The Sokols carry on similar work, but with a purer educational purpose. Similar activities have also been undertaken to some extent by the Communist, German, and Christian-Social groups.

In 1906 certain political parties and several prominent persons founded the Intellectual Union, the central body for popular education in Czecho-Slovakia. This organisation is entirely non-political and comprises several thousand local organisations, which yearly reach thousands of the people by means of lectures and popular courses, and which organises theatrical performances, concerts, exhibitions, etc.

For the rural population special courses have been organised under private initiative; they receive state subsidies. It is interesting to note that agricultural workers are especially interested in recreations of an intellectual type; the majority of the members of amateur dramatic societies are said to be agricultural workers. An organisation known as the Association of Young Country Workers has done much to organise facilities for the use of spare time of agricultural workers. Its chief interest is in encouragement of music and drama, and its activities are directed to organising musical societies, instrumental and vocal, and dramatic clubs.

By an Act of February, 1920, ten per cent of the net profits of mining undertakings must be deducted for the benefit of the workers and devoted to schemes of general interest to them. A considerable portion of the fund thus obtained has been spent on such facilities as public halls for lectures, performances, games, libraries, etc.

As to allotment gardens, an allotment movement took place in 1917, largely because of economic pressure. A central federation of societies for the making of allotments was founded, and since the war this activity has taken a firm place as a recreation. The sports associations encourage the garden movement.

In the matter of housing, it may be noted that the workers' co-operative societies usually build small houses with gardens rather than tenements.

On all questions involving the need of land the expropriation of large estates has had an interesting influence, since, aside from its relation to the housing policy, it has enabled the State Land Office to make grants of land for gardens, open spaces, allotment gardens, and athletic and playing fields. In accordance with the Act on the expropriation of large estates, the Land Office approved about 130 contracts of sale or gift, and also leases by which gymnastic and sports associations have acquired for purpose of physical education land which has been laid out in their spare time by workers who belong to the societies.

Town Planning.—The following information was given by a Government Official: All cities, towns, and large villages in Czecho-Slovakia have town plans to take care of a growth of a hundred years or more. These plans include spaces for parks and playgrounds. The municipalities buy at private sale, if possible, the space necessary for these; otherwise they acquire such space by condemnation proceedings. They also frequently adopt the principle of excess purchase or "excess condemnation"—the latter being a well-known technical term everywhere; that is, they buy or condemn the ground fronting on the proposed park and resell it, usually at such prices as to go a long way toward paying for the park itself out of the profit. This is most apt to occur when they can buy before the public knows about the proposed park, and sell afterwards.

Subsidies for Theatres.—The National Theatre is one of the most interesting cultural developments in Czecho-Slovakia. Under the administration of the National Theatre stands also the Stavosky Theatre. The system of running these theatres is simple: each year there is a deficit, which is met from State funds; there is a special department of the federal government which concerns itself with the matter. The theatres have a permanent staff of actors, singers, technical workers, etc., of about six hundred persons. They give plays and operas, and both are considered above all as cultural and educational agencies. At one time, the Stavosky Theatre employed only the German language, but since 1918, when the Czecho-Slovak Republic was formed, both theatres use the Czech language. There is, however, in Prague a New German Theatre for the German population, which is a private property of the Union "Deutscher Theater Verein." Its deficit also is met from State funds.

The Sokols.—The Sokols were founded in 1862 with the purpose of promoting physical education among all classes and the general education of young persons. They have a tremendously strong nationalistic spirit. The administration is in the hands of a central committee of representatives of the regional federations, and a secretariat divided into sections for gymnastics, education, hygiene, relief, youth, and press service. The organisation publishes some fifty periodicals.

The extent of the Sokol movement as authoritatively reported at the 1924 convention was indicated by the following figures: within the Republic of Czecho-Slovakia there were 3,120 societies consisting of 253,000 men, 98,000 women, 79,000 young people of both sexes, and 215,000 pupils of both sexes, a total of 645,000. In addition Sokols modelled on the Czech Sokols exist in neighbouring countries. Jugoslavia had four hundred and twenty-seven societies with over 47,-000 members; Poland six hundred and thirty societies with 58,500 members; Bulgaria fifty societies with over 15,000 members. The Sokol activities in Russia have been completely suppressed since the war.

In Czecho-Slovakia the local societies combine into regional organisations, of which there are fifty-three. Out of the regional organisations is created the central governing organisation with its several sections and committees. Most important of these is the Central Technical Section which guides and directs the whole physical education programme, establishing the principles, the methods and the activities which constitute the marvellous gymnastic exercises of the Sokols. In addition, there is a Central Section for Culture caring for intellectual education, organising historical celebrations and general conferences not only relative to the special activities of the Sokols but also to general intellectual development. This section, for instance, in 1923, organised over 57,000 educational conferences and meetings, over 4,500 educational tours and trips, and nearly 10,000 dramatic presentations, concerts, etc. The Central Sanitary Section organises sanitary and health courses and conferences for all of the societies. The Insurance Section provides accident insurance for all members in case of accident during the physical exercises. A "Central Section for the Minorities" gives a general supervision to the Sokol organisations existing outside of Czecho-Slovakia. An Architectural Section helps and advises in the planning of new gymnastic buildings. An Artistic Section controls the artistic character of the Sokol enterprises—decoration of the gymnasiums, etc. Other sections promote organisation work, record the statistics, furnish pictures, direct the publicity and provide a museum of physical education.

The spirit of the Sokols is above all earnest. The movement is marked by an intense and pure nationalism which, under the conditions of the country, is considered particularly fortunate and desirable. The gymnastic training is no more than an instrument for their serious purpose, which is to strengthen the sense of unity. In this connection, Josef Scheiner writes of the movement: "At first it was a modest step on the part of the sporting amateurs of Malypeter's private gymnastic institute who intended to form a society for the promotion of gymnastics; but as soon as public attention was aroused the leading national powers took up this resolution as a great promising means for arousing the exuberant vitality of the Czech nation. The society at its very beginning assumed a more important task, reaching far beyond the mere training of the body; in truth, it was only a few weeks after its appearance that during the precipitous rush of public life it was placed in the most exposed position as one of the first workers and fighters for the emancipation of the young nation.

"On the 26th of February, 1862, the constituting

general meeting of this first Czech gymnastic society was held in Prague. By the will of the nation the new society was immediately endowed with a chivalrous character; tasks were heaped on it; it was flooded with mottoes, in which the whole spirit of the people manifestly represents itself excited by the sudden events, the courage, manliness, demonstrative patriotism (a proud behaviour, showy uniform)—on the other side the democratic character, brotherhood, addressing each other by 'thou,' and all the signs of a vigorous youth, as well as of a generous movement which filled the heads and hearts of a people recovering its senses after a trance.

"This has also been expressed by giving the society the name 'Sokol,' by which especially in the Yougoslav songs of chivalry the noble character of heroes is designated."

In Prague a visit was paid to the elaborate headquarters of the organisation, which include a residence school for teachers, and to several training classes in the city. The excellence of the classes of beginners was almost incredible; there must indeed be some peculiar physical aptitude to account for the almost unhuman precision of the exercises. Apropos, it is interesting to note that the type of the athletic work of the Sokols has been adopted experimentally by leaders of movements who have an interest in promoting mass action and in discouraging the individualistic and exhibitionary trends in athletics. This gives rise to the question whether or not imitation for what might be called psychological purposes can have much value among other peoples. The majority of students in this matter incline to the belief that the value of such imitation is doubtful; a movement which is almost overwhelmingly the expression and indication of one people's racial character can hardly be transformed into a merely formative influence upon a totally different people. One doubts, for instance, that the Sokol movement could genuinely become a part of the life of any people temperamentally incapable of having toward it the attitude of fervid idealism reflected in this concluding paragraph of Josef Scheiner's article:

"The Sokol cause, therefore, serves the whole nation, its destination is to support its life, to make progress possible and to adapt its capabilities to the attainment of a powerful future. This conviction as yet rules the whole camp and directs all its steps; its spirit breathes in every one of its undertakings, in its entire press and primarily in every periodical of the Sokols. It is the concern of the Sokol Union to preserve this ideal character and aim. As long as it faithfully executes these prescripts and is led by enlightened and progressive men, without regard to temptations and without yielding to exterior pressure, it will be able to fulfil its noble mission to the nation and to secure for itself the merit of further development and progress."

AUSTRIA

In general, recreational and leisure conditions in Austria may be said to parallel those in . Germany, allowing for variations—usually not highly important —growing out of the difference between the Austrian temperament and the German; the Austrian temperament being probably less serious than the German, and less susceptible to certain mass enthusiasms. Everywhere in Austria, even in recreational matters, there is a certain picturesque and graceful quality,—a kind of charm—which is often lacking in Germany; and there exists in Austria a stronger enthusiasm for experiment in education. Noteworthy, too, is the fact that in Austria nothing lacks some touch of the æsthetic. The walls of a children's dental clinic, for instance, are considered an opportunity for the stimulation of appreciation of loveliness in colour and design; and in Austria there tends in these matters to be an invariable fine taste and simplicity. But the resemblances between Germany and Austria are in most respects more obvious than the differences; both are marked, for instance, by strong political divisions in private organisations, and by a tendency toward official provision for the numerous aspects of the leisure problem. This fact of Austria's strong similarity to Germany makes it unnecessary for us to devote to Austria the lengthy space which otherwise might be given to it.

Provision for Workers.—Vol. XVII, No. 6 of "Industrial and Labour Information," in February, 1926, printed the Report of the Austrian Government concerning the development of facilities for the utilisation of workers' spare time. It will be remembered that the eight-hour day has, since December, 1918, been generally observed in Austria, and that the 48-hour week is becoming the rule. Excerpts from the Report follow:

"In the provision of public baths, swimming pools, etc., the municipality of Vienna has taken measures which may be regarded as a model for the rest of the country. In other chief towns and industrial centres, the question is also being dealt with intelligently.

"In regard to fostered modes for the utilisation of workers' spare time, three distinct trends may be noted. First, the development of workers' gardens and allotments, poultry keeping, and the like are encouraged in Austria, especially by the trade unions whatever their

political leanings, by the local authorities of towns
and industrial centres, and by special voluntary organisations. Second, with a view to the development of the
physical health and strength of the workers by means
of games and sports, the trade unions have set up a
large number of gymnastic and sporting associations,
which are also encouraged by the government within
the limits of the means at its disposal. Third, in order
to encourage the development of general education, the
Federal Minister of Public Education has already done
useful work in giving advice to and subsidising the popular libraries and educational institutions which have
existed for many years, in organising theatrical performances, in encouraging the production of reputable
films, as also the cult for old customs, folk dances, and
folk songs, and in using his influence in favour of the
creation and development of popular educational and
other associations.

"The principle of the free use of institutions connected with the utilisation of spare time has always
been and is still observed in Austria. The great majority of these institutions were created by the trade
unions, and thus neither the Federal Government nor
(to any great extent) the employers, have any right
to interfere with their management. No pressure can,
therefore, be brought to bear on the working class in
regard to the use of these institutions. The trade
unions themselves exercise no constraint, but endeavour
to enlighten the workers so as to induce them to make
use of the institutions in question. No change of policy
in this direction is contemplated. It will, therefore,
continue to be a matter for the trade unions to set up
district or local committees, as suggested in the Recommendation, for co-ordinating and harmonising the ac-

tivities of the various institutions providing means of recreation."

It should be realised that, in Austria as in Germany, voluntary work for the trade unions and works-councils, activities in connection with the political party, administrative work, meetings of co-operative societies, involve great numbers of the workers during much of their free time, evenings and week-ends.

The movement for workers' education—the Union for Workers' Education in Vienna—founded in 1867, was the organisation from which all subsequent forms of workers' educational organisations developed. Education still is, as already stated, an important factor in the leisure occupation of Austrian workers. There is apparent, however, in the workers' educational movement as well as in other forms of organisation concerned with workers' leisure, a tendency to suspect outside influences. Thus the Labour Party's Central Education Institute (Zentralstelle für Bildungswesen) has succeeded in getting control of the majority of the workers' educational institutions. The main activities of this Institute, for the management of which trades unions are partly responsible, are in Vienna: lecturers are sent regularly to other industrial centres; it organises evening classes, lectures, and library work. Besides this Education Institute, the Labour Party carries on an Art Centre which is the largest and most efficient Austrian organisation providing opportunities for enjoyment of the theatre and of music; it gives special orchestral concerts for workers.

Among the educational developments which, although not exclusively for workers, are doubtless, in many instances, used by them, may be mentioned the important People's College Movement (Volkshochschulwesen), with its university extension evening lectures, and the

People's Institute (Volksheim) and the People's Educational Union (Volksbildungsverein); the two latter, with several centres of their own in Vienna, are very popular, particularly as they act as a medium for the arranging of excursions, expeditions, and concerts at the week-ends.

Active participation of Austrian workers in amateur drama and music is widespread. The Austrian Federation of Choral Societies numbers over 14,000 members, a large percentage of whom are workers.

The young workers naturally tend to go in for sport; the older workers go in for gardening. As in other countries, the allotment-colonies are dense with workers and their families at all week-ends and at evening.

Play Provision and Sports.—Austria, like Germany, tends to make wide provision for the recreation of the people. The recreation places visited in Vienna included a hall for athletics, belonging to the city, affording accommodations for athletic associations, class work, etc., and containing gymnasium rooms, apparatus, practice rooms for special sports, etc.; the Fasanen Garten, a fine outlay of playing fields then under construction for the use of the schools; the Augarten, accessible to a thickly populated district of Vienna and containing good playing fields; the Amalien Bad, a huge municipal natatorium, good-looking and complete; the Red Cross playing fields, including gymnasium and sun-bathing facilities; and the bathing beaches of the Danube.

As to sport, football is highly popular. It is interesting to note that the game was popular in Austria even before the war. There is eagerness to play it as well as to watch it, as is shown by the hundreds of football clubs. Swimming, too, is immensely popular; there is a workers' swimming club which has its own beach on the Danube, and similar bathing-places in great numbers are available for other organisations and individuals.

Individual opportunity for sport and outdoor life is afforded at all seasons by the resources of the mountainous country. The Naturfreunde originated in Austria. With them, walking, climbing, and winter sports are hugely popular. Local branches of the Naturfreunde arrange weekly Saturday-Sunday excursions, have special libraries of maps, guides, and scientific books, and frequently provide lectures on pertinent subjects. They maintain more than 150 * Herbergen and holiday homes throughout Austria.

ITALY

The "Dopolavoro" † *Leisure Movement.*—The movement in Italy which for the purposes of the present report at once claims our attention is called the "Dopolavoro." From the point of view of the American investigator, it is probably most expedient to regard the movement as an important experiment, on a national scale, in the matter of leisure provision for workers. To regard the movement as an experiment is not to imply any judgment as to its value or duration; it is merely to see it as an integral part and expression of Fascism, which, to the foreign observer, is itself an experiment, in the sense that the Russian Soviet Government is an experiment. In other words, one feels that the ultimate fate of the "Dopolavoro" movement is intimately bound up with the ultimate fate of Fascism. Of course, it may be that Fascism has acquired a momentum and direction that would insure

* Shelters.
† "Dopolavoro" means "after work."

its dominance in Italy independent of its leadership; likewise, it may be that even though Fascism should with the passage of time become moderately or even radically altered in nature, the "Dopolavoro" movement, having acquired an independent character and validity, would continue, under a new political régime, in its present form. It is, however, precisely because this whole question is so uncertain, so extremely problematical, that we feel justified in discussing the "Dopolavoro" movement as a profoundly interesting experiment in leisure-provision, rather than as a natural and instinctive Italian racial manifestation, in the sense, for instance, that the Sokol movement in Czecho-Slovakia may be regarded as a racial manifestation.

Our specific information on the "Dopolavoro" is taken from a "Report on the First Two Years of the Activity of the O. N. D." (Opera Nazionale Dopolavoro), published in Rome by that organisation in 1927. According to the "Premise" of the pamphlet, "The movement in favour of Welfare Work, known in Italy by the name of Dopolavoro (O. N. D.) which aims at promoting and co-ordinating the initiatives best suited to ensure the profitable employment of the workers' leisure time, has given way to such useful and imposing developments in the short course of two years, and has altogether received such a large tribute of commendations, that everywhere it appears to-day as one of the most characteristic manifestations of the Fascist Revolution, which under Mussolini's leadership is bringing the Italian nation toward the highest summits of power and greatness.

"It will be seen that the action that the O. N. D. performs in this country is vast and proteiform, and that the results so far obtained are worthy of careful study and consideration."

According to the pamphlet, the activities and initiatives promoted and encouraged by the Opera Nazionale Dopolavoro, now in operation, are as follows: (1) Popular Teaching—lectures and instructive conversations; libraries; reading rooms; courses in professional and manual work; (2) Propaganda for Hygiene and Welfare; (3) Agricultural and Forestry Propaganda; (4) Artistic Pastimes—musical bands; individual singing; choirs; dramatic amateur societies; concerts; classical and modern dancing competitions; meeting and playing rooms; matches and competitions; folklore; (5) Cinematography and Radio-Telephone; (6) Physical Training—Games in the open air; drilling; sport matches; lessons in physical training; (7) Excursions—organisation of excursions and journeys of local, regional, and national character; (8) Dwellings—workers' dwellings; propaganda for the decoration and fitting up of homes and furniture; furnishing competition for workers' home; hygenic measures; (9) Kitchen Gardens and Flower Gardens—practical teaching and schemes for the cultivation of vegetables, flowers, and trees, the rearing of bees and poultry; competitions and exhibitions; experimenting fields; (10) Economical Restaurants and provision stores; (11) Afterwork Industries—development and organisation of petty and domestic industries.

On the whole, it would seem that the "Dopolavoro" movement implies a radical modification of the psychology of both employers and workers, indicating a recognition of responsibility on the part of the workers who avail themselves of the provisions. Thus it becomes an instrument for attempted reconciliation between capital and labour. The movement is rooted in a belief in the paternalistic method; a belief that "the attentive cares of the employers should manifest themselves not only in the course of the working hours by solicitous inquiries and measures taken in matters of sanitary conditions, safety of factories, lighting, ventilation, etc., but should include also the forms of solicitude which make their beneficent effects felt during the hours of leisure to the advantage of the moral, intellectual and physical devotion of the workers and their families."

As to finances, "For the eminently social institutions of the 'Dopolavoro,' participation in the expenses must manifest itself in a public form, by means of important and generous subscriptions on the part of all constituted organisations and all classes of citizens. The workers, individually, are excluded from any contribution. Subsidy is demanded particularly from Employers' Associations and, in a limited degree, from communes and provinces."

Various branches of the "Dopolavoro" extend, of course, throughout Italy. Many of these have special "Dopolavoro" buildings, containing most elaborate equipment and provision. In many cases, these are old buildings—even, in some cases, palaces as in Venice,— that have been acquired by the O. N. D. of the particular locale and remodelled for their uses. The numerous illustrations of such buildings contained in the pamphlet include pictures of clubrooms, tennis grounds, buffets, skating-rinks, writing-rooms, gardens, dining-halls, kitchens, libraries, little theatres, gymnasiums, dormitories, asylums, apprentices-schools, concert halls, lecture halls, boxing rings, etc.

An indication that "Dopolavoro" leisure-provision is mainly in the interests of production may be seen in the following paragraph from the O. N. D. pamphlet:

"Therefore, under the protection of the O. N. D.

that spirit of unity is consecrated, that will reunite in harmony of intent and action all productive energies through the willing, spontaneous assistance of the different classes. Industrial men well know that the quantity and the quality of the production depends in a great part on the goodness of the workman; they well know the efficiency of the work is in relation with the good employment of the after-work hours; all this they have so well understood that in many factories by the side of the provisions enforced on them by social legislation, those of a Dopolavoro character have been added."

The attitude and response of the worker are indicated by the pamphlet as follows:

"On his side, the Italian workman is beginning to understand what is being done for him and appreciates much more the initiatives of the employers, the more active the assistance is that is given him. Materially and morally improved, the workman thus becomes an intelligent soldier, ready for the mute heroism of every day, to observe the continual unfailing sacrifice with which the great economic battles are won."

The whole spirit of the movement is summed up in the following paragraphs from the pamphlet's "Conclusion":

"The preparation of the wide Dopolavoro movement that might have taken several years, has been reduced by intense work to a minimum. The Fascist Régime creating such an intimate and healthy national solidarity, has pushed all into the great current pervaded by the fever of civil progress.

"It is the iron will of the Duce that is transfused into the will of these devoted followers—of all Italians —it is the renewed soul of the Nation that, awakened from its drowsiness, will tenaciously confirm, in the

name of Fascism, the aims of potency and the greatness of the country; it is the reborn conscience of the
mass of our marvellous people that, forgetting the sad
times of abjection and surrender, intends to rise again
to redeem itself from the mistakes of a sad past, and
regain the time lost.

"It is significant enough, for example, that the old
Case del Popolo that were the seats of the red organisation, have now become the much frequented seats of
the Dopolavoro Fascista for the admonishment and
example of the new healthy popular current bred in
the Sacred Love of the Country.

"And whilst the Venetian Dopolavoro gathers in the
ancient Palaces that remind us of the glories of the
Queen of the Sea, the workers adherent to our institutions in many other Italian cities are co-operating
to render the task of the beneficent institution easier.

"And a new life flourishes and will flourish still
more in the masses that, Fascism, with its institutions,
redeems; those masses that, strengthened in their
physical health, spiritually renewed, will take up again
in the name of our Race the glorious task reserved
to a Race that has a millenary civilisation."

Fascist Attitude Toward Sport.—The Paris edition
of the "New York Herald" in September 25, 1927, contained an article entitled "Fascists Believe Sport's Use
is Making Soldiers." We shall quote the article in
full as perhaps giving some indication of one angle
of the Fascist attitude toward sport and, possibly,
toward recreation in general.

"International university students at the Olympic
Games now in progress here have given rise to considerable discussion in the Fascist Press concerning
the value of sports in general. These discussions bring
into clearer relief the Fascist conception of athletics,

which falls into line with most other Fascist concep-
tions, which differentiate Fascism from all other forms
of government and systems of society.

"The principal point in the Fascist conception of
athletics revolves around the claim that the only reason for the existence of athletics is to develop soldiers.
Without this end constantly held in view sportsmanship
becomes an obnoxious form of snobbery. The point
is amply illustrated by an article published this week
by "Il Tevere," an ultra-Fascist newspaper, which says
boldly that the army manœuvres, also now in progress,
represent the sublimation of sport or, rather, its justification. The article goes on to say: 'The athlete who
offers his muscles and his sporting knowledge to the
mother country is a perfect sportsman—a Fascist
sportsman—because it is necessary to give our athletics
a Fascist character, which distinguishes it from athletics as an end in itself, sport for sport's sake, as we
would describe Anglo-Saxon athletics. This for us
means degeneration of sportsmanship, which must be
avoided with great care. Sports for sport's sake create professionalism, and all professionalism is pernicious. . . . Several observers have revealed that an
excessive passion for sports coincides almost always
with a decadence of the people who manifest this
passion.' "

We have noted in other European countries an occasional tendency—usually contested by other important voices in those countries—to see in sport a more
or less indirect method of effecting military fitness;
but the above quotation represents the only case we
have met in Europe of emphatic avowal that military
fitness is the only justifiable end of sport. It is interesting to the American recreation student to note that
in its assertion that "excessive passion for sports co-

incides almost always with a decadence of the people
who manifest this passion," the article makes no distinction between a passion for participation in sport
as against a passion for merely passively watching it.

Activities in Italian Cities.—Dopolavoro offices and
centres of activity were visited in Venice, Florence,
Rome and Naples. In Rome the O. N. D. maintains
its own cinema producing department, which provides
free outdoor entertainment to great numbers of the
people. Pictures are shown in the evening in the public squares of crowded districts; the subjects are generally of a Fascist-propaganda or nationalist-educa-
tional type. At the showing visited, the square was
thronged with spectators of all ages, observing with
enthusiasm. Everywhere excellent buildings have been
provided or reclaimed for the use of the Centres. In
Venice the provincial headquarters are housed in the
Palace of the Doges. Here, as in Florence, the emphasis seemed to be placed on recreational provision
"afterwork," implying a relative neglect of the child.
This condition would seem to prevail in all the great
cities, where the working population is varied and
dispersed. In the smaller towns, and especially in communities of purely industrial origin or development,
activities reaching the families, and thus all ages, of
the working people, have apparently been better developed. (This would seem to be the case where the
"afterwork" provision has been initiated by employers.) In Naples impressive sport grounds and a holiday beach colony for small children were visited. Here
the branch of the movement dealing with the encouragement of excursions has been especially well-developed;
possibly there is a particular interest here because
of the romance of the neighbourhood. At the time
of the visit (August, 1927), a most imposing Centre

was in process of construction and soon to be opened for use: a large property in a poor and greatly crowded district being rebuilt into a recreation-plant of vast size and varied provision—halls for gymnastics, games, and dramatic performances, class and club rooms, libraries, and offices. Everywhere a fine taste is manifest in the decorations and the architectural reconstruction of these centres, attaining sometimes to classic loveliness or grandeur. It is apparent that it is intended that the small child is to learn here, and the working man never to forget, the great cultural heritage of his country.

SUPPLEMENT

RECREATION IN THE UNITED STATES *

The first quarter of this century may be regarded by future historians as the dawn of recreational life in the United States. The productive power of the nation has brought increased leisure to every individual and has also set up inexpensive facilities for his play and entertainment. This applies to both commercial recreation and non-commercial recreation.

Motor cars in the United States have multiplied until there is one to every 5.13 persons,—practically averaging one to a family. One family in four has a radio set. At these 7,500,000 radios thirty-five million persons, it is estimated, listen in on the occasion of a national broadcast by the President or on a championship event in the world of sport. For the daily entertainment of

* This article was contributed by the Playground and Recreation Association of America.

millions of patrons there are twenty thousand motion picture houses. When professional baseball opened its 1928 season on a raw April day two hundred and two thousand spectators, including President Coolidge, were present.

Non-Commercial Recreation.—Equally remarkable is the rise of new movements or enlargement of old ones in the field of "participant" recreation under non-commercial auspices.

In 1906 when the Playground and Recreation Association of American was organised in Washington, D. C., under the leadership of Theodore Roosevelt, Luther Halsey Gulick, Henry S. Curtis, and others, only forty-one cities reported organised public playgrounds. Twenty years later, this number had grown to 790, which reported 10,123 separate play areas and 2,905 leaders employed the year round. In 1927, $32,191,763 were expended for the maintenance of public recreation. (These figures include about twenty Canadian cities.) More than a million and a half children and adults, on the average, daily make use of public recreation fields, according to a conservative estimate. This recreation has been enjoyed by the American public at a per capita tax of twenty-five cents a year. For this sum one cannot gain admission to a good motion picture show.

The Boy Scouts of America, launched in the United States in 1912, numbers 625,413 boys and 189,053 men, the latter leaders and officials. One boy in every eligible seven in the United States is a scout. The Girls Scouts have 167,925 members in good standing; the Camp Fire Girls a similar number. All these movements have sprung up since 1900.

The Y.M.C.A., an older organisation, had an enrollment in October, 1927, of 961,754 men and boys.

The Canadian membership brings the total to over one million. A sister organisation, the Y.W.C.A., counts 600,000 members.

Growth of Public Parks.—Municipal, county, state and national parks and forests have become an enormous recreational asset to the public. National parks, exclusive of the new Smoky Mountain reservation in Tennessee and North Carolina, comprise more than seven million acres; national forests, partly available for recreation, 161,648,000 acres. Forty-three of the forty-eight states in 1925 had state parks, with actual or potential value for outdoor recreation, totalling over 6,500,000 acres. In 1926, 1,681 municipalities reported nearly a quarter of a million acres in municipal parks. However, in few cities has the standard of one acre of parks for a hundred persons been attained.

There is a rapidly growing movement among municipalities to acquire parks outside the city limits. One hundred and nine cities have such areas.

Golf and tennis, until a few years ago the prerogative of the rich, are now on a public basis. In 1926 there were 6,900 public tennis courts. One hundred and fifty cities have provided municipal golf courses where anybody can play for a fee of twenty-five or fifty cents a round. The number of public courses is rapidly growing.

One hundred and thirty-six cities have municipal bands, and practically every village and town has a "town" band supported by contributions, proceeds of concerts, or other means. Community theatre groups connected with recreation departments of cities, settlements, scout troops, camp fire girls, and community centres flourish in hundreds of communities. These groups combine recreation with education. Fun, rather than technique, is the gauge of their success. In addition there are hundreds of little theatre groups which primarily aim at artistic production.

Chautauqua and Other Movements.—The Chautauqua has had a pronounced effect on the cultural life of America. This movement, so-named from its origin in an educational and recreational summer assembly at Chautauqua, New York, is a wide-spread movement of seven-day cultural programmes in the smaller communities. During the summer, by train and motor, players, singers, entertainers, orchestras, lecturers, and recreation leaders for children go about from town to town providing afternoon and evening programmes of good quality entertainment. They appear in tents which, at the conclusion of the weeks' sojourn, are struck and transported to the next community. The programmes are financed by citizens, some of whom stand year after year as sponsors or guarantors. Tickets are sold to cover the cost of the entertainment.

The Parent Teacher Association, which serves the social needs of its membership to some degree and actively promotes school and neighbourhood recreation, has one million and a quarter members. A considerable part of the programme of women's clubs, which have three million members, comprises dramatics, musical entertainments, teas, dances, bridge, story-writing contests, lectures and other recreational and educational activities.

To these organisations must be added numerous private golf and athletic clubs, fraternal orders, national sport organisations, choral groups of native and foreign born, hobby clubs, hiking and mountain clubs, organisations of hunters and fishermen, yacht and polo clubs, nature study societies, and other groups of a social or recreational nature, if one is to have a com-

plete picture of the organised recreational life of the
country.

Causes of the Recreation Movement.—The educa-
tional-recreational movement for children has been due
to a variety of conditions in American life. The
conflict of children's impulses with city conditions
causes juvenile delinquency, ill health, and street acci-
dents. Public playgrounds, settlements, scout organisations, Camp Fire Girls, boys' clubs, Jewish community
centres, Knights of Columbus clubs and the Y.M. and
Y.W.C.A. have been developed to meet these problems.

The outdoor recreation movement is also due to the
popular reaction against the cramping influences of
cities. The automobile has greatly encouraged this
trend by making it possible for people quickly to reach
the mountains, the shore, the country, outlying public
parks and golf courses.

Underlying the whole recreation movement, commercial and non-commercial, is the enormous produc-
tivity of American industry which has reduced the
average work day and yielded a wage that allows the
working man increased spending money for the good
things of life. In other words the industrial revolution has democratised recreation in the United States.
Working people own not only homes but cars, radios,
pianos, and victrolas, and have a surplus of leisure
and energy with which to enjoy these facilities.

Characteristic Trends in American Recreation.—
The trend in the United States is to public control and
direction of recreation. The majority of groups administering public facilities are municipal. Municipalities have made it possible for any individual
to play golf. They have also democratised tennis.
They have put public bathing beaches and swimming
pools within the reach of the multitude at nominal

fees. A beginning has been made in municipal opera, notably in St. Louis. Municipal drama is an accomplished fact in many cities and towns. In this connection the development of excellent symphony orchestras in nearly all important American cities is especially significant. Although there are short seasons of opera in various cities, American musical taste seems to find its satisfaction in the symphony rather than in opera.

The organised recreation movement has taken up good activities formerly enjoyed only by the rich and made them available to the general public through tax-supported recreation systems, and with no taint of paternalism.

Organised recreation has multiplied facilities for the people's recreation. When the movement began, the playground was the typical public facility. Now there are included the following: swimming pools, bathing beaches, athletic fields, tennis courts, picnic grounds, quoit courts, skating rinks, dancing pavilions, community houses, summer camp facilities, wading pools, parks, forests, lakes, ponds, gymnasiums and auditoriums. The recreation leader takes his service to the buildings that have equipment, like the schools, parks, clubs and churches, and carries out a good part of his programme through these institutions.

Privately supported recreation organisations, especially settlements, have done valuable pioneer laboratory work which has served as an effective demonstration for public officials. Manual training was first developed in a settlement in the north end of Boston. Now it is a commonplace in the public school curriculum throughout the country.

Fundamentals in Recreation.—Some 4,500 leaders in American life, including college presidents, school superintendents, labour leaders, manufacturers, senators, governors, authors and others have signed the following statement on "Fundamentals in Community Recreation" prepared by the Playground and Recreation Association:

1. That in nearly every community with a population of 8,000 or more there is need of a man or a woman who shall give full time to thinking, planning and working for the best possible use of the leisure hours of men, women and children.

2. That community leisure time programmes should continue throughout the entire twelve months of the year.

3. That it is the responsibility of the entire community to maintain recreation opportunities for all the citizens and that there ought, therefore, to be, as early as possible, support of the recreation programme through public taxation under some department of the local government.

4. That there should be in every state a home rule bill which will permit the people of any city or town to make provision under local government for the administration of their community recreation.

5. That there is need in every community, even though the municipal recreation administrative body be most effective, for private organisation of citizens in their neighbourhoods to make the fullest use of the facilities provided, to make sure that what is being done is meeting the deeper needs of the people of the neighbourhood.

6. That the emphasis ought to be not only on maintaining certain activities on playgrounds and in recreation centres but also and definitely on the training of the entire people in leisure time activities, so that within the home, in the church and throughout all natural, human relationships there shall be the best opportunity for wholesome good times.

7. That the purpose in training children and young people in the right use of leisure ought not to be merely to fill up the idle hours but also to create an active, energetic, happy citizenship.

8. That even though the beginning of a city or town recreation programme be children's playgrounds, other features ought to be added progressively from year to year until music, dramatic activities, and discussion of public questions, training for more intellectual uses of spare time, and other valuable activities have been included, so that all ages and all kinds of people may find vital interest.

9. That every boy and every girl in America ought to be trained to know well a certain limited number of games for use outdoors and indoors, so that there will never be occasion for any boy or any girl to say that he cannot think of anything to do.

10. That most boys and girls should be taught a few simple songs, so that, if they wish, they may sing as they work or play.

11. That all employed boys and girls should have opportunity in their free hours to enjoy companionship and wholesome social life.

12. That through the community recreation programme every boy and girl should come to appreciate the beautiful in life.

13. That adults, through music, drama, games, athletics, social activities, community and special day celebrations, should find in their common interests the opportunity for a common community service.

14. That every new school built ought to have a certain minimum amount of space around it provided for the play of the children.

15. That nearly every new school building ought to have an auditorium, preferably on the ground floor, and should be so constructed that it is suited for community uses.

16. That if a suitable meeting place for community groups is not available in the schools or elsewhere, a community building should be provided through community effort.

17. That each child, under ten years of age, living in a city or town, should be given an apportunity to play upon

a public playground without going more than one-quarter mile from home.

18.　That every community should provide space in sufficient area for the boys of the community to play baseball and football.

19.　That every community should provide opportunity for the boys and girls to swim in summer, and as far as possible to skate and coast in winter.

20.　That every boy and every girl ought to have opportunity, either on his own home grounds or on land provided by the municipality, to have a small garden where he may watch the growth of plants, springing up from seeds which he has planted.

21.　That in new real estate developments, not less than one-tenth of the space should be set aside to be used for play just as part of the land is set aside for streets.

Administration of Public Recreation Facilities.—In some instances playgrounds and recreational facilities and activities are administered by a private community recreation association; in others by the school board, park board, or some other municipal body. A summary made in 1926 showed that in four hundred and fifty-nine cities where recreation was administered by public recreation authorities, one hundred and seventy-four programmes were directed by recreation boards, bureaus, commissions or departments, one hundred and thirteen by school departments, and one hundred and eleven by park commissions or departments.

In a number of states there are home rule bills permitting cities to establish independent recreation commissions or boards, employ workers, and appropriate funds. It is of advantage where official boards exist to have back of them private groups of citizens known as community recreation associations or acting under some other title. These groups initiate activities which the official commission cannot immediately undertake, help in securing publicity, raise funds necessary for needed activities for which the budget cannot provide, and stand back of the commission in all its work.

Leadership.—It has been found in the United States that the most important element in the operation of a recreation system is leadership. The first playground leaders of America were untrained matrons in the sand gardens of Boston in 1885. To-day the staff of an up-to-date city recreation system includes a number of specialists. Houston, Texas, to cite an example of the latest leadership trend, has a staff of specialists in educational dramatics, neighbourhood organisation, athletics, playground leadership, and community music. Leadership is carried to the people in the neighbourhoods where they live. The dramatic service includes a library, costume chest, pageant and festival, organisation service, story-telling, and a drama course for volunteer workers. In addition, each playground and recreation centre has its own leaders.

There must be trained paid workers to direct activities. Experience has shown that a playground, however well equipped, will not attract children unless there is leadership to vitalise it. Without such direction, the playground falls into the hands of bullies and becomes a bad influence.

The kind of leadership that adults need might be called organisation guidance. For instance, some young men have the disposition to play baseball. To play the game satisfactorily, there must be assembled two teams, at least eighteen players, including two pitchers having a rather rare type of skill. A playing field is needed, bats and balls are required. Leadership for them means help in organising these groups and in arranging for these necessary facilities. Similar assistance is important in the case of a club wanting to have a sketch class, to organise a "little theatre group" to put on some plays, or to organise an orchestra.

The plan of leadership which is in effect in many cities and which is essential for the full functioning of a recreation programme involves, first of all, a year-round executive, either a man or a woman, who gives full time to planning programmes, organising and supervising activities, training workers, both paid and volunteer, organising neighbourhood groups and arranging community celebrations, being responsible to the community recreation commission or association for the conduct of the work. Such an executive is usually known as superintendent of recreation.

Every national organisation in the field of organised recreation of the educational sort conducts training courses to develop qualified workers or co-operates with colleges and universities in administering such courses. The training work of the Playground and Recreation Association of America may be outlined as an example.

First of all, the Association conducts in New York a National Recreation School, giving a nine months' course for college and normal school graduates for young men and women of high scholastic standing and of pronounced leadership in the social and athletic life of the institutions. In this school, to which a maximum of fifty students are admitted each year, learning is by discussion, demonstration and practise rather than theory. Some of the subjects in the course are: athletics, social recreation, community music, community drama, handcrafts, nature study, boys' and girls' clubs, camping, problems of city finance and management, and psychology of recreation. The instructors and lecturers have been drawn from the ablest recreation leaders of the country. In addition to the year's course of this school, the Association usually conducts a six weeks' summer session primarily for those already engaged in public recreation or physical education.

Institutes Reach Thousands.—Through the Association's specialists in games, dramatics and community organisation, several hundred institutes are carried on annually throughout the country. They reach thousands of paid and volunteer workers. For rural leaders, including teachers, ministers, home demonstration agents, and others, the Association conducts similar institutes in recreational methods.

Much energy is also given to the publication of studies and the preparation of manuals. Recently a two-year national survey of municipal and county parks was completed and the results were published in two large volumes, with a foreword by President Coolidge. Other typical handbooks are "The Design and Equipment of Playgrounds," "Municipal Golf" and "Eighty-eight Successful Play Activities."

The National Physical Education Service, organised in 1918, is a department of the Association's work devoted particularly to promoting and enriching school programmes of physical education. The wide-spread tendency to secure recreation areas in new schools and to provide more time for physical training in the school curriculum, is creating new opportunities for physical educators. In modern physical education in America, formal calisthenics and drills have largely given way to play-motivated activities.

Effect on American Institutions.—This movement has had pronounced effects upon fundamental American institutions. Parks, which used to be merely breathing places, have been thrown open to the people for active recreation. Formerly used only for relaxation and the satisfaction of the æsthetic nature, they are now used for athletics, games, skating, golf, tennis, nature study and picnics.

The public education system has been profoundly affected by the introduction of the "interest" or play element into the curriculum. Games, dramatics, music, and art have been added as extra curricula activities. Every new school in a progressive community has its playground; every high school its athletic field. The buildings must have gymnasia, stages, and community centre facilities, the latter for the use of adults after school hours. Modern physical education substitutes free, enjoyable games for formal, stiff calisthenics.

The churches, recognising the truth in the assertion of one of their leaders that "it is largely through the proper use of leisure that the kingdom of God will be realised," have set about promoting "church-centred" recreation. Summer camps, scout troops, and social programmes for young people, including dancing and games in parish houses, are fostered. Picnics, musical activities, and dramatics are encouraged. Training classes in these activities are a feature of the programmes of many conventions of religious bodies.

Industry has long felt the influence of the movement. Industrial recreation, however, has passed its peak. The number of industries fostering organised recreation has declined in recent years, due to the dislike of the workmen for paternalistic programmes and to the growth of municipal recreation. Manufacturers have seen that neighbourhood and community recreation are more satisfying to labour.

The family unit has been less affected by the educational recreational movement than by commercial recreation. It is claimed by some that the radio, the automobile, and the moving picture, have brought families closer together in their play than they were formerly. However, home play campaigns promoted by municipalities, have encouraged backyard playgrounds, home music, home reading, story-telling and conversation.

A partial by-product of the movement is the emergence of a type of city planning centring about open spaces and recreation facilities. This is typified in a new model community about to rise in northern New Jersey, called Radburn. Parks, playgrounds, walks and large yards are the dominating feature of this city, which is designed for a population of 25,000. "A town for the motor age" it is called. It will protect the children from the hazards of the street.

In seeking to understand the recreation movement in America one must recognise the part which organisation has played. Men and women drawn together by their common interest in recreation have formed local associations and also the national Playground and Recreation Association of America. Through organisation an exchange of experience between communities and between individuals has been made possible. Groups in different communities desiring to establish playgrounds, swimming pools, athletic fields, and provide adequate recreation leadership, have been able to obtain the advice and the help of the best trained individuals available because such local and national organisation existed.

Pretty generally throughout America there has been a demand on the part of the fathers and mothers for better play opportunity for their children. It has been recognised that children must play. Adults generally like to play. Because this hunger is real, the small groups in localities interested in recreation have grown larger and larger until there is a rather general acceptance in the cities of America of the idea that municipalities themselves should provide places for recreation and a certain minimum amount of leadership so that all property, public and private, that is open for recreation use may be utilised by the people so far as they have need.

Those interested in recreation, as they have tried to enlarge their own groups, have found it necessary to break through the crust of the hard work tradition, the puritanical reverence for the discipline of toil.

Much recreation in America has sprung from organised efforts to provide facilities and to train for specific activities. Yet entirely independent of all organised recreation activity, though sometimes growing out of such organisation, there is a tremendous amount of play and recreation which is entirely unorganised. Recreation in all its forms is making a substantial contribution to health and good citizenship in the United States.

THE END